The Household of God

SOCIETY OF BIBLICAL LITERATURE

DISSERTATION SERIES

William Baird, Editor

Number 71

THE HOUSEHOLD OF GOD:
THE SOCIAL WORLD OF THE PASTORAL EPISTLES

by
David C. Verner

David C. Verner

THE HOUSEHOLD OF GOD
THE SOCIAL WORLD OF THE PASTORAL EPISTLES

Scholars Press
Chico, California

THE HOUSEHOLD OF GOD
THE SOCIAL WORLD OF THE PASTORAL EPISTLES

David C. Verner

Ph.D., 1981
Emory University

Advisor:
Fred B. Craddock

Library of Congress Cataloging in Publication Data

Verner, David C.
The household of God.

(Dissertation series / Society of Biblical Literature ; no. 71)
Bibliography: p.
1. Bible. N.T. Pastoral Epistles—Criticism, interpretation, etc. 2. Sociology, Biblical. I. Title. II. Series: Dissertation series (Society of Biblical Literature) ; no. 71.
BS2735.2.V47 1983 227'.83067 82-25015
ISBN 0-89130-611-0

Printed in the United States of America

Contents

LIST OF CHARTS

ABBREVIATIONS

Abbreviations of the titles of ancient works and of collections of papers are found in G. Kittel and G. Friedrich (eds.), *Theological Dictionary of the New Testament.* The titles of periodicals, serials and reference works commonly cited in New Testament scholarship have been abbreviated according to the usage in the *Journal of Biblical Literature.* Other abbreviations used in this dissertation are as follows:

ANRW - H. Temporini, ed., *Aufstieg und Niedergang der römischen Welt*
CPJ - V. Tcherikover and A. Fuks, eds., *Corpus Papyrorum Judaicarum*
ESAR - T. Frank, ed., *An Economic Survey of Ancient Rome*
MAMA - *Monumenta Asia Minoris Antiqua*
OGI - W. Dittenberger, ed., *Orientis Graecae Inscriptionis selectae*

I

Introduction

In 1 Tim 3:14-15, the author informs his readers, "I am writing these things to you . . . in order that you may know how to behave in the household (οἶκος) of God, which is the church of the living God. . . ." This passage has supplied the impetus for the present study, in which the following will be argued: The author of the Pastorals sets forth in his composition a coherent concept of the church as the household of God. This concept is two-pronged, informing the author's understanding both of the household as the basic social unit in the church, and of the church as a social structure modelled on the household. This two-pronged concept is developed in such a way in the Pastorals that they contain information about the social strata, social structure and social tensions of the church to which they are addressed.

That the Pastorals contain material which deals overtly with social structure and social relations in the church will be readily seen by even the casual reader. This material, concentrated in 1 Tim 2:1-6:1 and Titus 1:5-9 and 2:1-10, concerns itself with proper conduct (in some cases, proper qualifications) of members of the church according to their various official positions (for example, bishop, deacon) or social stations (for example, women, slaves) within the church. Church members are thus instructed in the social requirements of their various positions within the official and social structure of the church. In addition, the Pastorals contain polemic against opponents who are accused of causing, among other things, social disruption in the church, an accusation which appears to indicate the presence of social tension in the church (2 Tim 3:6; Titus 1:10-11). Furthermore, it will be contended that the Pastorals reveal much about social strata in the church, the social standing of the author, and his perspective on social tensions in the church.

However, a major difficulty arises in interpreting the material in question. It is not immediately apparent that this material reflects a coherent perspective based on the concept of the church as the household of God, or any other concept. In the first place, the author has been viewed as a collector, whose arrangement of traditional material is for the most part haphazard.[1] Furthermore, the material in the Pastorals that is of greatest interest to the proposed investigation is paraenetic material. Since Dibelius, the prevailing view has been that paraenesis is moral exhortation of an extremely generalized nature.[2] Thus it has been understood as traditional material of the sort most unlikely to reflect the perspective of a particular author or to provide insights into particular situations in churches. Therefore, if the Pastorals are to be studied for indications of social features of the church to which they are addressed, then the issue of their coherence, and, more specifically, the coherence of their perspective on the social structure of the church and social relations within it must be addressed.

If the concept of the household of God is indeed central both to the author's presentation and to his understanding of the church, then a line of inquiry into the problems of social class, social structure and social tensions in the church of the Pastorals is suggested: If the church is the household of God, then what sort of household is envisioned? How is the household of God related to ordinary households[3] within the community, and how does its structure both reflect and differ from theirs? By the way in which the author conceives of the household, does he leave any clues as to his own social and cultural milieu, as well as that of the church which he addresses? In addition, can it be discerned why this particular image plays a dominant role in shaping the author's understanding of the church? Is it an image which he passively receives from church tradition and assumes without further ado in his presentation of the material, or is there evidence that he actively develops it as a vehicle for bringing to expression his own particular understanding of the church in its social aspect over against conflicting understandings? If the latter is true, what is at issue in this conflict, and what are the social implications of our author's stand for his church?

---

[1]M. Dibelius and H. Conzelmann, *The Pastoral Epistles* (trans. P. Buttolph and A. Yarbro; ed. H. Koester; Hermeneia; Philadelphia: Fortress, 1972), may be taken as representative of this approach to interpreting the Pastorals.

[2]*From Tradition to Gospel* (trans. from rev. 2nd. ed., B. L. Woolf; Cambridge: James Clarke and Co. Ltd., 1971) 238ff.

[3]The term "household" here designates the persons who live in a particular domicile. The question whether, when the Pastorals' author uses this term, he has a more specific conception in mind will be addressed in the course of the investigation.

PREVIOUS INVESTIGATION OF SOCIAL STATUS, SOCIAL STRUCTURE AND SOCIAL TENSIONS IN EARLY CHRISTIANITY

Social Status

During most of this century the common view among New Testament scholars has been that the early church drew its membership from the lower classes of the Roman Empire. This view was championed and developed by Adolf Deissmann, who directed attention to the significance of non-literary papyri, ostraca, etc., from the ancient world for study of the New Testament. Deissmann argued that the language of archeological remains which preserved information about the lives of common people in the Hellenistic-Roman period, closely paralleled the language of the New Testament. He thus drew on this material both to illumine the language of the New Testament and to describe the social circumstances of life in the early church.[4] This view of the social status of the early Christians is reflected in the work of such scholars as Ernst Troeltsch, A. D. Nock, and S. J. Case.[5] Recently, John Gager has reaffirmed this viewpoint, arguing that the church drew largely from the lower strata of urban society.[6]

Among the early dissenters from this near consensus were Ernst von Dobschütz and Ernst Lohmeyer. Von Dobschütz argued that the membership of the early church cut across a broad spectrum of social strata. He directed attention especially to 1 Corinthians, where he noted, for example, that differences of social position caused conflict in the common meal (11:20). Thus he observed, "Paul, it is true, speaks of 'not many wise after the flesh, not many mighty, not many noble.' We must distinguish, however, between 'not many' and 'not any.' "[7] Lohmeyer

---

[4]*Light from the Ancient East* (trans. L. R. M. Strachan; New York: Doran, 1927), especially pp. 9, 466.

[5]Troeltsch, *The Social Teaching of the Christian Churches* (trans. O. Wyon; London: George Allen and Unwin Ltd., 1931) 44; Nock, *Conversion* (London: Oxford U. Press, 1933) 187-211; Case, *The Social Origins of Christianity* (Chicago: U. of Chicago Press, 1923).

[6]"Religion and Social Class in the Early Roman Empire," in S. Benko and J. J. O'Rourke, *The Catacombs and the Colosseum* (Valley Forge: Judson Press, 1971) 99, 112-13. See also *Kingdom and Community* (Englewood Cliffs, NJ: Prentice-Hall, 1975), Chapter 4.

[7]Von Dobschütz, *Christian Life in the Primitive Church* (trans. G. Bremmer; ed. W. D. Morrison; New York: G. P. Putnam's Sons, 1904), especially pp. 14, 57, 61.

contended that the church originally drew on the same classes as Pharisaic Judaism: skilled craftsmen and professional people. This fact accounted in large measure for the hostility between the two movements. In addition, the church's membership included at least a small percentage from the upper classes, especially women. This basic social pattern held true for the whole period of the early church from its beginnings to the time of Hermas.[8]

In recent years a reassessment of the question of social class in early Christianity has been in progress. E. A. Judge reopened the discussion in *The Social Pattern of Christian Groups in the First Century*.[9] Judge maintains that the leadership of the Hellenistic churches came from "a socially pretentious section of the population of the big cities." The remaining membership was comprised largely of the household dependents of this leadership. Even these dependents are not to be identified with the lowest classes of society, which were to be found on the land. Thus Judge characterizes early Christianity as essentially a movement of the "owner and patron class," "who sponsored Christianity to their dependents."[10]

Gerd Theissen has arrived at similar conclusions with regard to the social spectrum present in the Pauline churches in his study of the Corinthian community, although he does not find the church to be constituted

---

[8]Lohmeyer, *Soziale Fragen im Urchristentum* (Darmstadt: Wissenschaftliche Buchgesellschaft, 1973, reprint of Leipzig, 1921 ed.) especially pp. 54, 87, 112. The interest of Luke in socially prominent converts has been noted by many, e.g., H. J. Cadbury, *The Book of Acts in History* (London: A. and C. Black, 1955) 43. However, this interest has not always been taken as evidence for the presence of a significant upper class element in the early church. Thus E. Plümacher finds this feature of Luke's presentation to be part of a more general tendency of Luke to depict the early Christian movement as one of significance and substance according to the standards of the Hellenistic-Roman world. Luke's point is expressed most succinctly in Acts 26:26: οὐ γάρ ἐστιν ἐν γωνίᾳ πεπραγμένον τοῦτο. Plümacher concludes, on the basis of sociolinguistic considerations, that neither Luke himself nor his intended readers actually come from the upper classes, but from the middle and lower classes, the real constituency of early Christianity. (See pp. 25, 30-31).

[9](London: Tyndale Press, 1960).

[10]Ibid., 59-60. Cf. Judge, "The Early Christians as a Scholastic Community," Part II. *JRelS* 1 (1960-61) 125-37, and "St. Paul and Classical Society," *JAC* 15 (1972) 19-36.

to such a great extent by patrons and their dependents. Theissen takes into account a variety of indicators of social status: mention of members of the community who have held offices in the larger society, mention of householders and thus households, mention of members who have given service to (= sponsored) Paul or the church, and mention of members who travel, an undertaking requiring money. Theissen finds that the majority of Corinthians whose names are mentioned in Paul's letters or in Acts are identifiable as belonging to the upper social strata.[11] He concludes from this, not that most of the membership comes from these strata, but that Paul addresses himself primarily to that element of the membership that belongs to the upper strata, the element from which the leadership of the congregation comes. Thus, in Theissen's view, the early church, as represented by the Corinthian community, consisted of members drawn from the highest to the lowest levels of urban provincial society.[12]

Part of the difference between this description and that of Gager, for example, is semantic. According to the Roman ranking system, Christians did not belong to the upper classes, namely, the senatorial and equestrian classes, nor is it likely that very many Christians belonged to the decurionates of provincial cities. However, these groups made up only a tiny minority of the provincial population. (See below, chapter II, pp. 47ff.) Thus Judge and Theissen turn their attention to the actual social strata present in provincial cities. A. Malherbe ventures to suggest the emergence of a new consensus on this subject: that early Christianity was indeed a movement that embraced people from a broad spectrum of social strata, including people from the upper strata of urban provincial society, and that, characteristically, the leadership of the churches came from these upper strata.[13]

---

[11]"Soziale Schichtung in der korinthischen Gemeinde," *ZNW* 65 (1974) 232-74.

[12]The presence of wide difference in social strata was, according to Theissen, not without its consequences for the social coherence of the community: "Das hellenistische Urchristentum ist weder eine proletarische Bewegung unterer Schichten gewesen, noch eine Angelegenheit gehobener Schichten. Charaktaristisch für seine soziale Struktur ist vielmehr, dass er verschieden Schichten umfasste--und damit verschiedene Interessen, Gewohnheiten, Selbstverständlichkeiten." ("Soziale Schichtung," 268.) See below, pp. 11ff. for a discussion of Theissen's interest in social conflict and tension.

[13]*Social Aspects of Early Christianity* (Baton Rouge: Louisiana State University Press, 1977) 31. Cf. H. Kreissig, "Zur soziale Zusammen-

Social Structure

A variety of institutions in Hellenistic-Roman society have been suggested as models for the social structure of the church. History of religions research in the late 19th and 20th centuries explored the possibilities of viewing the early church on the model of the mystery religions and the various types of associations. The former approach, which directed attention to the cultic and especially the sacramental aspects of the church, is represented by Wilhelm Bousset in *Kyrios Christos.*[14] The latter approach was taken by Edwin Hatch, who built on the work of G. F. C. Heinrici.[15]

In *The Organization of the Early Christian Churches,* Hatch described the church as a Christian association.[16] Like the church, pagan associations commonly possessed a more or less pronounced religious element and practiced regular common meals. Membership involved contributions to a general fund and members came from a variety of social categories: slave and free, men and women, aliens and citizens. What distinguished Christian associations, in Hatch's view, was the central place of charity in the church. While charity was practiced in other associations, it was of the essence of the church. Hatch's greatest interest, however, was not in the overall social structure of the church, but in the development of church office, especially the nature and relationship of the offices of bishop, deacon, and elder.[17]

---

setzung der fruhchristlicher Gemeinden im ersten Jahrhundert u. Z.," *Eirene* 6 (1967) 91-100, locates Christianity among urban artisans and tradespeople. W. Wuellner, "The Sociological Implications of I Cor. 1:26-28 Reconsidered," *Studia Evangelica* IV, Vol. 112 TU (Berlin, 1973) 666-72, argues that the actual meaning is "Are not many of you wise . . . ?"

[14]W. Bousset, *Kyrios Christos* (trans. J. F. Steely; Nashville: Abingdon, 1970).

[15]For the work of Heinrici, see references in Malherbe, *Social Aspects,* 87, n. 56.

[16]2d ed. revised (London: Rivingston, 1882).

[17]Hatch found the antecedents of these offices in the pagan associations and, in the case of elders, in the Jewish synagogue. He argued that the elders had their parallel in the governing councils of both pagan associations and the synagogue. The function of these councils was primarily judicial. The office of bishop, on the other hand, was one concerned with finance. Given the importance of charity in the Christian associations, this function, and with it the office, became increasingly

E. A. Judge argues in "The Early Christians as a Scholastic Community" that, according to the social categories of the Hellenistic-Roman world, Paul was a sophist, a travelling preacher sponsored by a variety of patrons, who are mentioned in his letters. The churches which he founded, therefore, belong to the social category of philosophical societies which formed in urban areas across the empire to receive instruction from travelling teachers. Thus the churches were concerned primarily with philosophy and ethics and not the cult.[18]

Robert L. Wilken, focusing on early pagan characterization of Christianity and the response of the Apologists, finds that the church was understood at times as a philosophical school, and at other times as an association by both Christians and pagans. The characterization as a philosophical school called attention to the religious ideas of the whole church. The characterization as an association called attention to the social and organizational structure of the local congregations. It can be seen that Wilken's description combines elements from the descriptions of Hatch and Judge.[19]

R. M. Grant, in *Early Christianity and Society*,[20] represents a slightly different approach, in which the social and political structure of the church is viewed against the background of the prevailing political model of the age, namely, monarchy. Grant pays particular attention to Paul's use of the metaphor of the body, a metaphor for a hierarchically ordered society which was often employed in explication of the political theory of monarchy. The political model for church structure is important in connection with the focus of the present study, namely, the significance of the household for the social structure of the church, because in

---

important. It was this aspect of Hatch's work that Harnack carried forward in his study of early church order. See the summary of Olof Linton, *Das Problem der Urkirche in den neueren Forschung* (Uppsala, 1932) 31ff. This line of research has been continued in such studies as H. von Campenhausen, *Ecclesiastical Office and Spiritual Power in the Church of the First Three Centuries* and E. Schweizer, *Church Order in the New Testament*, SBT 31 (1961).

[18]Op. cit., above p. 4, n. 9. Judge's emphasis here thus represents a rejection of the position of Bousset.

[19]"Collegia, Philosophical Schools and Theology," in *The Catacombs and the Colosseum*, 268-91. The type of association bearing closest resemblance to the church, Wilken finds, was the burial society.

[20](New York: Harper and Row, 1977) 36ff.

Greco-Roman political thought the structures of household and πολιτεία were closely related.[21]

In a brief article written in 1939 Floyd Filson emphasized the importance of the household for the social structure of the early church by directing attention to the fact that the early congregations consisted of one or more house churches. Filson noted that the organization of congregations in house churches shed light on such matters as social status of early Christians, church polity, and social tensions in the churches.[22] Similarly, Otto Michel, in his article on οἶκος in *TDNT* emphasized the importance of the household in the structure of early Christian communities. In addition, Michel traced the use of "house" as an early Christian image of community and its antecedents in Judaism.[23]

As noted in the discussion above, the importance of the household for the social structure of the church was a key point in Judge's description of early Christian groups. For Judge, the church of the first century consisted primarily of households of persons from the owner and patron class, households which included family members, slaves, and other dependents. The household was so prominent in the structure of the church, not only for this reason, but also because "the entrenched rights of the household as a religious and social unit offered the Christians the best possible security for their existence as a group."[24]

A. Strobel disputed this view of the early Christian household, arguing that the concept of the οἶκος (also οἰκία) in Greek paralleled that of *domus* in Latin, which designated a group of persons related by blood. By contrast, the Latin *familia* referred to a household that included slaves and real property. Thus the οἶκος of, for example, Cornelius (Acts 10:2; 11:14) would be, not the household of Cornelius in the sense in which Judge uses the term, but the kinspeople of Cornelius.[25] The inference is that kinship groups were more significant for the social structure of the early church than households. Strobel's findings have been called into question, however, by Theissen, who contends that, although Roman law does appear to distinguish between *domus* and

---

[21]See below, pp. 20ff., for discussion of the research of David Balch on this question.

[22]Filson, "The Significance of the Early House Churches," *JBL* 58 (1939) 109-12. See also the summary given by Malherbe, *Social Aspects*, 61.

[23]Michel, "οἶκος," *TDNT* V, especially sections 6-9.

[24]*Social Pattern*, 75.

[25]"Der Begriff des 'Hauses' im griechischen und römischen Privatrecht," *ZNW* 56 (1965) 91-100. Strobel is addressing the problem of infant baptism, not that of social structure and social class per se.

familia, Greek knows no such distinction. Theissen notes that at least on some occasions Greek distinguished a household that included slaves from one that did not by designating the former as a whole household or a complete household.[26] Thus it is likely that reference in the New Testament to baptism of whole οἶκοι (e.g., Acts 18:8) refers to households that included servants. In addition, references in 1 Timothy 3:4f. and 3:12 to wife, children, and household indicate that here οἶκος refers specifically to household servants. In such instances οἶκος appears to be at least roughly equivalent to *familia*. Theissen cites numerous instances in the New Testament in which the context reveals the high social status of persons identified as having households. Thus he surmises that even where such a context is missing, the designation of someone as a householder is a probable indicator of high social status.[27] The implication for the social structure of the church is that it was the upper class household as described by Judge which was significant for this structure, not the extended kinship group, and not the lower class family, which may not have been designated as a household at all in the literature of early Christianity.

Finally, Malherbe, while agreeing with this picture on the whole, suggests that further light can be shed on the social structure of the early church by investigation of the relationship between associations and household communities in Roman society. Thus it may be that the house church can be understood on the model of household associations.[28] It appears that study of the household in early Christianity has the potential for clarifying those aspects of the church's social structure that have been seen as analogous to those of other social institutions in Hellenistic-Roman society.

Social Tensions

Interest in social tensions in the early church has been provoked by various passages in the New Testament and the contemporary extra-canonical Christian literature. Thus tension between rich and poor is suggested, for example, in James and in the Beatitudes. Karl Kautsky, in

[26]E.g., Aristotle, *Pol.* 1253b, οἰκία δὲ τέλειος ἐκ δούλων καὶ ἐλευθέρων.

[27]"Soziale Schichtung," 246-49. See also H. Gülzow, *Christentum und Sklaverei in den ersten drei Jahrhunderten* (Bonn: Rudolf Habelt Verlag, 1969) 28, 51, 101ff.

[28]*Social Aspects*, 90-91.

Foundations of Christianity, argues that this tension was a basic ingredient in the transformation of the church from a revolutionary proletarian movement to a conservative institution which was supportive of the values of the established social order.[29] More recently, Martin Hengel has given careful treatment to the ethical compromise which was reached.[30] Tension between different types of leadership in the church, usually seen as the difference between charismatic and institutionalized leadership, is found, for example, in the Didache. This question has attracted the interest of scholars studying early church order.[31] Furthermore, passages such as 1 Cor 7:17-24, 1 Cor 11:1-16 and the various *Haustafeln* have raised the question whether there was an impulse for social liberation among Christian women and slaves that met with resistance from other elements in the church. Scholarship has been divided on whether or not the passages in question really indicate social tension of this type.[32]

In addition, it has occasionally been suggested that conflicts and tensions in the church which are less obviously social in nature actually have their basis in social conflicts and tensions. Thus S. J. Case wrote, in the *Social Origins of Christianity*, "Heresy was fundamentally a social phenomenon rather than an intellectual problem. Differences of opinion, that were always present even in the most peaceful community, never resulted in heresies until rival social attitudes crystallized around specific centers of interest and thus gave real vitality to the opinions in

---

[29]Kautsky, *Foundations of Christianity*, (authorized trans. from the 13th ed.; New York: International Publishers Co., 1925).

[30]Hengel, *Property and Riches in the Early Church* (trans. J. Bowden; Philadelphia: Fortress Press, 1974). Hengel's study takes him into the third century.

[31]See Did. 11-15 and above, p. 5, n. 11.

[32]This question will be addressed more fully below. Among scholars who recently denied or minimized such tensions are S. S. Bartchy, *Mallon Chrēsai* (Missoula, MT: University of Montana Press, 1973) and David Balch, *"Let Wives Be Submissive . . . ." The Origin, Form and Apologetic Function of the Household Duty Code (Haustafel) in I Peter* (Ph.D. dissertation, Yale, 1974). Defending the contrasting position is James E. Crouch, *The Origin and Intention of the Colossian Haustafel* (Göttingen: Vandenhoeck & Ruprecht, 1972).

question."[33] Unfortunately, Case did not follow up this observation with detailed investigation.

Despite the interest that New Testament scholarship has from time to time shown in the study of social tensions in the early church, there has been little interest in grounding this study in sociological theory. The type of sociological theory most clearly applicable to such study is conflict theory.

Karl Marx was the first social theorist among the forerunners of modern sociology to emphasize the importance of social conflict in social systems.[34] In the Marxist tradition this emphasis was continued as one of central importance. However, until recently, most sociologists and social historians outside of this tradition have tended to neglect social conflict. Biblical scholarship of the late 19th and early 20th centuries proved no exception to this pattern. Thus the most prominent analysis during this period of social conflict as a force within early Christianity came from the Marxist Karl Kautsky, who had no credentials as a biblical scholar.[35]

Recently, however, conflict theory has been applied to the study of social tension and social conflict in the early church by Gerd Theissen. Theissen explicated the theoretical basis of his work in the sociology of early Christianity in an article written in 1974.[36] According to the categorization of J. H. Turner, Theissen's theoretical perspective can be classified as that of conflict functionalism. Theissen is convinced of the heuristic value of seeking the function or functions of particular phenomena for the social whole within which such phenomena exist.[37] At the

---

[33](Chicago: University of Chicago Press, 1973) 199. Cf. A. H. M. Jones, *Were Ancient Heresies Disguised Social Movements?* (Philadelphia: Fortress Press, 1966). Focusing on heresies of the late Roman period, Jones counsels caution in viewing these heresies as disguised social movements.

[34]J. H. Turner, *The Structure of Sociological Theory* (Homewood, IL: The Dorsey Press, 1974) 78ff.

[35]*Foundations of Christianity,* op. cit.

[36]"Theoretische Probleme religionssoziologischer Forschung und die Analyse des Urchristentums," *Neue Zeitschrift für systematische Theologie und Religionsphilosophie* 16 (1974) 35-56.

[37]He hopes to avoid making an assumption for which functionalism has often been attacked, namely that the mere existence of a social phenomenon indicates its functionality for the social whole: Nicht dass alles functional ist, wird a priori behauptet, sondern dass es sinnvol ist, nach Functionalität zu fragen und dabei gegebenfalls auch Dysfunctionalität zu entdecken." (p. 40).

same time, he views social conflict and social tension (*Spannung*) as basic ingredients of social life. Thus, in describing the basic tasks of social life, he finds that the integrative functions, those which enable systems to cohere and persist, presuppose conflicts and tensions which require management. Furthermore, conflict and tension are of the essence of the antagonistic functions, which provide social systems with a means of bringing about needed changes.[38]

From this theoretical perspective, Theissen is especially sensitive to the presence of social tensions in the early church. Thus he finds in the conflict between the strong and the weak in Corinth a conflict of interests and perspectives between members of the church from the upper and lower social strata of the city.[39] The same social division underlay the problems which the Corinthians were having in connection with the Lord's Supper. Well-to-do members probably supplied the food for the common meals, and, in accordance with common practice in the feasts given by the associations, probably also provided themselves with more and better food than they provided the poorer members. This practice humiliated the poorer members and denied any sense of unity and fellowship in the church.[40]

The details of Theissen's sociological interpretation are not the focus of interest here. What is of particular interest is that he has applied sociological theory to the analysis of texts in the New Testament with results which on the whole succeed in bringing to light social tensions in the community to which these texts are related. In addition, he illuminates the social strata and social structure of the church in the process. Thus this theoretical perspective promises to be especially useful in the present study.

Implications for Pastorals Research

The Pastoral Epistles constitute a particularly appropriate focus for further study of social status, social structure, and social tensions in the

---

[38]Pp. 44-53. Theissen draws especially on the work of Ralf Dahrendorf for his analysis of conflict and tension in society. For a summary of Dahrendorf's theory, see Turner, chapter 6.

[39]"Soziale Schichtung," and "Die Starken und Schwachen in Korinth: Soziologische Analyse eines theologischen Streites," *ET* 35 (1975) 155-72.

[40]"Soziale Integration und sakramentale Handeln: Eine Analyse von I Kor. 11:17-23," *NovT* 16 (1974) 179-206. For a summary, see Malherbe, *Social Aspects*, 71ff.

early church. The Pastorals have been described as representative of an emerging "middle class" Christianity.[41] Given the revision which is taking place in the picture of social strata in the original Pauline churches, this reading of the Pastorals bears reexamination.[42] The prominence of the image of the household of God, together with the generally pronounced interest in household matters in the Pastorals suggests that further insight into the significance of the household for the social structure of the early church can be gained from this material.[43] Furthermore, much of the material in question is presented according to the *Haustafel* schema and it is precisely such material which has provoked debate about the presence and nature of social conflict and social tension in the early church.[44]

However, as it was noted at the outset, methodological difficulties arising from the nature of the material to be studied, stand in the way of a straightforward reading of the text for information on the social conditions in the church of the Pastorals. These difficulties have come to light in the history of interpretation of the Pastorals and in the history of the investigation of the *Haustafeln,* among which 1 Tim 2:1-6:1 and Titus 2:1-10 have been classed.

PREVIOUS STUDY OF THE PASTORALS AND OF THE *HAUSTAFELN*

1 Timothy 3:14 and Pastorals Research

The central literary question which must be addressed in order to analyze the Pastorals in the manner proposed above is this: has the image of the household of God in 1 Tim 3:14 shaped the author's conception of the social structure of the church as this social structure is presented in the Pastorals, especially in the *Haustafel*-like material of 1 Tim 2:1-6:1? 1 Tim 3:14-15 presents itself as a statement of the author's purpose: "I am writing these things to you . . . in order that you may know how to

---

[41]E.g., A. T. Hanson, *The Pastoral Letters* (Cambridge: Cambridge University Press, 1966) 2.

[42]In addition, a variety of scholars in recent years have contributed to the clarification of class structure in Roman provincial cities. The work of Judge, R. MacMullen, and G. Alföldy will be considered below.

[43]See p. 25 below.

[44]See above, p. 10, n. 31, and below pp. 20ff.

behave in the household of God. . . ." However, there is no unanimity among interpreters on the question of whether or not this passage should be regarded as a statement of purpose for 1 Timothy or the Pastorals as a group. Furthermore, those who take this passage as such a statement are divided as to the significance of the image of the οἶκος θεοῦ in it.

W. Lock considers 3:14-16 to be "the heart of the Epistle," and 3:15 as a statement, not only of the letter's purpose, but also of that of the Pastorals taken together.[45] This purpose is "to build up a high standard of Christian character and intercourse in the church as the family of God."[46] Accordingly, Lock understands the organization and ministry of the church to be that of "God's family."[47]

C. Spicq finds that 3:14-16 is the hinge between the two major sections of 1 Timothy and that 3:15 states the overriding purpose of the Pastorals.[48] Yet he does not attach as much importance to the image of the church as a household as does Lock. Noting that οἶκος can refer either to the physical structure or to the social entity, he concludes that the reference in 3:15 actually involves both notions: the "house of God" is conceptualized both as a building, a sanctuary (as in 1 Cor 3:16, 6:19, Eph 2:22, and Heb 3:2, 5) and as a family-like community (as in 1 Tim 3:4-5:12; 2 Tim 1:15; and Titus 1:11). For Spicq, however, the second image of the church in 3:15 proves to be the dominant one: the "pillar and bulwark of the truth." This latter image, combined with that of the church as the sanctuary or abode of God, suggests that for the author of the Pastorals, the church is, above all else, the bastion of orthodoxy, the defender of the true religion. The purpose of the Pastorals as expressed here is thus to "fight the good fight of the faith," to stand firm against all forms of eclecticism in the syncretistic atmosphere of urban Hellenistic-Roman society.[49]

---

[45] *A Critical and Exegetical Commentary on the Pastoral Epistles* (Edinburgh: T. & T. Clark, 1924) iii.

[46] Ibid., xiii.

[47] Ibid., xviii. Cf. E. Schweizer, *Church Order*, section 6b and J. Chrn. Beker, "The Pastoral Letters," *IDB* III, 674.

[48] *Les Épîtres pastorales* (4th ed., rev.; Paris: J. Gabalda, 1969) 32.

[49] Ibid., 464-66. Cf. C. K. Barrett, *The Pastoral Epistles in the New English Bible with Introduction and Commentary* (Oxford: Clarendon Press, 1963), and R. J. Karris, *The Function and Sitz im Leben of the Paraenetic Elements in the Pastoral Epistles* (Unpublished Harvard Th.D. dissertation, Harvard, 1971) 122-23.

Of course it is possible to proceed on the basis that both the image of the household and that of the pillar and bulwark play important roles in the Pastorals. This is in fact Spicq's approach. However, a question is thereby raised concerning the clarity and unity of the author's purpose, a question that is posed sharply indeed by interpreters who have placed more emphasis on the presence of traditional material in the Pastorals than either Spicq or Lock.

In the view of Dibelius/Conzelmann, the Pastorals' author is a collector of church traditions with no coherent scheme of his own.[50] Thus 3:14-15 cannot possibly reveal such a scheme. The images of the household of God and the pillar and bulwark of the truth are firmly rooted in the tradition and familiar to both author and church. He invokes them simply to emphasize the greatness of the church and its role as defender of the truth, the kernel of which is given in the creedal formulation in 3:16.[51]

H. W. Bartsch, who accepts the Dibelius/Conzelmann view of the Pastorals' author as essentially a collector, nevertheless argues that a pre-pastorals church order stands behind 1 Timothy and Titus, as the basic source from which their church order sections derive.[52] This source contained (1) rules concerning worship, (2) rules concerning church office, and (3) rules resembling the *Haustafeln* of Colossians, Ephesians, etc.[53] This source is sufficiently unified in perspective that Bartsch can identify the understanding of existence inherent in it as identical with that of the earliest church. This understanding of existence is marked above all else by eschatological expectation that makes the proclamation of the gospel to the world the principal and urgent task of the church. He identifies 3:14-15 as the heading or title of this hypothesized church order, arguing that this title expresses the notion that a properly ordered community leads to properly ordered worship, through which God is glorified and the gospel proclaimed. Thus Bartsch finds a coherent point of view and purpose, if not in the Pastorals themselves, at least in the main source which, he believes, lies behind 1 Timothy and Titus.[54]

R. J. Karris has carried this type of investigation further by attempting to discover a plan and purpose in the Pastorals, while at the

---

[50] Dibelius/Conzelmann, *The Pastoral Epistles*, 5-6.

[51] Ibid., 60-61.

[52] H. W. Bartsch, *Die Anfänge urchristlicher Rechtsbildungen* (Hamburg: Herbert Reich Evangelischer Verlag, 1965).

[53] Ibid., 160.

[54] Ibid., 162ff.

same time taking full account of the preponderance of traditional material which they contain.[55] He accepts the dictum of Dibelius that early Christian paraenesis is formulated, not in response to particular situations, but in response to the situation of the early church in general. Yet he also maintains that individual authors must have used paraenetic tradition for specific purposes and that the way in which they use such tradition will reveal these purposes.[56] He considers the paraenesis of the Pastorals under the major headings of (1) their vice and virtue lists, and (2) their *Haustafel* and *Gemeindeordnung*. He finds that the key to the author's purpose lies in the fact that he has juxtaposed and interwoven polemic against false teachers with traditional vice and virtue lists, and church order and *Haustafel* traditions.[57] Through his analysis, he comes to the conclusion that the author belongs in a milieu in which the truth of one's teaching is confirmed or denied by one's conduct. The author's intention, therefore, is to assert the truth of Christian teaching as he understands it against all other religious teaching and to exhort his addressees to witness to the truth of the Christian faith by exemplary conduct.[58]

Karris conscientiously resists the temptation to read too much about the situation of the Pastorals out of the paraenetic tradition which they contain, because of his understanding of early Christian paraenesis as a response to general rather than specific conditions of the church. One wonders, however, whether this understanding of paraenesis has not unduly restricted Karris' inquiry to generalities.

The Haustafeln *in Previous Research*

Karris's treatment of the *Haustafel* tradition is of particular interest for the topic under discussion here. He is indebted for his understanding of this material to Karl Weidinger, with whose study of the *Haustafeln* scholarly discussion is still obliged to deal today.[59] Weidinger, a student of Dibelius, argued that the New Testament *Haustafeln* are superficially Christianized versions of Stoic duty lists, which in turn give expression to

---

[55] *Function*. See also Karris, "The Background and Significance of the Polemic of the Pastoral Epistles," *JBL* 92 (1973) 549-64.

[56] *Function*, ix.

[57] Ibid., 83.

[58] Ibid., 123-24.

[59] See *Function*, 85ff.

a traditional code of unwritten laws stemming from ancient Greece.[60] This traditional code undergoes no real development wherever it appears in pagan and Jewish literature throughout the Greco-Roman era. Its use by early Christian writers represents, purely and simply, the adoption by the church of the time honored common social ethic of Greco-Roman society.[61]

The duties of the code as it is found in Hellenistic writers fall under the following categories: duties to gods, to country, to parents, to brothers and sisters, to wives and children, and to relatives.[62] With minor alterations the same schema is found in the Christian *Haustafeln*, for example, those in Col 3:18-4:1 and 1 Pet 2:13-3:7. Interestingly enough, Weidinger finds that the schema, although still recognizable in the later Christian *Haustafeln*, undergoes increasing "Christianization."[63] In other words, it undergoes development in accordance with particular conditions and concerns in the church. This development takes place chiefly through the addition of Christian motivations. Thus at first, ἐν κυρίῳ is added to the motivations to stress the importance of understanding the enjoined behavior as part of the total context of life in the Christian community. Later, more elaborate motivations are added. For Weidinger, however, these developments do not represent fundamental changes in the *Haustafel* schema, and in fact, are explainable by a trend in the overall development of Christian letter writing in which paraenetic tradition and ad hoc preaching were increasingly blended together. The *Haustafeln* of 1 Peter and 1 Timothy represent the schema in its most developed form.[64]

Dibelius/Conzelmann, Bartsch, and Karris separate out the *Haustafel* and church order material in the Pastorals, so that, according to Dibelius/Conzelmann, the actual household rules of the Pastorals are found in 1 Tim 2:8, men and women; 5:1-2, Timothy and various groups; 5:5f., widows; 6:1f., slaves; Titus 2:1-6, older men and women, younger men and women; 2:7f., Timothy; and 2:9f., slaves. These rules have been interspersed with church order rules according to no clear arrangement. No essential departure from the earlier *Haustafel* schema is found.[65]

---

[60]K. Weidinger, *Die Haustafeln: Ein Stück urchristlicher Paränese* (UNT 14; Leipzig, 1928).

[61]Ibid., 50ff.

[62]Ibid., 41.

[63]Ibid., 74ff.

[64]Ibid.

[65]Dibelius/Conzelmann, 6.

Thus Karris, who assumes the same classification of material, finds no special significance in the household rules of the Pastorals, but understands them as forming a segment of the general standard of behavior to which the Pastorals' author calls the church, a standard commonly accepted in the Hellenistic-Roman world.[66]

This understanding of the *Haustafel* tradition has been challenged by James E. Crouch.[67] Crouch accepts Weidinger's contention that the *Haustafel* tradition is rooted in the popular ethic of the Greco-Roman world, the unwritten laws (ἄγραφοι νόμοι), which are reflected in the Stoic duty lists. Thus he rejects the notion that this tradition originated in Pharisaic Judaism (E. Lohmeyer), on the one hand, as well as the contention that it is the specific creation of the church (K. H. Rengstorf) or of Jesus himself (D. Schroeder), on the other hand. Yet at the same time he argues against Weidinger and Dibelius that there is significant multi-staged development from the Greek unwritten laws to the Christian *Haustafeln*, and that indeed development can be discerned even among the latter.[68]

With A. Juncker,[69] Crouch observes that there is a substantial formal and conceptual difference between the Hellenistic and Christian codes: While the former deal with the individual's duty toward various classifications of people, the latter deal with the duties of different groups of people (above all, wives, children, and slaves) toward other groups (especially husbands, parents, and masters). The Hellenistic codes thus visualize the individual in his various relationships; the Christian codes, by contrast, envision social relationships within a community of persons of varying social status.[70]

Furthermore, Crouch argues that the tradition did not pass immediately from the Hellenistic world into the church, but was mediated to it through Hellenistic Judaism.[71] In Hellenistic Jewish propaganda, the unwritten laws, in the form of the Stoic schema, were incorporated into

---

[66]Karris, *Function*, 103-4, 113-15, 121-24.

[67]Op. cit., 15, n. 32.

[68]Crouch, 19-27. See also K. H. Rengstorf, "Die NT Mahnungen dem Manne unterzuordnen," in W. Foerster, ed., *Verbum Dei Manet in Aeternum. Festschrift für Otto Schmitz* (Wittenberg: Luther Verlag, 1955) 131-45. Rengstorf also pays attention to inner-Christian *Haustafel* development.

[69]*Die Ethik des Apostels Paulus*, Vol II (Halle: Verlag von Max Niemeyer, 1919) 206-7.

[70]Crouch, 19-20.

[71]Ibid., 102-7.

expositions of the Mosaic Law. In the process the unwritten laws began to take on certain Oriental-Jewish characteristics, notably, the characteristic of reciprocity.[72] Reciprocity is seen, for example, where the duty of a father toward his children is given alongside the duty of children toward their father. Crouch also notes, following Lohmeyer, that the most prominent groups in the New Testament *Haustafeln* (slaves, women, and children) are often lumped together in Jewish literature on the basis of their common inferior status in Judaism. Here, however, the purpose is to exempt these inferior classes of people from some of the legal requirements placed upon men, rather than to specify their social obligations.[73]

Both the reciprocity of the Hellenistic Jewish lists of social duties and the characteristic Jewish lumping together of wives, children, and slaves are carried over into the Christian *Haustafel* tradition. Yet at the same time, Crouch maintains, the Christian *Haustafel* as exemplified by Colossians 3:18ff. is a form unparalleled in either Jewish or Hellenistic literature, in that it displays the above mentioned characteristic elements together in one discrete unit in which the various groupings of people are directly addressed and exhorted.[74] Furthermore, it is a special characteristic of the Christian *Haustafel* that the duties of the subordinate member of each pair are stressed.[75] It is therefore possible for Crouch to speak of the specific origin, situation, and intention of the Christian *Haustafel* form as found especially in Colossians, and to seek to derive these factors directly from the form and content of the *Haustafeln* themselves.

On this basis he rejects the idea that the *Haustafeln* represent the accommodation of the church to the world as the result of waning eschatological expectation (Dibelius/Conzelmann), as well as the notion that they are a natural reflection of the central importance of the household in the early church (Rengstorf).[76] In fact, Crouch disputes that the *Haustafeln* are primarily concerned with the household at all. Instead, he argues, they are a conservative response to a brand of Christian enthusiasm, widely current in the earliest church, that defied established social conventions, especially in the cases of wives and slaves.[77]

---

[72]Ibid., 102.

[73]Ibid., 103-5.

[74]Ibid., 120.

[75]Ibid., 121.

[76]Ibid., 120, 103f.

[77]Ibid., 9, 19-22, 122ff. Thus he views them as a response to social tension in the church.

Crouch's findings, in turn, have been criticized, and, in some important respects, convincingly rejected by David Balch.[78] While Balch does not dispute Crouch's argument that the Christian *Haustafeln* are significantly different in form from the Stoic duty lists, he proposes another pagan antecedent for the *Haustafeln* that much more closely parallels the *Haustafel* form, namely, the topos on household management.[79] This traditional topos, which consistently treats husband-wife, parent-child, and master-slave relationships, is found as early as the writings of Plato and Aristotle, as a part of the larger traditional topos on the πολιτεία, and continues to appear in this literary context as late as the 4th century A.D. The topos on household management thus was regularly included in discussions of the political and social structure of society as a whole. Its inclusion in such discussions is illuminated by the fact that for most of the authors cited by Balch,[80] the household is understood to be the foundation of the πολιτεία, and, therefore, proper management of the household is a matter of fundamental political and social significance.

Balch shows that the topos on household management appeared not only in treatises on political philosophy, but also in the writings of popular rhetors such as Dio Chrysostom.[81] Therefore, this topos was probably widely declaimed and widely known in the Hellenistic-Roman world, so that it would have been easily available for use in the early church. The effect of Balch's research is thus to negate Crouch's basis account of the course by which the Christian *Haustafel* schema developed.

Balch, nevertheless, is unwilling to view the *Haustafeln*, and in particular the *Haustafel* in 1 Peter, as simply general moral exhortation that plays no specific role in the early Christian communities. He finds that the topos on household management was commonly employed for one of two purposes. On the one hand, spokespersons of the political establishment used this topos in propaganda intended to encourage good citizenship. On the other hand, the topos on household management was employed apologetically by various groups, especially religious groups, which were suspected of undermining the established political order. Evidently, foreign religions such as the cult of Isis and Judaism were commonly accused of subverting the πολιτεία by deviating from the

---

[78] Op. cit., 15, n. 32.
[79] Ibid. See especially pp. 49ff.
[80] E.g., Aristotle, Arius Didymus, Dionysius of Halicarnassus.
[81] Ibid., 47.

prevailing patterns of household management. Josephus thus uses this topos to defend the Jewish πολιτεία as fundamentally the same as that of the Romans.[82]

Balch concludes that the *Haustafel* in 1 Peter speaks to the same problem which Josephus encountered: the church is being falsely accused of promoting deviant behavior in households. Thus the function of the *Haustafel* is apologetic. Christians are being exhorted to exemplary behavior in order to refute the slanders of their antagonists in the larger society.[83] Thus Balch disputes Crouch's contention that the *Haustafeln* reflect the presence of social tensions within the churches. The real problem in his view is not Christian behavior, but pagan perceptions.

Among the consequences of Balch's findings for the understanding of the *Haustafeln* presented by Crouch are the following: (1) Crouch contends that the conception in the Christian *Haustafeln* of a community of people in relationship to one another is a Jewish and Christian emphasis, but not an emphasis in the pagan antecedents of the *Haustafeln*. Balch has shown that this conception is indeed emphasized in the pagan antecedents of the *Haustafeln*, not, to be sure, in the Stoic duty lists, but in the traditional topos on household management. The effect of this observation is clearly to weaken the case for understanding the *Haustafel* schema as a peculiarly Christian development reflecting peculiar conditions in the church. (2) Crouch argues that the *Haustafeln* are not particularly concerned with relationships in the household, but Balch's identification of the topos on household management as the antecedent of the *Haustafeln* provides strong evidence that relationships in the household are at the center of their concern. Thus at this point Balch's research lends plausibility to the contention of the present study, that the *Haustafel*-like material in the Pastorals reflects a strong interest in the household, on the one hand, and on the church understood on the model of a household, on the other.

Certain aspects of Crouch's work, however, still stand. Crouch conducted his investigation on the principle that particular conditions in the church called forth the *Haustafeln* and that these conditions could be inferred from the form and content of the *Haustafeln* themselves. Balch, although he reaches different conclusions about the conditions which gave rise to the *Haustafeln*, works on the same principle. Furthermore, Crouch is actually more attentive to the details of the Christian *Haustafel* form

---

[82]Ibid., 132-38.

[83]Ibid., 206-8, 214.

and the implications for the conditions under which it came into being. His view of the *Haustafeln* takes into account that they are paraenesis addressed to insiders. Balch, of course, is aware of this fact, but he nevertheless posits an apologetic function for the *Haustafel* of 1 Peter. The apology is made, however, not directly by the *Haustafel* itself, but by the behavior of Christians who obey its exhortations. Thus Crouch's argument that the *Haustafeln* reveal actual social tensions in the church at least deserves not to be dismissed out of hand.

Finally, there is an important issue which has not been resolved by the work of Crouch and Balch. Crouch views the various Christian *Haustafeln* as artifacts of a traditional schema that was employed and developed in the church over a period of time. Thus, for Crouch as for Weidinger it makes sense to speak of development from earlier to later forms of the *Haustafel*. In the case of Ephesians there may even be direct literary dependence on an earlier form, namely, that of Colossians. Balch, by contrast, rejects the notion of a distinctive traditional Christian schema, arguing that the various *Haustafeln* are independent responses to a common problem in the early church, namely, suspicion of Christian subversion of household and state. Their similarity in form stems from the fact that they all employ the topos on household management to address this problem.[84]

These opposing viewpoints underline the fact that there is still little clarity on the way in which the *Haustafeln* were composed and/or transmitted and on how they functioned. Did the author of the Pastorals, for example, compose rather freely, limited, perhaps unconsciously, by the necessity of including certain key motifs that characterized the topos on household management? Or was he the transmitter of firmly fixed traditions, who felt at liberty to add only a word here or an interpretive comment there? Or did the type of constraints which operated upon him fall somewhere in between these alternatives? If understanding is to be gained of how the Pastorals' author has used the *Haustafel* schema/topos[85] to express his conception of the household of God, then

---

[84]Crouch, 12, 34-35; Balch, 266, 67. Balch, in rejecting the possibility of literary dependence among the *Haustafeln*, appears to misunderstand Crouch's position here. Crouch is not, with the exception of Colossians and Ephesians, speaking of literary dependence, but of the common use of a traditional schema which had antecedents outside the church, but which took on a distinctive form within the church.

[85]The fact that Crouch refers to the *Haustafel* "schema" while Balch refers to the household management "topos," may indicate differing notions about the role of tradition in the *Haustafeln*. The issue of in what

comprehension of the nature of the traditional constraints which limited and channeled his self-expression is essential.

The Problem of 1 Timothy 2:1-6:1

No one disputes that the *Haustafeln* of 1 Timothy and Titus are different in both form and content from that of, for example, Colossians. In fact the *Haustafel* of 1 Timothy is so different in form and content from that of other examples that there is no general agreement on what does and what does not belong to it. As noted above, Dibelius/Conzelmann and Karris assign some portions of 1 Tim 2:1-6:1 to the *Haustafel* category and other portions to the church order category. Weidinger, Campenhausen, Crouch, and Beker consider this material together as either a *Haustafel* that has been expanded by material dealing with church order, or a church order that has incorporated *Haustafel* material.[86]

Clearly the division of the traditions of 2:1-6:1 into church order and *Haustafel* categories is made on the basis of whether the setting in which the rules apply is the church or the household. Thus Dibelius/Conzelmann discerns in the latter the appearance of a "religious family tradition," which is concerned with the "structuring of life under the ideal of good Christian citizenship." This tradition exhibits a "family ethic" which goes beyond the traditional rules for the household as seen in earlier *Haustafeln*.[87]

Those who view the material in 2:1-6:1 together as an expanded *Haustafel* or a church order just as clearly do not regard the two-fold setting as indicative of any fundamental division in this material as it is presented by the author. Beker, offering a more refined version of Lock's position, contends that a pattern of church order derived from the "regulations for family life," that is, the *Haustafeln*, is to be seen here, so that, in the Pastorals, "the structure of the house of God is built upon that of the family (3:15)."[88] Thus, in this view, household and church are not conceived in the Pastorals as separate settings, but are seen together as the unified sphere of the Christian community.

---

sense the traditional framework of the *Haustafel* may be viewed as a "topos" and in what sense, a "schema" will be explored in chapter III.

[86]Weidinger, 66ff. Campenhausen, *Polykarp von Smyrna und die Pastoralbriefe* (Heidelberg: Carl Winter; Universitatsverlag, 1951) 32-33; Crouch, 12; Beker, *IDB* III, 674.

[87]Ibid., 40. This point appears to be a movement away from the position that the *Haustafeln* are basically unchanging.

[88]Beker, *IDB* III, 674.

Campenhausen has made the observation that in early Christian literature this particular configuration of material occurs only in the Pastorals, in Polycarp to the Philippians and, in rudimentary form, in Ignatius to Polycarp. He uses this evidence to support his contention that Polycarp authored the Pastorals.[89] Yet this formal correspondence might just as well indicate that the configuration common to Polycarp and the Pastorals reflects conditions which were general in the church, but general only during a limited period and perhaps only a limited geographical area.

Implications for the Present Study

Previous investigations of the Pastorals and of the *Haustafeln* have established certain points. Much of the material in the Pastorals that deals with social structure and social relations in the church is organized according to the *Haustafel* schema. In their form and content the *Haustafeln* reflect particular concerns in the early church. The various *Haustafeln* are not all identical in form and content, and thus may not all reflect exactly the same concerns. 1 Timothy 2:1-6:1 represents the furthest departure from the *Haustafel* form as found in Colossians; however, Pol. Phil. 4:1-6:1 corresponds rather closely to the form found in 1 Timothy. These last two examples may therefore reflect concerns peculiar to the church at a particular juncture in its history in a particular geographical area.

Two key areas of continuing unclarity have also been uncovered. There is no real consensus on whether the author of the Pastorals presents a coherent understanding of the church. Symptomatic of the unclarity here is the disagreement on the question of whether 1 Tim 3:14-15 really should be viewed as the author's statement of purpose and whether the image of the household of God that is given here actually interprets the surrounding material in 2:1-6:1. Corresponding to this unclarity is the unresolved debate over the question of whether and how the Christian

[89] *Polykarp,* 33. Actually Campenhausen stresses that there are three facets of the configuration: *Haustafel* material, church order material, and polemic. It is the latter in its relation to the other two upon which Karris has focused attention. Indicative of the lack of agreement among scholars on the significance of the form of this material is the fact that Crouch regards 2:1-6:1 as the dissolution of the *Haustafel* form, while Campenhausen considers this same passage as its culmination and full realization.

Haustafeln are to be understood as developments of a traditional schema. One cannot speak with confidence about the concepts of the household and of the household of God which the Pastorals present unless it can be shown that the materials which the author presents have been shaped, at least in part, by these concepts. In turn, in order to understand the process by which these materials would have been shaped by such concepts, it is necessary to have some clarity about what kind of traditional materials the author was using, for example, fixed traditions or traditional paraenetic topoi, and how he went about placing his own stamp on them.

THE PRESENT TASK

The investigation will proceed in several stages:

1. A survey of the household in the Hellenistic-Roman period, focused on the structure and characteristics of Greek and Roman households, on differences in households according to social status, and on tensions related to the household as revealed in the literature of the period. The purpose of this survey will be to provide a social context within which the concept of household that emerges can be placed.

2. An investigation of the way in which the Pastorals' author has used the traditional *Haustafel* schema and traditional materials to express his concept of the household of God. This investigation will involve consideration of several issues: (1) What is the nature of the *Haustafel* form as a traditional paraenetic topos or schema? More especially, what is the nature of the literary constraints which such topoi/schemata impose on authors who use them? (2) In what ways does the author of the Pastorals show himself to be a transmitter of traditional material on the one hand, and a creative developer and interpreter of such material on the other, in particular as he employs the *Haustafel* schema? What role, if any, does the image of the household of God play in his shaping and interpreting of traditional material?

3. An attempt to identify social strata, social structure, and social tensions in the church of the Pastorals by examining the pertinent data from the Pastorals in light of the information gathered about the household in the general social context. Here the key passages in the Pastorals will be analyzed in detail for the information they contain about the social situation in which they have their setting. In the process attention will be given to locating the church of the Pastorals, by means of the social features which it displays, in the history of the developing church.

SIGNIFICANCE

The present study is intended to make several contributions to research in the field of New Testament. First, it should contribute to the discussions which have been taking place for some time on the nature of traditional paraenetic material and its transmission in early Christian literature. Secondly, it should clarify the social milieu from which the Pastorals come and the social concerns to which they speak. The notion that the Pastorals represent a Christianity that is emerging from its lower class beginnings onto a middle class plateau is fast becoming obsolete. As noted above, the work of such scholars as Judge, Theissen, and MacMullen is making clear (1) that from the beginning, Hellenistic Christianity drew at least its leadership from the urban upper strata, and (2) that the concept of "middle class" obscures rather than clarifies the social realities of urban Hellenistic society. Finally, the study will address itself to the vexing problem of placing the Pastorals in a history of the developing church. Various approaches to this problem have been taken. Bultmann, for example, understands them primarily as a development within the Pauline tradition, and, above all, as a development of Pauline theology.[90] E. Schweizer, in contrast, understands them primarily as representing a developing eschatology that has its roots, not in Pauline tradition, but in the primitive community.[91] Others, such as J. Jeremias, argue that the Pastorals belong in the genuine Pauline corpus and represent no more than a certain shift of emphasis in Paul's later writings.[92] Such discussions thus both presuppose and contribute to the lengthy debate concerning the date, authorship, and geographical location of the Pastorals. If the church of the Pastorals can be placed in the social history of the early church, then, although the problem of date, authorship, and location will not have been directly addressed, a new perspective on the place of the Pastorals in the history of the developing church will have been gained.

---

[90] *The Theology of the New Testament*, Vol. 2 (trans. K. Grobel; New York: Scribner's, 1955) 183ff.

[91] *Church Order*, section 6a.

[92] *Die Briefe an Timotheus und Titus* (Göttingen: Vandenhoeck und Ruprecht, 1953), 3ff. Cf. Spicq, *Les Épîtres pastorales*, and J. N. D. Kelly, *A Commentary on the Pastoral Epistles* (New York: Harper and Row, 1963).

II

The Household in the Hellenistic-Roman World

The task of this chapter is to investigate the household as a part of the social structure of urban society in the early Roman Empire. Where possible the investigation will focus on the early part of the second century and on the Greek cities of Asia Minor, especially Ephesus. Attention will be directed toward three principal areas of inquiry: (1) the social structure of households: what social categories, for example, "husband," "household slave," operate within households and on what bases persons of one category relate to persons of other categories and to society at large; (2) the relationship of household structure to social stratum: what similarities and differences are discernible between households belonging to different social strata; and (3) social tensions related to the household: what evidence exists of social tensions in household relationships, and what the nature of such tensions is, who feels them and what the social consequences are.

THE SOCIAL STRUCTURE OF HOUSEHOLDS

The Traditional Greek and Roman Households

A brief sketch of the traditional Greek and Roman households will provide a backdrop against which developments in the Hellenistic-Roman period may be seen.

Descriptions of the household in classical Greece tend to focus on classical Athens, since the sources for Athens are much fuller than the sources for other Greek city-states of the period. It is usually assumed that what was true of Athens generally held true in other Greek πόλεις as well.[1]

In classical Athens the οἶκος constituted, in an extraordinarily concrete sense, the basic socio-political unit. This, however, is not to say that the household in the modern sense (that is, a discrete residential grouping) held this position in Athenian society. Rather, the οἶκοι of Athens were the hereditary residential estates (houses and land) of the πόλις and the citizen families who owned and resided upon these estates.[2] The households of the numerous resident foreigners and the other classes of non-citizens in the city did not qualify as οἶκοι.

The οἶκος was also a religious unit. Everyone who became a part of it passed into the service and under the protection of its gods. Accordingly, when a woman married, she exchanged the religion of her father's οἶκος for that of her husband's. As a part of the marriage ritual she was introduced to the gods of her new household and brought under their protection. Newly bought slaves were similarly inducted into the household cult.[3] Children learned the requisite rites by watching their parents.[4] When a member of the family died, the οἶκος carried out the burial and mourning rites. The surviving kin were expected to attend to the grave in order ritually to minister to the deceased, who continued to be considered a member of the family.[5] It was the

---

[1]W. K. Lacey has collected evidence from widely scattered literary and inscriptional sources that supports the assumption that Athenian marriage and household law is representative of a pattern widely followed in classical Greece. This situation may have come about, as Demosthenes claims (Dem. 24. 210), because many city-states consciously adopted laws on the Athenian model. Certain important exceptions do exist, the most important of which are Sparta and Gortyn. See W. K. Lacey, *The Family in Classical Greece* (London: Thames and Hudson, 1968) 225ff. On Sparta and Gortyn, see ch. VIII. Cf. H. Blanck, *Einführung in das Privatleben der Griechen und Römer: Die Altertumswissenschaft* (Darmstadt: Wissenschaftliche Buchgesellschaft, 1976) 89ff.; S. B. Pomeroy, *Goddesses, Whores, Wives, and Slaves: Women in Classical Antiquity* (New York: Schocken Books, 1975) chaps. IV-VI; W. Goodsell, *A History of the Family as a Social and Educational Institution* (New York: MacMillan, 1930) chap. IV.

[2]See Dem. 44. 33-42; Lacey, 90f.

[3]See H. J. Rose, "The Religion of a Greek Household," *Euphrosyne* I (1957) 111-12.

[4]Ibid., 97.

[5]Ibid., 114-15; Lacey, 148.

obligation of the son who succeeded to the headship of the οἶκος to carry forward the οἶκος cult into the next generation.[6]

The importance of the οἶκος in Athenian society becomes evident when one takes into account that the principal source of wealth in Athenian society lay in real estate, the ownership of which was restricted to citizens. The most common way in which a citizen came into possession of real estate was through inheritance of the family οἶκος or a portion of it. Thus, from the heirs of the old Athenian families, the heads (κύριοι) of the established οἶκοι, came the citizens of means, who were able to undertake the civic duties necessary to the life of the πόλις.[7] Such duties included holding public office and undertaking liturgies for the πόλις, such as equipping war ships and underwriting the expenses of civic religious observances.

It is thus not surprising that Athenian law protected the integrity and continuity of the individual οἶκος. Normally the οἶκος passed as a matter of course from father to son. If there was more than one son, the οἶκος could be divided into shares, or, if the οἶκος was too small to be divided, one son would find some other means of livelihood such as serving in the military or volunteering to go as a colonist to a new settlement.[8] However, if there was no male heir, the problem of continuity in the οἶκος became more complex. Daughters and wives could not inherit since women in Athens were not citizens in a full sense and could not own property. In such a case the law offered several options to provide for the continuity of the οἶκος: (1) the κύριος of the οἶκος could adopt a son, by one of several methods, to become his heir;[9] (2) he could divorce his wife on the grounds of infertility and marry another;[10] (3) if the κύριος died without leaving an heir, his daughter became an ἐπίκληρος, that is, she was empowered to retain the οἶκος in trust until she herself, by marriage, could provide it with a legitimate head. To this end her father's nearest male relative was obliged either to marry her himself or to provide a dowry for her marriage, so that an heir might be provided.[11]

Some indication of the internal social structure of the Athenian οἶκος has already been given. The οἶκος was headed by its

---

[6]Lacey, 15.
[7]Ibid., 76, 96-99, 146.
[8]Lacey, 126.
[9]Ibid., 145.
[10]Ibid.
[11]Ibid., 139; Pomeroy, 60-62.

κύριος, who possessed authority over the estate, and over his wife, his children and his slaves.[12] Aristotle described the role of the κύριος in the household according to a tripartite scheme: As master (δεσπότης), husband (πόσις), and father (πατήρ) he was involved in the three fundamental social relationships of the household as the dominant party in those relationships.[13]

The master's authority over his slaves reflects a dual conception of slavery. On the one hand, slaves were classified as property. Aristotle discusses the slave as "live property" and a "living tool" of the master (*Politics*, 1253b). In this description Aristotle is reflecting a view widely held in classical Greece. G. R. Morrow notes that slaves were frequently called ἀνδράποδα, "human-footed stock," analogous to τετράποδα, "four-footed stock."[14] In the *Laws*, Plato discusses slave ownership in the context of a general section of property rights (Book 6). On the other hand, the law also recognized the slave as a person in certain respects. The concept of the slave as a person is reflected in the fact that the master's authority over his slaves was often conceived on a political model.[15] Thus another common term for slave is οἰκέτης, a term reflecting the notion of the slave's membership in the household. The householder thus had a moral obligation to rule justly in the case of his slaves, just as in that of his wife and children. Slave owners guilty of ὕβρις (wanton insult and injury) toward their slaves could in fact be prosecuted.[16]

A male child remained under his father's guardianship (κυριεία) until he reached the age of majority.[17] A female child remained under her father's κυριεία until she was transferred to that of her husband, or until her father died, in which case someone else, usually her nearest male relative, was designated as her κύριος.[18] A childless widow or divorcee passed back into the κυριεία of her father's οἶκος, while a widow with adult sons might choose to remain with them in her husband's

---

[12]Aristotle, in his famous exposition of the subject in *Politics*, indicates that a "complete household" (οἰκία τέλειος) consists of both slaves and free persons. (1253b)

[13]Ibid.

[14]*Plato's Law of Slavery in Its Relation to Greek Law* (Urbana: University of Illinois Press, 1939) 31-32.

[15]Ibid.

[16]Morrow, 40.

[17]Age 18. Pomeroy, 74; Goodsell, 82.

[18]Pomeroy, 63.

οἶκος under their κυριεία.[19] In any event, Athenian women in whatever circumstances remained under the authority of a κύριος for as long as they lived.

The nurture and education of children actually fell to their mother and her servants through the sixth year of life. At age seven boys, whose supervision was at this time normally entrusted to a slave called a παιδάγωγος, began to attend school. Girls, who remained at home in the women's quarters, were taught to read and write, the remainder of their education having consisted in learning the traditional domestic skills such as spinning and weaving.[20]

The wife's subordinate position in the Athenian household is reflected in the form which betrothal and marriage took in classical Athens. Legally recognized marriages could take place only between citizens and the daughters of citizens. The betrothal, called an ἐγγύησις, consisted of an agreement between two citizens: the husband-to-be and the father of the prospective bride.[21] In the ἐγγύησις, the father formally pledged his daughter's hand and specified the dowry, and the prospective groom formally accepted the father's pledge. The prospective bride was not a party to the contract at all, but only its object. She was given in marriage by her father to her husband (ἔκδοσις). At the time of her marriage, the young woman was transferred from the guardianship of her father (or whoever had become her κύριος, in the event that her father had died) to that of her husband.[22]

Married women from respectable families were obliged to conform to a social code that severely restricted their activities and freedom of movement. They were expected for the most part to stay at home and supervise the household. A woman who was forced to work outside the home to help support the family or to do her own shopping in the marketplace, because she had no servants to do these chores, suffered social stigma.[23] A woman who willfully and unnecessarily went out in public risked her reputation as a faithful wife. Even within the οἶκος itself,

---

[19]H. J. Wolff, "Marriage Law in Ancient Athens," *Traditio* 2 (1944) 47.

[20]Pomeroy, 74; H. Blanck, *Einführung*, 89; Lacey, 163.

[21]C. Vatin, *Recherches sur le mariage et la condition de la femme mariée a l'epoche hellenistique* (Paris, 1970) chap. 1, pp. 115-18; Lacey, 105-6.

[22]Apparently the normal marriage age for young women was fourteen years, whereas the normal age for husbands was thirty. See Pomeroy, *Goddesses*, 64. Xen. *Oec.* 75.

[23]Lacey, 170; See Dem. 58. 31-4.

women were expected to retire to the women's quarters when their husbands gave dinner parties.[24]

As noted above, women were not allowed to own and control property independent of male oversight, nor did they possess direct inheritance rights. Provision was made for married women, however, through their dowries. While the husband possessed the right to use the principal, he was obligated to support his wife from the income, for which a standard percentage was set by law. In addition the dowry was to be used for her support in the event of her divorce or the death of her husband.[25]

However, the husband's κυριεία over his wife was not absolute. Her father could, if he chose, dissolve the marriage and reassert himself as her κύριος. Furthermore, she herself could initiate a divorce, although it was considerably easier for husbands to divorce their wives than vice versa. A husband could divorce his wife simply by sending her away. A wife could divorce her husband, however, only if she could persuade her father or another male citizen to register her divorce with the ἄρχων.[26]

Aristotle depicted the primary household relationships as those of master and slave, husband and wife, and father and children. The structure of actual household relationships in ancient Athens was, no doubt, more complex than Aristotle's scheme would indicate. Thus, for example, although marriage in Athens was in a strictly legal sense monogamous, married men often had concubines as well as wives. This practice was apparently viewed by the citizens as perfectly acceptable. The only drawback, from the citizen's point of view, was that he could not sire citizen children by his concubine. If he attempted to claim citizenship for her children, he was subject to heavy legal penalties.[27] In addition it was apparently a common practice for elderly citizens to relinquish the κυριεία of their οἶκοι to their sons, who then took legal and practical responsibility for management of the οἶκοι.[28] Under these

---

[24]Lacey, 159; See Isaeus 3. 13-14.

[25]Pomeroy, 63; Lacey, 110. Dem. 27. 5, 13-14, 18.

[26]Pomeroy, 64; Lacey, 108-9; A. R. W. Harrison, *The Law of Athens*, Vol. 1 (Oxford: Clarendon, 1968) 39ff. See Dem. 30.17.26; 41.4; Isaeus 3.8, 35, 78.

[27]E.g., see Apollodorus' accusation against Neaira, in which he cites a law that calls for enslavement or a heavy fine for persons found guilty of fraud in such a matter. See Dem. 59.16-17; Lacey, 112.

[28]See Lacey, 106-7, 130. Aristotle mentions the retirement of elderly citizens in *Pol.* 1275a, comparing their status to that of the children of citizens. Apparently, however, retired citizens did not

circumstances, the οἶκος would consist of three generations, from the middle of which the κύριος would come.

The traditional Roman household (*familia*) belonged to an agrarian setting. The ancient sources picture the life of the *familia* as a simple one in which the members were closely bound together in the daily routine. Slaves, who worked as farmhands, ate their meals at the master's table. They also participated together with the free members of the *familia* in the household cult of the *Lares*. At the head of the *familia* stood the *pater familias*, who possessed almost unlimited power over wife, children, and slaves.[29]

The power of the *pater familias* over his wife came about through the traditional Roman marriage with *manus*. In marriage with *manus*, which could be accomplished by several different procedures, the bride was freed from her father's authority (*patria potestas*) in order to become subject to the authority of her husband (*manus*).[30] *Manus* gave the husband power to divorce his wife, but deprived her of power to divorce him.[31] His power over her included even the right to take her life. In early Rome the only sanctions against the abuse of *manus* were religious ones. Later, serious abuses of this power were subject to the supervision by the censor.[32] Not surprisingly, the power of *manus* extended to the property of the wife as well as her person. In Roman law, in contrast with Athenian law, women could in principle own property. However, in marriage with *manus* a woman transferred all her property to her husband. He was required only to return her dowry upon divorce.[33]

The paternal authority (*patria potestas*) of the *pater familias* was almost unlimited. He had the power of life and death over his children, subject only to religious and moral restraint, and, in later times, the

---

relinquish the right to vote in public assemblies or to serve as jurors. See Lacey, 131; Aristophanes, *Wasps*, 508ff.

[29]Cf. Max Kaser, *Roman Private Law* (2d ed., trans. R. Dannenbring; Durban: Butterworths, 1968) 61, 69. F. Bömer, *Untersuchungen über die Religiones der Sklaven in Griechenland und Rom* I (Wiesbaden: Franz Steiner Verlag, 1957) 32-33, 57. Cato, Agr. 143.2. Horace, Iamb. 2.65f. *serm*. 2.6.65ff.

[30]C. J. Carcopino, *Daily Life in Ancient Rome* (ed. H. T. Rowell; trans. E. D. Lorimer; New Haven: Yale U. Press, 1940) 77; Kaser, 61.

[31]P. E. Corbett, *The Roman Law of Marriage* (Oxford: Clarendon, 1930) 182ff.; Kaser, 247.

[32]Kaser, 61.

[33]Ibid., 252.

review of the censor.[34] His children could, in a sense, "own" property, but he possessed the sole right to dispose of it. Daughters continued under his *potestas* until they married and came under the power of *manus*. Sons continued under the *potestas* of their *pater familias* indefinitely, either until his death, or until they were emancipated from it through an involved legal process. Since the *pater familias* had sole right of proprietorship over all property held by members of his family, adult sons under his *potestas* could not own property in the full sense. Instead he granted them a *peculium*, an estate, which he allowed them to manage.[35]

Slaves were subject to the sweeping authority of the *pater familias* by the power of ownership.[36] As in ancient Athens, the law reflects a dual concept of the slave, both as property and as a person. Slaves could not contract a legal marriage and their children became the property of the mother's master. Yet a slave was allowed to accumulate and manage a separate property (*peculium*). However, it was impossible for him to own any property, so everything he acquired belonged to his master.[37]

It should be noted that, like the Athenian marriage, the Roman marriage as described above was an institution essentially for citizens only. In a slave marriage, commonly called *contubernium*, neither man nor woman had any legal rights or obligations with regard to the other. Similarly a slave father possessed no authority over his offspring. Marriages of free non-citizens (*peregrines*) were acknowledged under the provisions of their own laws. A fully legal marriage, in the eyes of Roman law, could only be contracted by Roman citizens, or by a Roman citizen and someone who possessed the right of intermarriage (*conubium*). During the Republican period *conubium* was gradually extended to an increasing

---

[34]Ibid., 61.

[35]In classical Roman times the rights of adult sons to such property were increasingly fortified. The institution of *patria potestas* often gave rise to the situation that adult sons still in their father's *potestas* married and had children. In such instances husband, wife, and children were all subject to the power of the *pater familias*. See Kaser, 256-59.

[36]According to Kaser's classification, p. 70. Bömer views the *potestas* of the *pater familias* over slaves as essentially the same as that over children (p. 57, n. 1), while W. L. Westerman, *The Slave Systems of Greek and Roman Antiquity* (Philadelphia: American Philosophical Society, 1955) 947, distinguished the two forms of authority.

[37]Kaser, 70-71. The master might, nevertheless, bequeath or give a slave his *peculium* upon manumission.

number of Italian municipalities, whose citizens possessed Latin citizenship.[38]

Developments in the Hellenistic Period

As noted above, in classical Athens, legally recognized marriages could be contracted only between Athenian citizens. Only from such unions could citizen children be produced. Thus the marriage institution acted as a guarantee that the future citizenry would come from citizen stock. In the Hellenistic period citizenship in Greek cities became less severely restricted. Accordingly the range of marriages that possessed full legal status was expanded. Thus by the third century many cities were enacting agreements of "isopolity" with one another, that is, agreements in which the citizens of one city came to enjoy potential citizenship in another city. For instance, Axos enjoyed isopolity with the Aetolian League. If a citizen of Axos settled in one of the Aetolian cities, then he received Aetolian citizenship. By this agreement, he could settle in Aetolia, marry an Aetolian, and have children who could become citizens.[39] Furthermore, under certain conditions in certain places, non-citizens could marry and have children who would become citizens. Thus, in Rhodes, epigraphical evidence indicates that it was possible for non-citizens who possessed the right of residence, ἐπιδαμία, to marry and have children who would grow up to become citizens.[40]

At the same time the status of women was improving. One area in which such improvement can be seen is that of capacity to own and manage property. In classical Athens women could not own property at all. In Hellenistic Egypt, however, Greek women bought and sold real estate as well as movable property. They borrowed and loaned. They inherited from their fathers on an equal basis with their brothers. With

---

[38]Extra-legal cohabitation was also possible for citizens without social stigma. The children of such unions, however, did not possess Roman citizenship. Kaser, 242; Corbett, 24ff; J. P. V. Balsdon, *Roman Women* (London: The Bodley Head, 1962) 176.

[39]Tarn, 64; Vatin, 124.

[40]Vatin, 124. Nicasion of Cyzicus (1st century B.C.) married a woman of Soli. Rhodes had granted him ἐπιδαμία. Their son Nicasion was considered for all practical purposes a citizen.

some important exceptions,[41] they also were able to make wills.[42] Many marriage contracts prevented both husbands and wives from disposing of property unilaterally. Women in other parts of the Hellenistic world were also becoming owners of property. For example, in third century Tenos both married and unmarried women were buying and selling land and houses.[43] Such women could have possessed a degree of independence over against their husbands and their families never dreamed of by women in classical Athens.

The improving status of women is also reflected in changes in the form of the marriage contract. It will be recalled that the form of betrothal found in classical Athens, ἐγγύησις, involved an oral agreement before witnesses between a woman's κύριος (normally her father) and her prospective husband. She herself took no part in the agreement. ἐγγύησις apparently continued as a form of betrothal during the Hellenistic period.[44] However, other forms of betrothal and marriage developed from and alongside ἐγγύησις.

The fullest evidence of developing Greek marriage contracts comes from Egypt. Greeks in Egypt contracted marriage according to various forms. What is significant for the present study, however, is that in all of the various forms there was an increasing tendency for the bride herself to become an active party to the contract. One such contractual form, συγγραφὴ συνοικισίας, preserved the ancient custom of ἔκδοσις, by which the bride's κύριος gave her to her husband. However, in an instance of marriage by συγγραφὴ συνοικισίας dating from the early second century B.C., the young woman Olympias gave herself in marriage, while her father only assisted her in the

[41] ἀσταί could not make wills. The meaning of this term in Hellenistic Egypt is not entirely clear. Apparently it refers at least to citizen women of the autonomous Egyptian cities. Cf. R. Taubenschlag, *The Law of Greco-Roman Egypt in the Light of the Papyri: 332 B.C.-640 A.D.* (2d ed.; Warsaw: Panstowe Wydawnictwo Naukowe, 1955) 18.

[42] Claire Preaux, "Le statut de la femme a l'Epoque hellenistique, principalement en Egypte," *Recueils de la Societe Jean Bodin* XI, *La Femme* I, 1959, 143-44. Taubenschlag, 127.

[43] Vatin, 188.

[44] See Vatin's discussion, 157-60. Diodorus Siculus 9.10 appears to indicate the persistence of the form. Vatin has assembled inscriptions from Myconos, Tenos, and Delphi which attest to the continuing practice of ἐγγύησις in the Hellenistic world.

process.[45] Another popular form, συγγραφὴ ὁμολογίας, contained no provision of ἔκδοσις at all, but concerned itself with dowry and with rights and duties of husband and wife.[46] In Alexandria during the first century B.C., marriage was contracted by συγχώρησις, a form which sometimes included ἔκδοσις. More often, however, the bride and the groom contracted the marriage directly with each other. Thus in one such contract, Isidora, assisted by her brother, contracted to marry Dionysius. The extent to which Isidora acted on her own initiative is indicated by the fact that Dionysius has received the dowry directly from her rather than from her family.[47]

The Greco-Egyptian marriage contracts in all of the various forms normally included an enumeration of the marital obligations of both husband and wife. The sanctions for failure to live up to these obligations usually included divorce and forfeiture of the dowry, and perhaps an additional financial penalty. P. Eleph. 1 (311 B.C.) lists the husband's duties as follows: he is required to maintain his wife in a manner suitable to her dignity as a free woman (not a concubine), he must not bring another woman into the house (in such a way that he commits ὕβρις against his wife) nor beget children by another woman, and he must not mistreat his wife.[48]

The provisions regarding the husband's sexual behavior are most interesting. It is assumed that the husband possesses the freedom to engage in extra-marital sex. He must not, however, go to such lengths that he brings shame or injury to his wife. Therefore, he must not bring another woman into the household with his wife and he must not beget bastard children who might lay claim to his estate.[49] Later marriage

---

[45]Vatin, 170. P. Giess. 2: ἐξέδοτο ἑαυτὴν ᾿Ολυμπίας μετὰ κύριου . . . ᾿Ανταίωι . . . .

[46]A. J. Wolff, *Written and Unwritten Marriages in Hellenistic and Post Classical Roman Law*, 5, 15ff. The origin and relationship of συγγραφὴ συνοικισίας and σ. ὁμολογίας are debated. For differing views see Wolff, op. cit., or Taubenschlag, 113-14; Vatin, 164-71.

[47]*BGU* IV 1050, Vatin, 175. Some evidence exists that marriage by mutual agreement was also becoming popular in the Seleucid realm. See Vatin, 175-79.

[48]See Vatin, 202; Pomeroy, *Goddesses*, 128, gives a translation. Jews in Egypt apparently made use of the same forms, e.g., συγγραφὴ ὁμολογίας, as illustrated in Philo, *Spec. Leg.* 3.72-82. Cf. E. R. Goodenough, *The Jurisprudence of the Jewish Courts in Egypt* (New Haven: Yale U. Press, 1929) 94.

[49]Exactly what is meant by the provision regarding the bringing of another woman into the household is uncertain. Vatin interprets it as a

contracts deprive the husband of the right of extra-marital sex altogether. In P. Giess. 2, for example, the husband is not only forbidden to bring another woman into the house or to sire bastard children, but he is also forbidden to have a concubine (παλλακή) or boy lover (παιδικόν) on any terms.[50] This development reinforces the impression that marriage in Hellenistic Egypt was gradually becoming less of a patriarchal institution and that the chasm between the legal and social positions of married women and their husbands was narrowing.[51]

In view of this apparent trend toward the liberation of married women, one might expect to find a similar line of development when it comes to the wife's marital obligations. This, however, is not the case. In P. Eleph. 1, her obligations are not spelled out in detail. It is merely stipulated that she must not do anything to injure her husband's honor. This prohibition surely intends to proscribe adultery on the wife's part; in addition it may include other kinds of behavior which would have been viewed as disgraceful.[52] It should be noted that the vagueness of this stipulation leaves the wife vulnerable to a wide variety of possible charges.

In marriage contracts of the second and first centuries, the lists of the wife's obligations adhere with great consistency to a stereotypical form. Vatin summarizes the injunctions found in these contracts:

1. the wife must be submissive to her husband;
2. she may not leave the marital residence without his permission;
3. she may not engage in social contact with other men;
4. she must not bring financial ruin upon the household;
5. she must not do anything to shame her husband.[53]

From these injunctions it is clear that despite the movement toward greater rights for married men noted above, the wife's freedom of

---

prohibition of extra-marital sex for the husband under his own roof (p. 202). Pomeroy views it as directed against the possibility that the husband might try to establish a second "quasi-legal marriage." (p. 128).

[50]Vatin, 206; P. Giess. 2.

[51]In the συγχωρήσεις of Alexandria, however, husbands retain the implicit freedom of sexual activity. Thus the development cited was not universal in scope.

[52]P. Eleph. 1. See Vatin, 200.

[53]Vatin, 200-201. Examples include P. Giess. 21; P. Tebt. I, 104. Similar injunctions are found in the συγχωρήσεις of Alexandria although the last point above does not appear. See *BGU* IV, 1051, 1098, 1101.

movement and social activity continued to be subject to severe restriction. The injunctions have three purposes: (1) to forestall the possibility of adultery on the part of the wife; (2) to prevent her from becoming a drain on the financial resources of the household; and (3) to discourage her from any publicly embarrassing conduct. The basic method of insuring all these purposes is to keep her sequestered in the house. Thus it continued to be expected of her that she would be obedient and submissive to her husband and that, like the wives of classical Athens, she would for the most part live out her life within the confines of the household.[54]

Rome and the Eastern Provinces During the Early Empire

By the period of the early empire most marriages were being contracted without *manus*. In such a marriage the wife remained a member of her paternal household under *patria potestas*. She retained any property which she happened to have except for the dowry. Accordingly, as in the Hellenistic world, it became possible for a woman to accumulate wealth and for wealthy matrons to maintain a great degree of independence over against their husbands.[55] Martial witnesses this social phenomenon with dismay: " 'Why am I unwilling to marry a rich wife?' Do you ask? I am unwilling to take my wife as husband." (*Ep.* VIII 12.)[56]

However, at least in a technical sense it was the woman's paternal family rather than the woman as an individual that exercised independent power over against her husband. In marriage without *manus*, she could divorce him, but only with the consent of her father or guardian, who was usually one of her male relatives. It was even possible for her *pater familias* to effect a divorce against her will.[57] Furthermore, although she could hold property which her husband could not control, she could not dispose of it herself without her guardian's consent. Furthermore, up to the time of Hadrian she could not write a will without the approval of her guardian.[58]

---

[54]Vatin, 200-202. He summarizes, "Une certaine emancipation de la femme dans la domaine juridique ne doit pas nous faire oublier qu'elle reste strictement tenue dans la vie sociale. . . ." (p. 202).

[55]L. Friedländer, *Roman Life and Manners under the Early Empire*, Vol. 2 (trans. L. A. Magnus; New York: E. P. Dutton & Co., 1913) 236ff.; Carcopino, 97; Corbett, 202-3.

[56]Cf. Juvenal who complains, "There is nothing more intolerable than a wealthy woman" (VI, 460).

[57]Corbett, 223.

[58]Carcopino, 84; Pomeroy, "The Relationship of the Married Woman to Her Blood Relatives in Rome," *Ancient Society* 7 (1976) 220, 224.

The extent to which this dependence upon her paternal family was a real restriction is not entirely clear. At least among the upper classes most marriages were arranged by the families involved. Thus, especially in a first marriage, when the bride was likely to be only fourteen or fifteen years old, she must usually have had little to do with the choice of her husband. One of Pliny's letters provides a glimpse of what must have been a typical procedure among the upper classes. The uncle of the prospective bride has asked Pliny whether he knows of anyone who would be a suitable match for her. Pliny sends what amounts to a letter of recommendation for a friend, in which he gives information about his friend's home town and his family, his career and his financial situation, his character and his appearance.[59] Many a marriage must have been made in this way. However, divorced men and women probably took more of the initiative themselves when they remarried. Pomeroy cites the example of Valeria who, while attending a gladiatorial contest, slyly initiated a romance with the dictator Sulla, which culminated in their marriage.[60] In addition, women sometimes did take the initiative in divorce. Juvenal portrays women, no doubt with much exaggeration, as able to divorce their husbands at will. A typical wife "flits from one home (*domus*) to another, wearing out her bridal veil. . . . Thus does the list of her husbands grow; there would be eight of them in the course of five autumns."[61] Of course a woman needed the cooperation of her guardian in order to initiate a divorce. However, it had become relatively easy for her to have a new guardian appointed if she desired.[62]

Yet an indication that guardianship was not a mere formality is found in the Augustan legislation which granted exemption from it to a free woman who had had three children or to a freedwoman who had had four. If guardianship had not involved real restrictions upon women, then this legislation would have provided little incentive for compliance, and thus would have made little sense.[63]

---

[59] Pliny, *Ep.* 1.14. The groom in a first marriage might well have been only a few years older than the bride and probably took no more initiative in the match than she did. The fact that marriage was arranged did not mean that no concern existed for the personal happiness and compatibility of the couple (Balsdon, 173ff.). The idea of romantic love in marriage was also not unknown (e.g., see below, pp. 55ff.).

[60] Pomeroy, 157. The account is from Plutarch, *Sulla*, 35.

[61] *Sat.* 6. 225ff.

[62] Carcopino, 84.

[63] As Pomeroy argues in "Relationship," 225. This is a different position than that which she took in *Goddesses*, 151-52, where she noted

In any event, the social freedom of the Roman matron, which had always been greater than that of her Athenian counterpart, had reached a new level. As noted above, Roman girls customarily became brides in their early teens, just as did the daughters of Greek households. However, Roman brides were probably, on the average, nearer the age of their husbands than Athenian brides.[64] Thus on the basis of age differential alone, there was likely to be less social disparity between husband and wife in Rome than in Athens. Roman girls also entered marriage with a better general education. Both boys and girls went to elementary school or else were tutored privately, beginning at age seven.[65] By the time of Juvenal, privileged Roman women were benefiting from higher education as well. They studied law, grammar, rhetoric, and philosophy, and did not hesitate to enter into debates with men, as Juvenal sourly notes.[66] Such women also enjoyed a varied social life. They gave and attended banquets with their husbands, took part in sports such as hunting and fencing, and attended gladiatorial contests at the Colosseum, choosing favorites among the combatants.[67] Thus despite the fact that women continued to suffer significant legal disabilities, they were experiencing more power as wives and more freedom to participate in all kinds of social activities outside the household than ever before.[68]

Striking social changes were taking place in other respects as well. Whereas in early Rome slaves had made up a relatively minor portion of the population, in the late Republic and early Empire slave

---

that women with a real desire for liberation had achieved it without the help of the law and that women who had gained the formal exemption sometimes continued to rely on male assistance in legal matters.

[64]Pomeroy, *Goddesses*, 164. Augustan legislation penalized unmarried and childless women at age 20; men at age 25 (Pomeroy, 166). H. J. Leon, *The Jews of Rome*, 230, notes six inscriptions which record the marriages of Jewish girls in Rome at ages from 12 to 17.

[65]Pomeroy, 170-71; Marquardt, 57ff.

[66]Juvenal, *Sat.* 6.398-412; 434-56.

[67]Ibid., 6.24ff. Juvenal alludes to the scandalous behavior of a senator's wife, who ran off to Egypt with a gladiator (6.82ff.).

[68]In this connection it is also interesting to note that by the early Imperial period it was against the law for a man to have a wife and a concubine at the same time. Thus, as in Hellenistic Egypt, the gap between sexual standards for men and women was narrowing. See B. Rawson, "Roman Concubinage and Other *De Facto* Marriages," TAPA 104 (1974) 288.

numbers reached heights greater than in any previous society.[69] Furthermore, manumission of slaves, often at a comparatively early age, became so common during this period that legislation was enacted to discourage this practice.[70] As a result of the great numbers of manumissions, freedpersons (*liberti* and *libertae*) came to constitute a sizable segment of the total Roman population.[71]

---

[69]According to Keith Hopkins, *Conquerors and Slaves* (Cambridge: Cambridge U. Press, 1978) 99, societies in which slaves played a central role in the economy have been few. The only documented slave societies in this sense in the ancient world were in classical Athens and in Roman Italy. Certain eastern cities such as Pergamum and Ephesus may have had slave populations approaching that of Rome on a percentage basis (see below, pp. 60-61).

[70]A. M. Duff, *Freedmen in the Early Roman Empire* (Rev. ed.; New York: Barnes and Noble, 1958) 84. Carcopino, 60. But for Asia Minor, see p. 63 below.

[71]Manumission did not dissolve all ties with the former master. Rather the relationship continued as one of patron to client. Often, under the conditions of his manumission, the freed slave continued to be liable for specified services to his former master. In addition, he was likely to emerge from slavery in his master's debt. Furthermore, even if he was not under such obligations, he was still bound to his former master by the duties of *obsequium* and *officium*, which together connoted filial respect, deference and allegiance. These duties, which had had a long history among the social customs of Roman society, received the force of law under Augustus. *Obsequium* proscribed certain kinds of behavior against one's patron. E.g., it barred a freedman from bringing a lawsuit against his patron, unless he could obtain special permission from the praetor; and it prevented him from bringing criminal charges against his patron, except for treason. *Officium* obligated the freed slave to perform various kinds of services for his patron at the patron's bidding. The patron could, for instance, request his freedman to take care of his children. Freed slaves also had the obligation to provide material assistance to patrons in financial trouble. Thus it is not surprising that many freed household slaves remained in the household in the same positions which they had held before their manumission. S. Dill, *Roman Society from Nero to Marcus Aurelius* (New York: Meridian Books, 1956) 117-19; Carcopino, 59-60; Duff, 36-46, especially 39-42. The successful householder counted many others besides his freed slaves among his clientele. For the ubiquity of the client-patron relationship and the degraded position of clients in general, see Dill, 93ff.; Friedländer, 195ff.; Juv. *Sat.* 5.

By the time of Martial, Pliny, and Juvenal, the Greek cities of Asia had been under Roman rule for more than 200 years.[72] Unfortunately, however, one cannot assume that what was true of Roman society had become true of such cities as Pergamum and Ephesus. In general, Roman policy had always been to make use of local laws, customs, and institutions wherever possible. This was especially true in the case of the so-called "autonomous" cities. Pliny's correspondence with Trajan regarding the autonomous city of Amisus in Pontus illustrates this policy at work. The citizens of Amisus have petitioned Pliny to allow the formation of benefit societies (ἐράνοι), a practice which the city's own laws permit. This practice is, however, against general Roman policy for the provinces. Trajan advises Pliny not to interfere with the laws of Amisus in this case, but to forbid the formation of such societies in cities directly subject to Roman law.[73]

In Roman Egypt this same general policy resulted in different laws for Egyptians, Greeks, and Romans, respectively. When one inquires about marriage law for Greeks in Egypt under Rome, one finds, for the most part, a continuation of the law of Hellenistic Egypt. Thus, although the terminology for the marriage contract itself changes,[74] the practice of ἔκδοσις continues, while at the same time, some women continue to marry independently.[75] Both husband and wife continue to be able to divorce each other and the wife continues to be able to recover at least the dowry.[76] Furthermore, the practice continues of including a provision forbidding either husband or wife to dispose of property without the other's consent.[77]

---

[72]The territory which, roughly speaking, makes up the Roman province of Asia had come under Roman rule by the action of Attalus III of Pergamum who bequeathed his kingdom to Rome at his death in 133 B.C. (Tarn, *Hellenistic Civilization*, 130, 136.)

[73]Pliny, *Ep.* 10.92, 93.

[74]The major distinction is between "written" and "unwritten" marriages, which correspond to earlier forms of Greek and Egyptian marriage. Taubenschlag, 117; Wolff, "Written and Unwritten Marriage."

[75]Taubenschlag, 140. Taubenschlag also notes that the practice of ἔκδοσις is also attested for Dura (Dura no. 74, 232 A.D.).

[76]Ibid., 122-23. See also *CPJ* 144 (13 B.C.), a deed of divorce involving a Jewess and her husband.

[77]Ibid., 127. While the currently available data from Asia Minor is much scantier, there is at least evidence that women there continued to accumulate wealth and reach positions of social prominence. (See below, pp. 51-52).

One further observation on the subject of women in marriage may be made: The evidence adduced above indicates that analogous changes in the status of women had taken place in Hellenistic and Roman society. Generally speaking, in both Hellenistic society and Roman society a woman was no longer totally subject by law to any man, whether it was her husband, her father, or her guardian. Both among the Romans and among the Greeks it had become regularly possible for a woman to obtain a divorce when she wanted it. In both Greek and Roman law, she could recover her dowry when her marriage ended. Furthermore, she could accumulate and control property of all kinds, even if she could not everywhere own property in the full sense. Thus both Greek and Roman women of the early empire, especially women from the upper classes, enjoyed at least potentially a considerable degree of power and independence.

A similar question arises in connection with the place of freedpersons in the Greek cities under Rome. In Roman Egypt, the Greek and Roman laws on manumission of slaves differed in certain particulars. Yet both recognized a continuing obligation of the freed slave to his patron.[78] The data on slaves and freedpersons in Asia Minor has yet to be fully collected and classified. However, there is little evidence in the sources for the manumission of slaves. Thus it is unlikely that the freed segment of the population in Asian cities was as large and significant an element as it was in Rome.[79]

Hellenistic Judaism

Like the traditional households of Greece and Rome, the traditional Jewish household was a patriarchal structure in which the constituting event, marriage, was brought about by a contract agreed upon by two men, the father of the bride and the groom. (Cf. Tobit 7:12-14.) However, Jewish law and custom related to the household differed in a number of respects from that of the Greeks and Romans.

In certain ways the patriarchalism of the Jewish household was even more pronounced than those of Greece and Rome. According to

---

[78]Taubenschlag, 99-100.

[79]H. Heinen, "Zur Sklaverei in der Hellenistischen Welt (I)," *Ancient Society* 7 (1976) 140, 142-43. Heinen's two-part article (the second part appears in *Ancient Society* 8 (1977) 121ff.) is a review of a work by three Russian scholars: T. V. Blavatskaja, E. S. Golubcova, and A. I. Pavolovskaja, *Die Sklaverei in der hellenistischen Staaten im 3-1 Jh. v. Chr.* (trans. M. Brauer-Pospelova, et al.; Wiesbaden, 1972). A series of gradations existed between slavery and freedom (p. 139).

rabbinical and Mishnaic tradition a man could divorce his wife for any reason, although rabbinical leaders like Hillel and Shammai debated what constituted the grounds for divorce based on differing interpretations of Deut 24:1-4 (M. Gittin 9.10).[80] However, a wife could not divorce her husband at all, although she could bring charges against him in the court and the court could force him to divorce her (M. Nedarim 11.12).[81] Adultery was defined as sexual intercourse between a married woman and a man other than her husband. From this definition it followed that unfaithful wives had committed adultery, but that unfaithful husbands had not done so, unless the other woman happened to be married. Female children remained under the guardianship of their fathers until they married, at which time the father's authority was transferred to the new husband.[82] Furthermore, responsibility for the education of the children was not shared between husband and wife as in Greece and Rome, but was allotted to the father alone.[83]

Yet in certain other ways women had greater freedom and power in traditional Jewish households than in traditional Greek and Roman ones. On the one hand, women possessed significant legal rights. Under Jewish law women possessed the right to sue at law without the assistance of a guardian, a right unknown to Greek or Roman women.[84] Jewish law also permitted women to own and manage property and allowed wives to retain property over which their husbands had no control and no inheritance rights.[85] Furthermore, in most circumstances, widows and divorcees were able to recover at least a portion of their dowries.[86] On the other hand, Jewish women traditionally possessed greater social freedom in the communities in which they lived than did Greek women. They were not

---

[80]However, J. A. Fitzmyer, "Divorce Among First-Century Palestinian Jews," *Eretz-Israel* 14 (1978) 104 *f., 110 *, argues convincingly on the basis of 11QTem 57:17ff. and CD 4:20f. that divorce was prohibited altogether at Qumran.

[81]Cf. the practice in the households of classical Athens as noted above, p. 32. Roman marriage with *manus* also deprived the wife of the right to divorce her husband. See above, p. 33.

[82]See Z. W. Falk, *Introduction to Jewish Law of the Second Commonwealth*, vol. 2 (Leiden: Brill, 1978) 290; M. Kethuboth 6.51.

[83]See Falk, 323.

[84]Falk, 327. Sifre Numbers 2.

[85]Falk, 300.

[86]Ibid.

expected to remain sequestered at home, but to visit the marketplace and to take active part in the general social life.[87]

It should also be noted that Jewish household law and custom differed dramatically from Roman and Jewish law in two other respects, namely, on the question of polygamy and exposure of infants. While in Greek and Roman society monogamy was the only legitimate form of marriage, polygamy remained, at least in theory, an accepted form of marriage in Jewish society, with the apparent exception of the community at Qumran.[88] In this connection, Jewish law featured the institution of levirate marriage, which called for the marriage of a childless widow to her brother-in-law, even if he already had a wife.[89] Jewish society remained the only society in the Hellenistic-Roman world in which exposure of infants was condemned.[90]

However, there is considerable evidence[91] to suggest that in household matters the Jews of the Hellenistic-Roman Diaspora tended to adopt the laws and customs of the larger society of which they were a part, forsaking in the process many of the laws and customs peculiar to Jewish tradition. The Egyptian Jewish community had apparently discontinued the practice of levirate marriage by the time of Philo.[92] Alexandrian Jews contracted marriages according to the Greek form of ὁμολογία.[93] They adjudicated divorces in Greek courts according to Greek laws, so that Jewish women, with the assistance of their guardians, could divorce their husbands by mutual agreement.[94] Jewish women

---

[87] *CPJ* I, 35.

[88] See Fitzmyer, op. cit., and 11QTem 57:17ff. and CD 4:20f.

[89] Falk, 317. Deut 25:5ff.

[90] See A. Oepke, "παῖς," *TDNT* V, 646.

[91] Most of the specific evidence on matters related to the household comes from Egypt. However, there are strong indications that Jews all over the Hellenistic world had become highly acculturated to Greek culture. Cf. F. Blanchetiere, "Juifs et non-Juifs," *RHPR* 54 (1974) 367-82; G. Kittel, "Das Kleinasiatische Judentum in der hellenistisch-römischen Zeit," *ThLZ* 69 (1944) 9-20; W. M. Ramsey, "The Jews in Graeco-Asiatic Cities," *Exp.* Ser. 6, 5 (1902) 19-33, 92-109.

[92] Falk, 317, draws this conclusion based on the fact that this law does not appear in Philo's *Special Laws.*

[93] See E. R. Goodenough, *Jurisprudence,* 94; Philo, *Spec. Leg.* 3.72-82.

[94] For a good example see *CPJ* 144, a deed of divorce involving a Jewish woman named Apollonia and her husband Hermogenes. The deed

inherited according to Greek rather than Jewish law.[95] They were sequestered at home, away from the public eye, like Greek women, but unlike their Jewish sisters in Palestine.[96] Thus for the most part Hellenistic Jewish households must have closely resembled the pagan households by which they were surrounded.[97]

HOUSEHOLDS WITHIN THE CLASS STRUCTURE OF THE CITIES

Class Structure in the Cities of the Roman Empire

Most studies of Greek and Roman households tend to concentrate attention on upper class households. This tendency reflects the fact that the literary sources are concerned almost exclusively with the life of the upper classes in general. Since the present study seeks to shed light on the social strata present in a particular community of Christians, a description of upper class households only will not suffice.

However, differences in the households of the various strata of urban society in the early empire can only be understood against the backdrop of the class structure of that society.

Recent studies have emphasized the extreme "verticality" of Roman society. The upper classes (*honestiores*) made up a tiny minority at the top of a steep social pyramid. Most members of the lower classes (*humiliores*) were separated by a huge social and economic gulf from the upper classes. However, even here there were wide differences in accumulation of wealth and social status.[98]

At the top of the social pyramid, just below the emperor and his family, stood the senatorial order. MacMullen estimates that the senatorial class accounted for two-thousandths of one percent of the total

---

reads, in part: "To Protarchos from Apollonia . . . with her guardian . . . and from Hermogenes. . . . Apollonia and Hermogenes agree that they have dissolved their marriage."

[95]See Goodenough, *Jurisprudence*, 58; Philo, *Vit. Mos.* 2. 242-43.

[96]See Philo, *Spec. Leg.* 3.169-71; *Flacc.* 89.

[97]For the influence of the Roman *patria potestas* on the Hellenistic Jewish household, see G. Schrenk, "The Father Concept in Later Judaism," *TDNT* V, 974-75.

[98]Cf. the studies of Ramsay MacMullen, *Roman Social Relations* (New Haven: Yale University Press, 1974) chap. IV; Geza Alföldy, *Römische Sozialgeschichte* (Wiesbaden: Franz Steiner, 1975) chap. V.

population.[99] One could not ordinarily enter the ranks of this aristocracy unless one possessed the proper family background. However, with or without family background no one could become a senator unless he possessed an estate of 1,000,000 sesterces (= 250,000 denarii).[100] Many senatorial families possessed fortunes far in excess of the minimum requirement. Pliny, who declined to rank himself at the top of the scale, had an estate valued at about 20,000,000 sesterces.[101]

Next in rank came the equestrian order. The equestrians constituted a larger group than the senators, yet probably less than one-tenth of one percent of the total population.[102] The financial qualification for admission to the Equestrian order was an estate of 400,000 sesterces. Scholarly opinion has differed widely over the question of the significance of this qualification. Carcopino notes that an estate of this size would have yielded a yearly income of 20,000 sesterces at the normal interest rate. Carcopino takes this level of income as the "vital minimum" for a Roman citizen.[103] Thus in Juvenal's ninth satire, Naevolus, a ruined, aging degenerate, pines for an income of 20,000 sesterces in his old age to keep him from "the beggar's staff and mat . . . ," (135ff.) and in the fourteenth satire Juvenal advises his readers to renounce wealth and live simply. If they are not able to live as frugally as Socrates and Epicurus, then they should be satisfied with "a sum so big as that which Otho's law deems worthy of the fourteen rows . . . ," that is, an estate equal to the Equestrian census of 400,000 sesterces (14. 323f.). The equestrian census requirement, Carcopino concludes, is designed to insure that no one who is unable to maintain minimal middle class respectability will be able to enter the ranks of the *equites*.[104]

---

[99]MacMullen, 88.

[100]Ibid., 89.

[101]See Alföldy, 103.

[102]MacMullen, 89. On the basis of data from the end of the republican period, Alföldy estimates that there were about 20,000 *equites* during the reign of Augustus, and that the total number grew during the following two centuries (p. 108). J. Gagé, *Les classes sociales dans l'Empire romain* (Paris, 1964) 41, offers an estimate in the same range. Furthermore, the Equestrian population was concentrated in Rome and in Italian centers such as Padua and Cadiz, which had more than 500 *equites* each, according to Strabo 3.5.3, probably about one percent of the population of each city. See MacMullen, 183, n. 1; Alföldy, 108.

[103]Carcopino, 66.

[104]Ibid.

This view of the *equites* as a Roman middle class, however, is open to serious question. T. P. Wiseman notes that according to the Augustan census of 7 B.C., there were only 215 Roman citizens in the entire city of Cyrene with a census rating of 10,000 sesterces or more, that is, a rating as much as one-fortieth of the Equestrian census. Thus, at least in Cyrene a little more than a century before Juvenal, anyone with an Equestrian-sized estate would have been wealthy far beyond the hopes of most of the population.[105] MacMullen estimates the actual subsistence level for a laborer supporting a small family at 250 denarii (1,000 sesterces) per year.[106]

How, then, are the references in Juvenal cited by Carcopino to be interpreted? A second look at the passages in *Sat.* 9. 135ff. and 14. 316ff. reveals that they are susceptible of more than one interpretation regarding what they indicate about the cost of living in Rome. Naevolus, the character whom Juvenal portrays in *Sat.* 9, is an aging degenerate who, it is suggested, has made his living for the most part by selling his sexual services to both men and women (27ff., 70ff.). He has grown embittered because, unlike some others who have followed this trade, he has not been able to amass an estate of any size (27ff.). For this unhappy circumstance he blames his miserly patron who has not rewarded him justly for his services, which extend even to the point of having secretly fathered the patron's supposed children (70ff.). Now he longs, he says, for something to keep him from poverty in his old age. "Twenty thousand sesterces well-secured" will do nicely, along with some silver vessels, a

---

[105] T. P. Wiseman, "The Definition of 'Eques Romanus' in the Late Republic and Early Empire," *Historia* 19 (1970) 67-83.

[106] J. Szilagyi, "Prices and Wages in the Western Provinces of the Roman Empire," *Acta Antiqua* 11 (1963) 347-48, gives the following figures: In Pompeii preceding the destruction the standard daily wage was 5 asses (1 1/4 sesterces). In Matthew's parable of the workers in the vineyard, the daily wage is one silver coin (4 sesterces). In 160 A.D. Dacian gold miners earned 70, 90 and 105 silver denarii (x4 = sesterces) for a half-year's work. Szilagyi estimates that during the first and second centuries workers earning 87.5 to 100 sesterces per month would have spent about half of this sum to feed a family of four. T. Frank, *ESAR* I, 386, gives a somewhat higher estimate for food costs: 2 1/2 sesterces per day (ca. 75 sesterces per month). The base pay for a private in the Roman army was 225 denarii per year (1000 sesterces) plus food. D. Sperber, "Costs of Living in Roman Palestine," *Journal of the Economic and Social History of the Orient* 8 (1965) 250f., lists wages in first and second century Palestine ranging from 1/4 denarius to 8 denarii per day.

couple of "stout moesian porters" to bear him to the circus, an engraver, and a painter in addition to the pair of slaves he already owns (135ff.). Juvenal never comments directly on Naevolus' self-portrayal. However, Juvenal's repeated condemnation of the inordinate taste for luxury in Roman society of his day and his reverence for the old Roman virtues of a simple life should not be forgotten in this context.[107] Does he really expect the reader to take seriously Naevolus' claim that 20,000 sesterces a year, a set of silver vessels and six slaves are necessary to keep him from the beggar's mat? Surely not. Rather Juvenal is portraying the softness and vanity of a pathetic old scoundrel who persists in the belief that the world owes him a life of luxury. A direct condemnation of Naevolus would have been superfluous. His own words portray his character clearly enough.[108]

The second passage (*Sat.* 14. 316ff.) comes at the conclusion of a section in which Juvenal has been inveighing against greed. The question arises, With how much should one be satisfied? Juvenal answers, "With as much as supported Epicurus and Socrates." If, however, his readers find this answer too severe, he will accommodate himself to current Roman manners. They should be satisfied with the estate of an *eques*, or, if that is not enough, the estate of two or three *equites* put together. If they desire greater wealth than this, then they will never be satisfied no matter the size of their fortune. Once again it is possible to interpret Juvenal's remarks here to indicate that he considered an Equestrian estate to be sufficient only for a modest living. However, it may be significant that he suggests this sum as an accommodation to Roman manners. It will be recalled that he consistently portrays current Roman manners as flawed by a taste for luxury. Thus it is probable that he equates an Equestrian-sized estate not with modest means, but with moderate wealth. When one remembers that Juvenal himself probably fell into the latter economic category, this interpretation appears all the more likely.[109]

---

[107]See e.g., *Sat.* 1.90ff. a life in which retired soldiers were content with 2 acres of land, an allotment which, Juvenal jibes, modern day Romans would hardly find adequate for a garden.

[108]See G. Highet, *Juvenal the Satirist* (Oxford: Clarendon Press, 1954) 101-21 for discussion of this method in Satire.

[109]Juvenal was enough a man of means that he was able to live in Rome and at the same time own a Tiburtine farm managed by a *vilicus* (overseer). This farm produced fare for banquets in Rome. Juvenal also travelled to Egypt (*Sat.* 11. 56ff.).

It appears, then, that in Roman society of the early empire, a person with Equestrian census possessed considerable wealth compared with the vast majority of the population, although, compared with some of the senatorial fortunes, an estate of 400,000 sesterces must have seemed small. Thus in Rome itself and in other exceptionally prosperous centers such an estate probably signified only moderate wealth. In other areas someone possessing an estate of this size no doubt stood at the top of the local economic scale.[110]

The members of the municipal councils (*curiae*) of cities and towns throughout the empire comprised the lowest order within the upper classes. It is misleading, however, to think of the decurionate as a single class spanning the empire. Rather, the decurionate constituted a homogeneous social stratum only within individual municipalities where they were drawn from the local aristocracy.[111] The fact that the decurionate was recognized in Roman law reflects the Roman policy of governing wherever possible through already existing but carefully regulated local leadership. In Italy the *curiae* were regularly comprised of 100 members. In the older cities of the eastern provinces such as Ephesus, where city councils had been long established, the traditional number of councillors was generally maintained. As in the case of the Senate and the Equestrian order, the Romans set a financial requirement for entry into the decurionate. With decurions, however, this requirement was not a uniform one across the empire. Pliny indicates that the required census for decurions in his home town of Comum was 100,000 sesterces.[112] In certain African municipalities an estate of 20,000 sesterces sufficed.[113]

The path to membership in the *curiae* normally involved discharging public liturgies such as building a public monument or a civic building at one's own expense, or underwriting the cost of athletic contests; and holding a series of magistracies, in which one was also required to make considerable expenditures of time and energy for the city's benefit. By engaging in such activities a citizen displayed his wealth and his public spiritedness and thus accumulated the recognition and prestige necessary for entry into the *curia*.[114] In this connection it is interesting to note the growing participation of women in politics. Even in the Greek

---

[110]See MacMullen, 91-92 and below for discussion of the wide variation in wealth among the municipalities of the empire.

[111]Cf. Alföldy, 112.

[112]J. Gagé, *Les classes sociales*, 163.

[113]Alföldy, 113.

[114]Gagé, 165; MacMullen, 61f.; Hammond, 291.

cities of the eastern provinces women were beginning to discharge liturgies and to hold important magistracies.[115] It is debatable whether they actually carried out the duties of their offices or held those offices as honorary positions. However, in any event, being awarded the office and bearing its title was the real indicator of high social status and political influence.[116] There then can be no doubt that in the Greek cities of the East, some women were rising to positions of wealth, social prestige, and political influence. Apparently, however, no women actually succeeded in becoming decurions.

Some towns had trouble finding enough citizens who could meet the financial requirement for decurions.[117] In other places a seat in the *curia* was a coveted status symbol for which men who met the financial requirement competed fiercely. In such a situation the existing *curia* would usually try to draw new membership from the "curial" families (that is, those families which had in the past supplied the membership of the *curia*) and thus to exclude men who possessed the requisite census rating but did not come from one of the established aristocratic families.[118] Rich social upstarts did regulary succeed in invading the decurionate, however. Decurions were expected to bear a considerable financial burden toward the upkeep and improvement of the city. Understandably a decurion whose financial resources were being strained might welcome a rich newcomer to whom some of the burden could be shifted.[119] Thus, although rich freedmen were forbidden entry into the municipal councils,

---

[115]A. J. Marshall, "Roman Women in the Provinces," in *Ancient Society* 6 (1975) 123. Julia Severa, who may have been Jewish, held the important post of archon jointly with her first husband and then went on to hold other offices independently. See F. Blanchetiere, "Juifs et non-Juifs sur la diaspora en Asie Mineur," *RHPR* 54 (1974) 379.

[116]Marshall, 125. For the other view, see D. Magie, *Roman Rule in Asia Minor* (Princeton, NJ: Princeton University Press, 1950) 649f.; 1507, n. 34; 1518, n. 50.

[117]Gagé, 163; Alföldy, 113.

[118]See Gagé, 165-66.

[119]See Peter Garnsey, "Aspects of the Decline of the Urban Aristocracy in the Empire," *ANRW*, Pt. 2, Vol. 1, p. 241. Garnsey finds evidence that less wealthy decurions were experiencing financial strain and occasionally financial ruin as early as the first half of the second century A.D. For the growing power of the council including its power to control admittance to its own ranks during the second century see D. Magie, 639ff.

their sons had good hope of becoming decurions.[120] During the early empire, senators, *equites*, and decurions taken together numbered perhaps 200,000 individuals. Along with their families they constituted, in all probability, less than one percent of the empire's total population.[121] This fraction of a percent constituted the group which during the second century A.D. came to be officially recognized as the *honestiores*, the upper classes. Everyone else belonged to the *humiliores*, the lower classes. Thus, in any given locale anywhere in the empire almost the entire population belonged to the lower classes.

As could be expected, the urban lower classes exhibited great social diversity. They included freeborn citizens and non-citizens, freedpersons and slaves. Within their ranks wealthy freedmen like Trimalchio stood at one economic extreme. At the other extreme were to be found free and freedpersons so destitute that they made their beds in public monuments and grain warehouses.[122] Beggars, menial slaves, and poor laborers stood at the bottom of the social scale. Wealthy freedmen and imperial slaves who held important administrative posts sometimes attained such a high degree of prestige that they came to be regarded unofficially as belonging to the upper classes.[123]

The wealth of the upper classes tended to be concentrated in land. Farming, politics, and military command were the approved vocations.[124] Lower class occupations were much more various. Many free and freedpersons worked as artisans and merchants. It was also not uncommon for a slave to run a small business as his master's representative. Factories owned by large scale entrepreneurs made use of slave labor as well as the labor of free and freedpersons.[125] In the lesser provincial cities non-slaves often earned their living as small farmers.

---

[120]For the exclusion of freedmen from the decurionate, see Pliny, *Ep.* 10.7.

[121]Figures given by Alföldy, 130.

[122]J. E. Packer, "Housing and Population in Imperial Ostia and Rome," *JRS* 57 (1967) 86.

[123]Alföldy, 130; MacMullen, 92; P. R. C. Weaver, *Familia Caesaris* (Cambridge: University Press, 1972).

[124]MacMullen, 99.

[125]How large a part large-scale manufacture played in the economy of the early empire is disputed. See MacMullen, 184, n. 2, for bibliography.

Many slaves and freedmen of the wealthy were teachers, philosophers, artists, doctors, and financial advisors and administrators.[126]

Within the lower classes people had ample opportunity to experience differences in social status and in some cases to entertain realistic hopes of social advancement. Many individuals gained a sense of social importance through participation in associations. On the one hand, an individual artisan could gain a sense of public recognition unavailable to him as an individual through identification with his craft association. Thus prominent citizens often displayed their wealth and generosity by becoming patrons of associations and politicians welcomed the endorsement of associations. On the other hand, individuals could experience social advancement within the associations to which they belonged. The organizational structure of many associations mimicked that of municipal governments. Thus while one might not have the remotest chance of becoming an important municipal magistrate such as an aedile, one might well become the aedile of one's association.[127]

Upper Class Households

As noted above (p. 42) in the late Republic and early Empire the slave numbers in Rome and Italy were greater than in any previous society. Many slaves lived on the land, supplying the labor force for huge slave farms (*latifundia*). Many others were industrial slaves. In addition, there were greater numbers of slaves to be found in the households of the wealthy than ever before. The picture given by Petronius of the household of Trimalchio suggests the numbers of slaves and the minute division of labor that could characterize a wealthy household, in this case the household of a wealthy freedman.[128] A porter stands at the door of Trimalchio's house to greet and screen visitors (28). Water-pourers cool the feet of his guests and manicurists attend to hangnails (31). Ranks of servants bring course after course to the dinner table and entertain the diners (34-7). In his dining room, Trimalchio keeps a clock and a uniformed trumpeter to mark the passing hours (76). As he travels to and

---

[126]Alföldy, 121.
[127]Macmullen, pp. 76-78, n. 70, p. 178.
[128]Petronius, *Satyricon*.

from the baths in a slave drawn litter, a slave musician plays a miniature set of pipes in his ear (27). In all Trimalchio owns 400 slaves (47).[129]

The matrons of such households wielded considerable power in the household itself and possessed a large measure of practical independence both inside and outside the household. They supervised the work of the domestic staff generally, and, in addition, had their own personal retinue to attend to their needs. Juvenal portrays such women as overbearing and cruel toward their slaves, having their hair-dressers flogged because a curl is out of place and their chair-bearers beaten on the false charge of being late (*Sat.* 6.47ff.). Whether or not most wealthy Roman matrons were this cruel toward the slaves in their households, Juvenal leaves the reader with no doubt that such women possessed the practical authority to manage household affairs and to have servants punished as they saw fit. In addition, the description given above of the full social life of Roman women applied mainly to women of privileged families (p. 41). These were the women who studied law, rhetoric and philosophy; dabbled in politics; and accumulated a sufficient amount of property to achieve financial independence.[130]

A glimpse of upper class households in Ephesus is provided by the "Ephesian Tale" of Xenophon of Ephesus.[131] Habrocomes, a sixteen year old *ephebe*, and Anthia, a fourteen year old maiden, fall in love when they catch sight of each other during the annual festival of Artemis (1.2.2; 2.5. Hadas, 102-3). When the respective sets of parents discover what has

---

[129]There is ample evidence to show that this picture is not simply the product of the satirist's imagination. Mima Maxey, in a study on the occupations of the lower classes in Rome, found 23 different kinds of household occupations listed in inscriptions. Mima Maxey, *Occupations of the Lower Classes in Roman Society* (Chicago: U. of Chicago Press, 1938), reprinted in *Two Studies on the Roman Lower Classes* (New York: Arno Press, 1975). See pp. 40-66. Susan Treggiani, "Domestic Staff and Rome in the Julio-Claudian Period, 27 B.C. to 68 A.D.," *Histoire Sociale* 6 (1973) 241-55, paints a similar picture.

[130]Cf. Baldon, 45ff.; Pomeroy, 149ff.

[131]This romance may date from the second or third century A.D., but could also have been written during the Hellenistic period. See M. Hadas, *Three Greek Romances* (Garden City, NY: Doubleday, 1953) opposite title page; K. Schneider, *Kulturgeschichte des Hellenismus* I, 685. The Greek text is available in the edition of A. D. Papanikolaou, *Xenophon Ephesius: Ephesiacorum* (Leipzig: BSB B. G. Teubner, 1973). The English quotations below are from the translation of Hadas, *Three Greek Romances*, 101-70.

happened, they arrange for the two young people to be married. An elaborate set of marriage rites follows, at the climax of which Anthia and Habrocomes are left together in the bridal chamber on a golden couch (1.8; Hadas, 108). A description of the two lovers' passion follows (1.9; Hadas, 109). It is of particular interest here that husband and wife are portrayed as approaching each other on an equal basis: "Their emotions were identical. . . . Their bodies trembled, their souls were agitated" (1.9.1; Hadas, 109). Habrocomes finally embraces Anthia and makes a speech. Then she takes the initiative: "Timid and fearful lad, how long will you delay in your love making?" (1.9.4; Hadas, 109). In this manner the author describes the two lovers alternately leading and being led. He summarizes approvingly, "The whole night they spent in eager rivalry with one another, contending which should appear the more ardent lover" (1.9.9; Hadas, 110). After a brief interval, the young couple sets off with an entourage of servants on a voyage to Egypt, travelling on a ship commissioned for them by their parents (1.10; Hadas, 111).

The families of the bride and groom arrange this marriage just as upper class Romans would have done, although the groom is perhaps a little younger than one would expect a Roman groom to be. The narrow age differential between bride and groom does represent a parallel to Roman marriage patterns. Habrocomes and Anthia approach each other in the marital relationship as equals, not as superior and subordinate.[132] One would also expect to find such an approach to marriage among some upper class Romans. The abundance of servants and the expensive household furnishings also recall the upper class Roman household. Thus one gains the impression that upper class households in Ephesus during the early Empire would have closely resembled those of Rome in basic characteristics.

Lower Class Households

The sketch of the household in early imperial Rome given above draws mainly upon literary sources, which concerned themselves primarily with the upper classes. Information about lower class households comes for the most part from other kinds of sources. Hints about the characteristics of lower class households can be found in the types of housing in which the lower classes lived.

---

[132]See also their mutual vows of faithfulness (1.11.4-5; Hadas, 112), which both lovers go to great lengths to keep during the course of their adventures.

James E. Packer has made an extensive study of housing in Ostia in the second century A.D.[133] Two basic types of housing are to be found in Ostia: private mansions (*domi*) and multi-storied apartment houses (*insulae*).[134] The *domi* of Ostia were the houses of wealthy and prominent people. *Domi* were built according to a traditional Roman plan in which a number of rooms were clustered around a central atrium. A typical *domus* was expensively furnished and decorated and possessed an enclosed, columned yard (peristyle) on the Greek model. It was designed to house not only the owner and his family, but also a considerable number of household servants, and to accommodate private social gatherings.[135] A typical Ostian *insula*, by contrast, contained a row of shops facing the street on the ground floor. These shops, which were as likely as not to have a mezzanine or a backroom, also served as living quarters for the proprietor and his family. The upper floors probably contained additional one and two room apartments. On the ground floor of some of the *insulae* were factories with mezzanines, which housed factory workers. Most apartments contained neither kitchen nor latrine facilities. Furthermore, they were too small to be used for socializing with friends. Thus, their inhabitants must have done most of their eating, drinking, and socializing in public places.[136]

Some of the *insulae* contained so-called "luxury apartments" on the ground floor and probably on upper floors as well. A typical luxury apartment, which contained a number of rooms, including several bedrooms, was large enough to accommodate a household that included several servants. It was also large enough for modest social gatherings. One should not, however, be misled by the designation of these dwellings as "luxury apartments." Life there did not begin to approximate life in a great *domus*. Like the more numerous one and two room apartments few

---

[133]"Housing," see above, p. 53, n. 122; *The Insulae of Imperial Ostia: Memoirs of the American Academy of Rome* 31 (1971).

[134]The standard height in Ostia was four stories.

[135]It will be recalled that in classical Athens the οἶκοι of the city were the households of the established citizen families and their estates. To what extent and under what circumstances "οἶκος" and "*domus*" carried an upper class connotation during the period in question is an intriguing question that has not yet been fully explored. E.g., the use of οἶκος in certain passages in Plutarch (cf. *Moralia* 140 A) and of *domus* in Pliny (cf. *Ep.* 8:16) suggests a certain snobbery connected with these words.

[136]Packer, *Insulae*, 72-73.

luxury apartments had latrines or kitchens. Thus, whereas the inhabitants of a *domus* might to some extent preserve the ancient ideal of the household as a self-sufficient society, the tenants of a typical luxury apartment were forced to meet some of their most basic daily needs outside its confines. The furnishings of luxury apartments, which were generally cheap imitations of the furniture, art, and sculpture to be found in the great *domi*, reveal the social aspirations of their tenants.[137]

With two thirds of Ostia excavated, 22 private mansions have been discovered. Packer thus estimates that in the entire city there were perhaps 33 private mansions, accounting for 660 persons. 58 *insulae* with luxury apartments on the ground floor and perhaps on upper floors have been found. Packer estimates that 1306 persons lived in this type of housing.[138] Out of a total estimated population of 27,000, then, less than 2,000 lived in either *domi* or luxury apartments. The majority of the population lived in one or two room apartments. Finally, perhaps 5,000 of Ostia's inhabitants were too poor to rent any kind of apartment and thus slept in and around public buildings and other structures.[139]

Was the Ostian pattern typical of urban areas in the early Empire or atypical? The evidence is inconclusive. The Ostia studied by Packer was a product of a thorough rebuilding program during the second century A.D. Packer finds, however, that Pompeii and Herculaneum, which were destroyed during the first century, contain numerous examples of the multiple dwelling, especially *insulae* containing rows of shops with backrooms. The *insula* was a common feature of architecture in Rome itself by the time of Livy during the late third century B.C. Packer thus theorizes that the multiple dwelling was an indigenous development in Rome, which then spread to smaller Italian cities like Ostia, Pompeii, and Herculaneum.[140]

This theory suggests that one should look for a different pattern in the housing of eastern cities. However, A. G. McKay has noted some intriguing evidence for the existence of multiple dwellings in Ephesus, where two adjacent *insulae* have been unearthed.[141] The two *insulae*

---

[137]Packer, *Insulae*, 72.

[138]Ibid., 70-71. In Packer, "Housing," the estimate is somewhat higher. At any rate, less than ten percent of the population, in all probability, lived in this type of housing.

[139]Packer, "Housing," 84-86; Packer, *Insulae*, 70-71.

[140]Packer, *Insulae*, 43ff.

[141]A. G. McKay, *Houses, Villas and Palaces in the Roman World* (Ithaca: Cornell University Press, 1975) 213ff.

were originally constructed in the first century A.D. and were built up the slopes of a terraced hillside to the height of three stories. Access to the upper stories was provided by a set of steps in between the two *insulae*. The eastern *insula*, of particular interest here, was sixty yards wide as it faced the street, and contained twelve shops on the ground level. Above the shops were small rooms which could be reached by a corridor leading from the stepped passageway at the end of the building. These garrets probably housed the proprietors of the shops below and their families. McKay theorizes that this combination of living and working quarters, so common among the lower classes of Ostia and Rome, may have been equally common in eastern cities.[142] If this hypothesis is true, then one can imagine the lower classes of Ephesus living in conditions very similar to their counterparts in Ostia.

Certain features of the eastern *insula* depart markedly from the pattern found in Ostia.[143] The second level of the eastern *insula* harbors a private two-story mansion, surrounded by apartments of varying size on the second and third levels. Clay piping still exists which once conveyed water up the hillside and into the apartments at every level. A drainage system was also concealed under the steps. Thus the inhabitants of this building had more home conveniences and probably more privacy than the tenants of the typical Ostian *insula*.[144]

---

[142]McKay in fact goes so far as to suggest that Rome imported the *insula*, together with the workshop-garret plan, from the East (pp. 213-14). F. Miltner, *Ephesos* (Vienna: Verlag F. Deutke, 1958) 79, drew back from the conclusion that Ephesian housing was dominated by the *insula* pattern. When Miltner wrote, the site discussed above had not been excavated. However, Miltner was aware of the site and guessed correctly that the buildings there were apartment houses.

[143]The western *insula* contained five large apartments. One of these units, e.g., contained twelve rooms on the ground floor and had a second story as well. Frescoed walls and an ornamental mosaic floor decorated a number of the rooms. Like the eastern *insula*, the western *insula* was served by water and drainage systems. Living quarters such as these five units could indeed justly be called "luxury apartments." How large a percentage of the Ephesian population could have afforded to live in housing of this type is a matter of conjecture, based on present data. However, assuming that the standard of living in Ephesus was not significantly higher than in Ostia, one would have to conclude that a smaller percentage of Ephesians lived in apartments like these than did Ostians in the so-called "luxury apartments" of their city. (See McKay, 217).

[144]McKay, 213-14, 217. McKay calls the second and third level apartments, which are generally larger than the garrets below, "middle class" apartments.

An interesting question arises with respect to the inhabitants of such dwellings as the one and two room apartments and workshop apartments of Rome, Ostia, Pompeii, Herculaneum, and Ephesus: how commonly did such "households" include household servants? In the case of the *domi*, and even in that of the luxury apartments, one easily conceives of slaves and freedpersons living on the premises and attending to the needs of the master and his family. One does not so easily imagine household slaves crowding the already cramped and sparsely furnished one and two room apartments so numerous in Ostia. This impression could result from a failure of a modern westerner's imagination. However, other evidence also suggests that most lower class households did not include household servants.

In the American South, at a time when slaves made up almost one third of the total population (a figure similar to that of Roman Italy) about one fourth of the free families owned slaves.[145] In classical Athens, another slave society, existing data suggest that about one fourth of the citizens and resident aliens together possessed slaves.[146] A study of census data from Roman Egypt compiled the following figures: Among 98 families, 21 families owned a total of 85 slaves, that is, about one family in five owned slaves. Slaves constituted an estimated ten percent of the total population in Roman Egypt, a figure approximated in the census data cited here.[147] Thus there were probably fewer slaves on a percentage basis in Egypt than in some other parts of the empire. The percentage of families owning slaves, however, may not have differed too greatly from that in other parts of the empire. Great numbers of slaves in Italy worked on slave farms (*latifundia*) and considerable numbers worked in industry and in the Imperial bureaucracy (see above, pp. 42, 54). This was not the case in Egypt. Furthermore, large numbers of household slaves in Rome were concentrated in the hands of a relatively small number of extremely wealthy householders. In the Egyptian census data, no one family was listed as owning more than sixteen slaves in

---

[145]See M. I. Finley, "Between Slavery and Freedom," *Comparative Studies in Society and History* 6 (1964) 239; *The Ancient Economy* (Berkeley: University of California Press, 1973) 77. Finley believes that the number of slave owners in ancient society was proportionately greater.

[146]See A. H. M. Jones, "Slavery in the Ancient World," M. I. Finley, ed., *Slavery in Classical Antiquity* (Cambridge: W. Heffer, 1960) 1-3; Blanck, 100; Finley, "Between Slavery and Freedom," 239.

[147]M. Hombert and C. Preaux, *Recherches sur le recensement dans l'Egypte romaine* (Lugdunum Batavorum: E. J. Brill, 1952) 152-54, 170.

all.[148] Thus the percentage of households including slaves in Rome itself may not have been much higher than the percentage of households with slaves in Egypt. From these figures it thus appears unlikely that more than twenty-five percent of households included slaves, even in the slave centers of the empire.

Basic financial considerations also support the view that a large majority of the population could not have afforded to buy and keep slaves. The price for unskilled slaves (children and adults) ranged from 800 to 2500 sesterces, roughly speaking.[149] For legal purposes slaves were commonly valued at 2000 sesterces.[150] Alföldy estimates that at such prices even individuals who met the census of a decurion (100,000 sesterces) could have afforded no more than a few slaves.[151] The highest paid of the rank and file Roman soldiers, who received 675 denarii per year,[152] would have had to spend nearly one third of a year's salary to buy even the cheapest slave. According to Dio Chrysostom, during the early second century a sizable element among the residents of Tarsus, a group whom he calls the λινουργοί (linen workers), were excluded from the citizen body of the city by their inability to pay an entrance fee of 500 drachmae (= denarii).[153] One thus has difficulty imagining that anyone in this group could have afforded to buy, feed and clothe a slave.

There is, then, broad evidence to indicate that the household which possessed even one slave stood higher on the socio-economic pyramid than most of its neighbors. The households of the one and two room apartments and workshop-quarters in the Ostian, Roman or Ephesian *insulae* were thus for the most part households which consisted of husband, wife and a child or two, but no slaves.

Burial inscriptions provide another kind of testimony about lower class households. Data depicting family life at the lower levels of society in early imperial Rome has been collected and interpreted by Beryl

---

[148]Ibid., 170.

[149]Alföldy, 122. For a list of slave prices, see Westermann, *Slave Systems*, 101; *ESAR* II, 280 (Egypt).

[150]R. Duncan-Jones, *The Economy of the Roman Empire* (London: Cambridge University Press, 1974) 348.

[151]Alföldy, 122.

[152]R. MacMullen, 94.

[153]Dio Chrysostom 34.21-3. See D. Kienast, "Ein vernachlässigtes Zeugnis für die Reichspolitik Trajans: Die Zweite tarsische Rede des Dio von Prusa," *Historia* 20 (1971) 66.

Rawson.[154] Rawson focuses attention on "the most humble of the Roman citizens--the fringe citizens--and their families."[155] Her observations on families of slaves and freedpersons are especially interesting. Since legal marriage was possible only for citizens, a conjugal union in which one or both parties were slaves produced illegitimate children. Such children took their status from that of the mother at birth. Thus the child of a freedman and a female slave was born into slavery. Such a child was at the disposal of the *pater familias*, who thus could break up the family at his whim. For example, one epitaph records the death of a three-year-old child who had been sold away from her parents into another house. By the time of the epitaph, both parents had won their freedom in different houses.[156] Once both parents had attained freed status, they could contract a legal marriage and establish a real *familia*. Rawson's study indicates that this did in fact happen.[157] In such circumstances, however, one's children might well still be slaves at the disposal of one's former owner. Thus, slaves and freedpersons often found it a difficult and lengthy task to establish a real family life. Certainly many slaves were never able to do so.

Juvenal portrays marriage as an extremely unstable institution, representing only the most casual of commitments, among Romans of all classes.[158] However, epitaphs such as the one noted in the previous paragraph suggest that strong family ties could persist in lower class families under the most discouraging of circumstances. I. Kajanto, in a study of divorce among the lower classes, finds little in the burial inscriptions that would indicate a high divorce rate.[159] What these inscriptions do record is the high value placed on stable marriages and faithful marital relationships. Thus the duration of extraordinarily long marriages is

---

[154]"Family Life Among the Lower Classes at Rome in the First Two Centuries of the Empire," *Classical Philology* 61 (1966) 71-83.

[155]Rawson, 71.

[156]Ibid., 79.

[157]Ibid., 78.

[158]See above, pp. 54ff. for the upper classes. For lower class marriages, cf. Juvenal's reference to the woman who asks the fortune teller "whether she shall throw over the tavern keeper and marry the old clothes man." (6. 591)

[159]"On Divorce Among the Common People of Rome," *Revue des etudes latines* 47 (1970) 103ff. Kajanto notes that since divorce as such was almost never recorded in an epitaph, the burial inscriptions provide only indirect and incomplete evidence on divorce among the people they commemorate. Even so, they provide strikingly little evidence of divorce.

proudly recorded.[160] In addition, *univirae*, women married only once, hold an especially honored place.[161] It appears, then, that the Roman lower class marriage was a rather stable institution, despite the legal and practical handicaps which such unions often faced.

To what extent such a picture would apply to the cities of Asia cannot easily be determined at present. Some data is available, however. According to Galen, there were as many slaves as citizens in Pergamum in his day.[162] On this basis slaves would have made up something less than one-third of the adult population including women and resident aliens.[163] This percentage would approach that of the slave population of Rome. Presumably other Asian cities of comparable size and importance, such as Ephesus and Smyrna, would have had similar numbers of slaves. As noted above (p. 44), manumission seems to have taken place less frequently in the cities of Asia Minor than in Rome. Accordingly, freedpersons would have constituted a smaller segment of the population in urban Asia Minor.[164]

---

[160]Ibid.

[161]Ibid., 112. Kajanto finds about fifty inscriptions praising *univirae*. H. J. Leon notes a Jewish inscription of this type, *Jews*, 232. J.-B. Frey first collected and evaluated the inscriptions dealing with the *univirae* in "La signification des terms *monandros* et *univira*," *Recherches de science religieuse* 20 (1930) 48-60. Frey argues that *univirae* were women who pre-deceased their husbands, having been married only once. Thus they were being praised as women who had never divorced. Leon, 129f., argues against Frey that widows who never remarried were also honored as *univirae*. Recently M. Lightman and W. Zeisel have re-affirmed the view of Frey in "Univira: An Example of Continuity and Change in Roman Society," *Church History* 46 (1977) 19-32, especially 22-27.

[162]Galen, "The Diagnosis and Cure of the Souls Passions," in *Galen on the Passions and Errors of the Soul* (trans. P. W. Narkins; Ohio State U. Press, 1963) 63; Carcopino, 65.

[163]Estimates of the actual percentage indicated by Galen's remark vary considerably. Galen gives the figure of 40,000 citizens, and thus 40,000 slaves. How large a percentage of the population slaves made up cannot be figured exactly apart from a knowledge of how many women, children, and resident aliens of various categories resided in the city. T. R. S. Broughton, "Roman Asia Minor," *ESAR* IV, 816-17, estimates a total population for Pergamum of ca. 200,000, in which case slaves would have made up about twenty percent. Carcopino assumes a total population closer to 120,000.

[164]Nevertheless freed slaves made up a large enough segment of the population in Pergamum to be included among groups promised special

SOCIAL TENSIONS RELATED TO THE HOUSEHOLD

Social tensions related to the household in this period appear to have centered around the changing position of women in society.[165]

The evidence from the Greek marriage contracts of Hellenistic Egypt (given above, pp. 35ff.) suggested a likely source of tension between husbands and wives. Greek women in Egypt were making gains in their legal and social status. Often they took the initiative in contracting their own marriages. They were placing greater demands on their husband's sexual fidelity. And they were marrying with the expectation of being able to effect a divorce if the marriage were not satisfactory. In addition, increasing legal capacity in the area of property ownership and management gave them, at least potentially, a degree of economic independence which they had not experienced before. However, the

---

concessions in return for their support of the city during the political crisis that followed Rome's acquisition of the Pergamene (Attalid) kingdom. See S. Dickey, "Some Economic and Social Conditions of Asia Minor Affecting the Expansion of Christianity," in S. J. Case, ed., *Studies in Early Christianity* (New York: Century, 1928) 398.

[165]One might expect social tension to have been a prominent and pervasive feature of the relations between master and slaves in the household since it was an institution founded on the most blatant exploitation of a subordinate group by a dominant group. However, this does not appear to have been the case. Certainly such tension existed. As noted above, pp. 30, 34, in both Greek and Roman law and tradition slaves were regarded as property. At the same time, neither the Greeks nor the Romans were able entirely to eradicate from their minds the idea that slaves were human beings. Thus, in both Greek and Roman society the institution of slavery involved a most serious value conflict. It may be significant, in this connection, that there was a general popular movement toward more humane treatment of slaves during the first and second centuries A.D., (cf. S. Bartchy, *Mallon Chrēsai*, 67) and, at least in some quarters, an apparently heightened resentment among slaves of poor treatment (cf. Juvenal, 4. 110-117). Nevertheless, in classical antiquity, slavery as an institution went essentially unchallenged, whereas, by contrast, the institution of marriage did not escape such challenge. See Bartchy, 63ff.; J. Vogt, *Ancient Slavery and the Ideal of Man* (trans. T. Wiedemann; Cambridge, MA: Harvard U. Press, 1975) 40. On the challenge to the institution of marriage, see below, pp. 71ff. K. Gaiser, *Für und Wider die Ehe* (Munich: Heimeran, 1974), has collected texts representing both sides of the question.

marital obligations of wives in the marriage contracts of the period continue to place the same restrictive social expectations as wives in an earlier period. Wives are expected to be domestic, socially retiring, chaste, and submissive to their husbands. Anything less is likely to bring dishonor to the household.

Husbands and wives, therefore, were caught amidst contradicting social forces. While women were experiencing increasing actual power and independence within marriage and without, they were still expected to behave as the relatively powerless wives of classical Athens, practically as if they were their husband's slaves.

The evidence for Hellenistic Asia Minor is much scantier. However, surviving descriptions of the Attalid queens Apollonis and Stratonice provide some important clues. Polybius summarized the life of Apollonis, the wife of Attalus I, as follows:

> Apollonis, . . . was a native of Cyzicus, and for several reasons a very remarkable (ἀξία μνήμης) and praiseworthy (παρασημίας) woman. For the fact that being a simple citizen (δημότις) she became a queen and preserved this dignity (ὑπεροχήν) until the end without employing any seductive and meretricious art (οὐχ ἑταιρικὴν προσφερομένη πιθανότητα), but always exhibiting the gravity and excellence (σεμνότητα καὶ καλοκαγαθίαν) of a woman strict in her life and courteous in her demeanor (σωφρονικὴν καὶ πολιτικήν), makes her worthy of honorable mention. Add to this that having given birth to four sons, she cherished (διεφύλαξε) for all of them up to her dying day an unsurpassed regard and affection, although she survived her husband for a considerable time. And the sons of Attalus on their visit to the town showed due gratitude and respect (καθήκουσαν χάριτα καὶ τιμήν) to their mother. For, placing her between them and taking both her hands, they went round the temples and the city accompanied by their suites. All who witnessed it applauded and honored the young men for this. . . . This all happened in Cyzicus after the peace with King Prusias (Polyb. 22.20).

Polybius thus portrays Apollonis as an exemplary mother and her sons as models of filial piety, whose behavior won the enthusiastic approval of the populace.

A similar description of Apollonis and her sons is given in an inscription from the Attalid city of Hierapolis. The inscription records a decree passed by the citizen assembly in memory of the Queen soon after her death. The opening lines summarize her virtues:

> Queen Apollonis Eusebes, wife of the god-king Attalus and mother of King Eumenes Soter, has crossed over to the gods, after a life in which she made splendid and publicly conspicuous demonstration of her own virtue. (ἔνδο[ξον κ]αὶ πρέπουσαν ἐν ἀνθρώποις ἀπόδειξιν τῆς ἰδίας ἀρέτ[η]ς). For she behaved reverently (εὐσεβῶς) toward the gods and piously (ὁσίως) toward her parents; she lived with her husband in a manner befitting greatness (μεγαλοπρεπῶς); and she instilled in her children a spirit of true and complete harmony (προσενενήνεχθαι δὲ καὶ τοῖς τέκνοις μετὰ πάσης ὁμονοίας γνησίως). (*OGI* 308: translation mine)

Here again, Apollonis is presented as the embodiment of matronly virtue; her piety toward the gods and her parents and her relationships with her husband and her children are all exemplary.

The decree went on to declare that her good memory lived on in her noble sons and in the testimony they continued to bear to her life, no doubt, as in the following inscription of her second son: "Attalus to Queen Apollonis, his mother, because of her tender affection for himself" (*OGI*, 301: my translation). As their most spectacular tribute to their mother they erected a temple to her memory in her native city of Cyzicus and decorated it with a series of relief sculptures on the theme of filial devotion.[166] Thus it may be seen that the sons of Apollonis were at pains to keep the memory of their mother and of their own exemplary relationship with her alive after her death.

In this connection it is interesting that the next queen, Stratonice, the wife of Eumenes II, is portrayed in similar terms. Her son, Attalus III, celebrates his filial devotion by giving himself the surname Philometor.[167] In addition, an example of his testimony to her virtue has survived in a letter which he addressed to the people of Pergamum. In this letter he writes, "Queen Stratonice, my mother, was the most pious (εὐσεβεστάτη) of all people and the most affectionate (φιλοστοργοτάτη), especially toward my father and toward me."[168] Essentially the same virtues are attributed to Stratonice as to Apollonis before her:

---

[166]For a summary of the content of each scene, see K. Schneider, *Kulturgeschichte des Hellenismus*, Vol. 1 (Munich: C. H. Beck, 1967) 92-93.

[167]Vatin, 109.

[168]In C. B. Welles, *Royal Correspondence in the Hellenistic Period* (Chicago: Ares Publishers, 1974; reprint of 1934 edition), # 67.

exemplary piety toward the gods and model behavior as a wife and mother.

As Vatin points out, the evidence strongly suggests a deliberate campaign on the part of the sons of Apollonis to promote and utilize her public image as a paragon of domestic virtue, and thus to represent themselves as the defenders of traditional Greek notions about relations in the family.[169] The fact that Stratonice enjoyed an almost identical public image, although she may not have been nearly so well suited to the role personally,[170] suggests that the portrayal of the queen and the royal family in these terms had become a consistent Attalid policy.[171]

However, such a policy only makes sense on the assumption that traditional Greek notions of family relations enjoyed a significant degree of popularity among the general populace.[172] Thus it is likely that the same kind of patriarchalism evident in the wifely obligations of the Greco-Egyptian marriage contracts also had currency in the Attalid kingdom. At the same time, that the Attalids represented themselves as defenders of traditional values in connection with the family suggests the existence of a popular perception that these values were being threatened. Therefore, one is led to conclude that tensions related to the growing power and independence of women existed here as they did in Hellenistic Egypt. This conclusion holds special significance for the present study, since the Attalid kingdom was soon to become the Roman province of Asia, the province in which the Pastorals were probably written.

---

[169]Vatin writes, p. 106, "Nous n'avons pas de raisons de douter des vertus de femme, mais il est évident que ce concert de louonges a été soigneusement orchestré." Actually Apollonis was an activist queen, e.g., in commissioning a number of building projects (see Hansen, 240-41, 267), and not at all a submissive, sequestered wife and mother on the traditional Athenian model. Thus one detects in the projection of her public image an attempt to appeal to old values that were no longer quite at home in the contemporary setting.

[170]Stratonice may have been an adulteress, and Attalus III, her originally illegitimate son. See Vatin, 108ff.

[171]Royal women in the other Hellenistic Kingdoms projected a very different public image. See Vatin, 106-7; Schneider, 1:79ff.

[172]Vatin suggests that the emphasis on proper and harmonious family relations may also have served Attalid public relations with the Romans (p. 107).

In the Roman period we find basically the same attitude toward wives in Plutarch's "Advice to the Bride and Groom," although Plutarch is much gentler in his approach. In fact Plutarch's approach suggests one way in which the conflicting forces mentioned above could be accommodated in genteel fashion. Plutarch's basic attitude and approach to husband/wife relationships is revealed in the following comment: "Every activity in a virtuous household is carried on by both parties in agreement, but discloses the husband's leadership and preferences" (139A). The husband is clearly the head of the household in Plutarch's view, yet there is also an attempt here to recognize the wife as a person with her own thoughts: Plutarch seems to be suggesting that the best way is for husband and wife to reach a genuine consensus. This dual emphasis is apparent in the specific advice that he gives: A wife should not take the initiative in love-making, but should respond to her husband's advances (140C). She should be content with her husband's friends as well as his gods, who are his most important friends, and should not embrace "queer rituals and outlandish superstitions" (140D). Property ought to be combined so that the whole is said to belong to the husband, even if the wife contributed the larger share (140EF). The woman should be content to stay at home and should remain silent except in talking to her husband (142C D). In sum, the wife ought to subordinate herself (ὑποτάττουσαι), and the husband ought to govern (ἀρχεῖν) her (142E). On the other hand, Plutarch makes certain concessions to the times that run counter to the older Greek practice. In Athens it was frowned upon for wives to dine with their husbands. Plutarch writes, however, "Men who do not like to see their wives eat in their company are teaching them to stuff themselves when alone" (140A). Furthermore, he argues against the practice of sexual freedom by men in marriage and he recommends that the husband should study philosophy and instruct his wife in the most useful parts (τὸ χρήσιμον) (144D-F).[173]

Plutarch's basic tone in this essay is calm and optimistic and one gains no strong sense of social tension in the household. Several brief references to women who dominate their husbands do, however, briefly interrupt this calm. 139B refers to women who gain dominance over their husbands by magic or by sexual manipulation. Such women make fools out of their husbands and end up with bad marriages. Plutarch also makes

---

[173]Nevertheless, he advises the bride to overlook any sexual infidelity on her husband's part (143F).

passing reference to unfaithful wives in this same section. Thus one can see that his reaction to a wife who does not fit his mold is strong.

One senses that many couples would have found Plutarch's compromise acceptable and workable. One might think of it as a moderate's approach to the question: basically conservative, but with some concessions to the changed status of women. At the same time one would not expect this compromise to be workable for all. Thus Plutarch's essay reveals the same potential for social tensions found in the others.[174]

Juvenal's portrait of the Roman matron (*Sat.* 6) attests that such tension was a notable feature of Roman society in his day. The main problem, in Juvenal's view, is that Roman women take every opportunity to subjugate, shame and plunder their husbands. Thus Juvenal warns, "If you are honestly uxorious, and devoted to one woman, then bow your head and submit your neck to the yoke. Never will you find a woman who spares the man who loves her . . . " (206-8). Such a woman will be sure to control the finances in every detail: "No present will you ever make if your wife forbids; nothing will you ever sell if she objects; nothing will you buy without her consent" (212-13). She will choose her husband's friends for him, turning away old comrades from the door (214-15). She will make him include her paramours among the beneficiaries, when he writes his will (116-18). She will usurp his position as master of the household by ordering slave executions against his will (219ff.). Then, once she has gained complete mastery over her husband and his household, she is likely to desert him for a new man and repeat the entire performance (224ff.). In a word, given the opportunity, the Roman matron "lords it over (*imperat*) her husband" (274). Thus Juvenal illustrates the dangers of ignoring the warning earlier given by Martial: "Let the matron be subject (*inferior . . . sit*) to her husband, Priscus; in no other way do woman and man become equal (*fiant poles*)" (*Ep.* 8.12).

Other parts of *Sat.* 6 complete this composite portrait. Some of this material has been referred to above (pp. 47ff.). The typical Roman matron feels free to deplete the family fortune on the most ridiculous and thoughtless extravagances: "Ogulnia hires clothes to see the games; she hires attendants, a litter, cushions, female friends, a nurse and a fair-

---

[174]Xenophon's "Ephesian Tale" reveals a somewhat more liberal attitude, in that here husband and wife appear to relate to each other on a more nearly egalitarian basis, and the same interest in mutual consideration of husband and wife for one another and an interest in their "relationship" in the modern sense is seen. Their marriage would have been a little too "modern" for Plutarch. See above, pp. 55f.

haired girl to run her messages; yet she will give all that remains of the family plate, down to the last flagon, to some smooth-faced athlete" (352ff.). She enters unashamedly into such traditional male pursuits as athletics and politics (398ff.). She joins the worshippers of the Great Mother or Isis in their exotic rites and she orders her life according to the advice of a Jewish dream interpreter, a Chaldean astrologer and the like (511ff.).

Juvenal's Roman matron violates almost all of the traditional canons of wifely behavior as presented by Plutarch: Instead of practicing conjugal fidelity and suffering her husband's affairs quietly, she complains loudly about his infidelity while shamelessly indulging in complete sexual freedom herself. Instead of accepting his friends as her own, she reconstructs his entire social circle. Rather than allow him to control the finances, she has the last word on every expenditure. She ignores his gods, preferring exotic and outlandish foreign religions. She makes a public spectacle of herself in athletic contests and political battles, rather than stay home and take care of the household.

Juvenal and Plutarch not only share the basic idea that wives should be subordinate to their husbands, but they also have a very similar notion of what wifely subordination means in practical terms. While Plutarch portrays the ideal marital relationship in straightforward fashion, Juvenal paints, in bitterly satirical terms, that which violates the ideal. Juvenal's 6th Satire thus provides the modern reader with the reactions of a Roman traditionalist to women in Roman society who were experiencing and exercising increased social freedom and power. No doubt, Juvenal exaggerates both their number and their non-conformity to traditional standards. However, he reveals the suspicion and hostility with which feminine emancipation was regarded in certain quarters.[175]

---

[175]The same tensions that come to the surface in Juvenal's 6th Satire may also be observed in Seneca, who was capable of invective against the women of his day to rival that of Juvenal (cf. *Ap.* 98.20-21). Yet at the same time, Seneca could argue for the essentially equal moral capacities of men and women (*Ad. Mar.* 16.1), advocate a single standard of sexual morality for husbands and wives (*Ep.* 94.26), and approve the concept of thoroughgoing education for women as well as men (*DeCong. Sap.* 14.1). For a fuller discussion see A. L. Motto, "Seneca on Women's Liberation," *Classical World* 65 (1972) 155-57.

The Traditional Household and the Larger Society

Both Plato and Aristotle treat marriage and family as the concern of the πόλις.

Plato regards marriage as a civic duty that one should undertake with the interest of the πόλις in mind. He thus writes, "Regarding marriage as a whole, there shall be one general rule: each man must seek to form such a marriage as shall benefit the state (τὸν συμφέροντα τῇ πόλει . . . γάμον) rather than such as best pleases himself" (οὐ τὸν ἥδιστον αὑτῷ) (*Laws* 6.773 B). Thus, according to Plato, when people follow their natural tendency to marry people like themselves in wealth, power, and temperament, the πόλις becomes unbalanced both morally and materially. Therefore, for the sake of the stability of the state, rich men should avoid choosing wives from rich families and men with quick tempers should marry even tongued women (*Laws* 6.773 BC).

The most important function of marriage is to provide the πόλις with the next generation of citizens. Thus Plato would require all men to marry by a certain age (*Laws* 4.721 AB) and he would give the power to dissolve marriages that had produced no children after 10 years (6.784 AD), entrusting the oversight of marriages to elected inspectresses. Similarly the education of children would be placed in the hands of officials of the πόλις (7.794 B).[176]

Aristotle directs the better part of the first book of the *Politics* to an exposition of proper household management (1253b ff.; see above discussion, pp. 30ff.). He concludes this exposition promising to return to the question of proper conduct in husband-wife and children-father relationships, when he discusses the various forms of constitutions (πολιτεῖαι). It is significant that he here explicitly links relationships in the household to the well-being of the πόλις:

> For since every household (οἰκία) is part of a state (μέρος πόλεως), and these relationships[177] (husband-wife; father-

---

[176]Cf. Vatin, 18-24, for analysis of the various ways in which Plato's legislation regarding women on such questions as marriage, dowry, divorce, and inheritance is designed for the benefit of the state (πόλις).

[177]Literally the text says "these are part of the household" (ταῦτα δ' οἰκίας). Rackham understands ταῦτα rightly as referring to the subject matter of the question which Aristotle has articulated in the previous sentence: "The question of the virtue generally belonging to man and woman and children and father, and of the right and wrong mode of

> children) are part of the household, and the excellence (ἀρέτη) of the part must have regard to that of the whole, it is necessary that the education both of the children and of the women should be carried on with a regard to the form of the constitution (πολιτεία), if it makes any difference as regards the goodness of the state (πόλις) for the children and the women to be good. And it must necessarily make a difference; for the women are a half of the free population, and the children grow up to be the partners in the government of the state (ἐκ δὲ τῶν παίδων οἱ κοινωνοὶ γίνονται τῆς πολιτείας 1260b).

While Aristotle does not make good on his promise to return to these particular concerns, he does discuss matters related to marriage and children in Books VII and VIII, where he considers various kinds of constitutions (πολιτεῖαι). Like Plato, he regards the birth and education of children as a major concern of the πόλις. Thus, for example, he would regulate the marriage age of men and women so as to insure optimum physiological conditions for the production of strong and healthy children (*Pol.* 1334b-35b); and he would require that all deformed infants be exposed (1335b). He would also lay the responsibility for the education of children upon the πόλις, which should establish a system of public education (*Pol.* 1337a ff.).

In addition, in an often noted instance, Aristotle considers the consequences for the πόλις, when the conduct of women is improperly regulated. He writes:

> For just as man and wife are part of a household (οἰκία), it is clear that the state (πόλις) also is divided nearly in half into its male and female population, so that in all constitutions in which the position of women is badly regulated, one-half of the state must be deemed to have been neglected in framing the law (*Pol.* 1269b).

In Aristotle's view, the historical example of Sparta reveals the folly of such neglect. In Sparta women gained a great deal of power and independence because Spartan men were so often engaged in military campaigns away from home. The women began to live "dissolutely and luxuriously" (ἀκολάστως . . . καὶ τρυφερῶς) and to control "many things" (πόλλα διωκεῖτο) during the period of the Spartan Empire. Then, in Sparta's hour of crisis, during the Theban invasion, she had to pay the

---

conducting their mutual intercourse and the proper way of pursuing the good mode and avoiding the bad one. . . ."

consequences for failure to discipline the women. They proved to be worse than useless, causing "more confusion than the enemy" (θόρυβον . . . πλείω τῶν πολεμίων) (*Pol.* 1269b). Aristotle here takes a stand against female emancipation in general. However, he does not specifically address the question of women's behavior in the context of their household relationships.

Similar ideas were alive among the Roman ruling class at the beginning of the empire. Arius Didymus, who served Octavian as a teacher and counselor,[178] outlines the proper content of the topoi on household management (οἰκονομικός) and on civic affairs (πολιτικός) in his *Epitome*. Like Aristotle, Arius Didymus places the two topoi in close conjunction, calling the household "a primary πολιτεία" (p. 148,5). Also like Aristotle, he is clear that the man has the rule of his house (p. 149,5ff.) and not the wife, children, or servants. "The man has the rule (ἀρχή) of this [house] by nature. For the deliberative faculty in a woman (βουλευτικόν) is inferior, in children it does not yet [exist], and is completely foreign to slaves" (p. 149,8ff.). Thus the man's rule over his household is justified by his superior natural capabilities.[179]

In light of Arius Didymus' views, certain attitudes expressed in a speech attributed to his pupil, Octavian, gain significance. The speech is found in Cassius Dio's account of the events leading up to the battle of Actium. Before the battle, Octavian addresses his troops, attempting to bolster their confidence and zeal by discrediting Anthony and his forces. For this purpose Anthony's relationship with Cleopatra is fully exploited. According to Dio's Octavian, it is not really Anthony but Cleopatra who commands the opposing forces, who expose their contemptible weakness by the very fact that they submit to the rule of a woman.[180]

Thus Octavian demands,

> Should we not be acting most disgracefully if, after surpassing all men everywhere in valour, we should then meekly bear the insults of this throng who, oh hearers! are Alexandrians and Egyptians . . . , who worship reptiles and beasts as gods,

---

[178]Balch, 133. Plutarch, *Anth.* 80.1. Cassius Dio 51.16.4.

[179]The parallels between Arius Didymus and Aristotle are noted by Wachsmuth in his edition of Stobaeus in the apparatus. Balch has marked these parallels and some others pointed out by Henkel in his translation of this material (p. 67).

[180]Among Greeks and Romans, Egypt was notorious for reversing the proper relationships of men and women under the influence of Isis. (See Diod. Sic. *Lib. Hist.* 1.27.1-2. Balch, 128-29.)

> who embalm their own bodies to give them the semblance of immortality, who are most reckless in effrontery but most feeble in courage, and who, worst of all, are slaves to a woman and not to a man. . . ? (50.24.5-7).

Anthony himself "pays homage to the wench as if she were some Isis or Selene . . ." (50.25.3).

> He is either headless or mad--for indeed I have heard and believed that he has been bewitched by that accursed woman--and therefore pays no heed to our generosity or kindness, but being a slave to that woman, he undertakes the war and its self-chosen dangers on her behalf against us and his country (40.76.4-5).

Anthony's behavior has made him effeminate and unfit for command. "For it is impossible for one who leads a life of royal luxury and coddles himself like a woman to have a manly thought or do a manly deed . . ." (50.27.4). Therefore, Octavian's forces will be fighting

> to maintain the reknown of your forefathers, to preserve your own proud traditions, to take vengeance on those who are in revolt against us, to allow no woman to make herself equal to a man (10.28.3).

What is peculiarly offensive about Anthony's Egyptian alliance is not simply that it is an alliance with a foreign power, but that it is an alliance in which Anthony has become enslaved to a woman. This presumed fact is presented as indicative of Anthony's weakness and effeminacy and of his betrayal of Roman values. By extension, anyone permitting or encouraging woman's emancipation would be violating Roman traditions and undermining the strength and stability of the Roman order. One cannot be certain from Octavian's speech that Octavian, or even Dio, himself a representative of the Roman ruling class some 200 years later,[181] drew this generalized conclusion.

However, the fact that this notion had currency in the early empire comes to light clearly in a passage from Dionysius of Halicarnassus, a contemporary of Octavian. Like Cassius Dio, Dionysius, who was the protegé of the senator and historian Q. Aelius Tubero, represented the viewpoint of the Roman ruling class.[182] In the *Roman Antiquities*,

---

[181]See Fergus Millar, *A Study of Cassius Dio* (Oxford: Clarendon, 1964) 6.

[182]See F. Millar, ibid.

Dionysius presents an apologetic encomium[183] of Rome in which he discusses Rome's history, institutions, and achievements. In 2.24 he introduces the subject of Roman law regarding the household. He prefaces his remarks in this section with the following comment:

> I will first observe that all who have established a politeia (πολιτεία), barbarian as well as Greek, seem to me to have recognized correctly the general principle that every state (πόλιν ἅπασαν), since it consists of many houses (ἐκ πολλῶν οἴκων), is most likely to enjoy tranquility when the lives of individual citizens (οἱ τῶν ἰδιωτῶν . . . βίοι) are untroubled, and to have tempestuous time when the private affairs of the citizens are in a bad way . . . (224.2).[184]

Thus here Dionysius explicitly ties the well-being of the πόλις to the right ordering of the private lives of the citizens.

He goes on to say that nevertheless it has not been equally well understood everywhere by what laws the private lives of citizens may best be regulated. Roman law, however, is exemplary in this regard. In Dionysius' view the cornerstone of this law is the authority given to the male head of the household over his wife and children. On the subject of the husband's rule of his wife, Dionysius writes as follows:

> (The Roman law of marriage) obliged both the married women, as have no other refuge, to conform themselves entirely to the temper of their husbands (τὸν τοῦ γεγαμηκότος ζῆν τρόπον) and the husbands to rule (κρατεῖν) their wives as necessary and inseparable possessions (225.4 —*LCL*).

In the case of children Dionysius praises Roman law for giving "virtually full power to the father over his son (ἅπασαν ὡς εἰπεῖν . . . ἐξουσίαν πατρὶ καθ' υἱοῦ . . .) even during his whole life" (226.4). Thus the traditional Roman *familia* under the rule of the *pater familias* is held up as a continuing source of strength and stability in Roman society.

---

[183]For a detailed description and analysis of this rhetorical form see Balch, 140ff.

[184]The above translation is Balch's, pp. 152-53. Balch's translation follows that of *LCL* except that "πολιτεία" is left untranslated and "οἶκοι" is translated "houses" instead of "families."

Balch concludes convincingly from this and other similar evidence that members of the Roman ruling class of the early empire did indeed regard the traditional patriarchal family as a positive force in maintaining the stability of the political order and that, conversely, they would have viewed departures from the patriarchal pattern as subversive of that order.[185]

However, it would be a mistake to limit this viewpoint to the Roman ruling class. One has only to recall the enthusiasm with which subject peoples across the empire received and celebrated the *pax romana*[186] to realize what a large stake ordinary people felt themselves to have in the stability of the political order. In fact, in popular belief as well as in official propaganda rulers were commonly conceived of as God's functionaries for the preservation, not simply of political order in the modern sense, but of cosmic order. Plutarch expresses this concept as follows:

> . . . rulers (ἄρχοντες) serve God for the care (ἐπιμέλειαν) and preservation (σωτηρίαν) of men, in order that of the glorious gifts which the gods give to men, they may distribute some and safeguard others (780 D) . . . . the ruler is the image (εἴκων) of God who orders all things (τοῦ πάντα κοσμοῦντος) (780 E).

Paul expresses basically the same concept in more restrained fashion in Romans 13:1-7, where he describes the governing authorities (ἐξουσίαι) as "instituted by God" (ὑπὸ θεοῦ τεταγμέναι) to punish evil and approve good, and as "ministers of God" (λειτουργοὶ . . . θεοῦ). Thus the legitimate governing authorities and the government they represent are identified with the orderliness of life in its most profound sense.[187] Accordingly, one would expect people who held such a conception to view their own well-being as dependent on the stability of the political/cosmic order.[188]

---

[185]See Balch, chaps. V, VI, and especially pp. 155f.

[186]Cf. G. Bowersock, *Augustus and the Greek World* (Oxford: Clarendon, 1965) 85, 112ff.; Clinton Morrison, *The Powers That Be* (London: SCM Press, 1960) 90-93.

[187]For a full discussion of this subject matter, see Morrison, especially, pp. 63-101; see also E. R. Goodenough, "The Political Philosophy of Hellenistic Kingship," *Yale Classical Studies* 1 (1928) 53-128.

[188]Of course the established order had its enemies as well. See e.g., R. MacMullen, *Enemies of the Roman Order* (Cambridge, MA: Harvard University Press, 1966); Bowersock, *Augustus*, 101ff. The example of

Furthermore, it was not only the ruling class that perceived a threat to the stability of this order in departures from traditional family structures and violations of traditional male/female role boundaries. Role reversal in the areas of grooming and dress often appeared as a topic of controversy and condemnation in writings of the period.

For instance, in *Pseudo-Phocylides*,[189] a Jewish wisdom poem probably written at some time during the first two centuries A.D., the reader is admonished,

> If a child is a boy, do not let locks grow long on his head. Braid not his crown nor make cross-knots at the top of his head. Long hair is not fit for men, but for voluptuous women (210ff.).

The same attitude is evidently encountered by Apollonius of Tyana, who is confronted with the charge that he "wears his hair long on his head" (*Ep.* 8). Similarly, this is a topic of controversy in the first generation of the Corinthian church, where Paul asks, rhetorically, "Does not nature (φύσις) itself teach you that for a man to wear long hair is degrading to him, but if a woman has long hair, it is her pride?" (1 Cor 11:14f.) In Paul's view, for a man to wear long hair violates the natural order of things because this practice oversteps the "natural" distinction between men and women.[190]

In the above examples it may be seen that certain patterns of behavior in men and women became symbolic of right order, or alternatively, the fundamental violation of right order. It is only a small logical step to apply this symbolism in the realm of the political order.

In two passages Epictetus explicitly makes such an application of this symbolism. In the first passage he confronts a young man who has plucked out his hair after the fashion of a woman: "Shall we make a man like you a citizen of Corinth (Κορινθίων), and perchance a warden of the city (ἀστυνόμον), or superintendent of epheboi (ἐφήβαρχον) or

---

Philo illustrates how one could be deeply opposed to the present political order, yet at the same time be the defender of a more profound cosmic order, which involved traditional patriarchal notions of sex roles. For Philo's opposition to the Roman order, see E. R. Goodenough, *The Politics of Philo Judaeus* (New Haven: Yale University Press, 1938); R. A. Baer, *Philo's Use of the Categories Male and Female* (Leiden: Brill, 1970), especially p. 42.

[189]Trans. P. W. van der Horst, *The Sentences of Pseudo-Phocylides* (Leiden: Brill, 1978).

[190]See H. Koester, "φύσις," *TDNT* IX, especially pp. 266ff., 271ff.

general (στρατηγόν), or superintendent of the games (ἀγωνοθέτην)?" (3.1.34). The implication is that men who flout the traditional symbols of the male role weaken the governing structures by becoming unfit to take their place in the citizen body.

In the second passage Epictetus attacks the Epicureans for opposing marriage:

> In the name of God, I ask you, can you imagine an Epicurean state (πόλις)? One man says, "I do not marry." "Neither do I," says another, "For people ought not to marry." "No, nor have children, nor perform the duties of a citizen." And what do you suppose will happen then? Where are the citizens to come from? Who will educate them? . . . Take me a young man; bring him up according to your doctrines. Your doctrines are bad, subversive (ἀνατρεπτικά) of the state (πόλις), destructive to the family (οἶκος), not even fit for women. Drop these doctrines, man (3.7.19-20).

Epictetus makes the accusation directly: opposition to marriage involves opposition to traditional household structure; it implies neglect of a citizen's duties to take part in civic affairs and raise children properly; and it is tantamount to subversion of the political order.

In this case Epictetus' surface logic may be deceptive. The line of argument is clear enough; the logical results of the doctrine that people ought not to marry or have children is the extinction of the πόλις through lack of new citizens. However, one senses that Epictetus does not envision this result as a real possibility. Rather, rejection on principle of traditional family life symbolizes for him rejection of the rightful order which life in the πόλις should follow. Thus he finds this teaching deeply offensive.

It is significant that Epictetus does not speak as a member of the Roman ruling class or as its representative.[191] Rather he speaks from the point of view of a private citizen concerned about civic affairs and the well-being of the πόλις. Whoever defied traditional family structures and sex roles in the society of which Epictetus was a part surely must have risked the wrath not only of the Roman overlords, but also of the many ordinary citizens who understood their own well-being as dependent upon the stability of the political order.[192]

---

[191]For Epictetus' background, see the introduction of the LCL edition.

[192]Wayne Meeks, "The Image of the Androgyne," *HR* 13 (1974) 179, observes, "Among those who advocated the preservation of the status quo,

This conclusion will prove important to our understanding of the political atmosphere in which the *Haustafeln* of the Pastorals have their place.

Conclusions

Traditional Greek and Roman households showed important structural similarities. In both societies the household (οἶκος, οἰκία; *familia, domus*) was in the most basic sense of the concept an institution for the citizenry. Both householders and their wives came from the citizen ranks and it was only in such a fully legal conjugal union that citizen children could be produced. Non-citizens could claim to possess households only in a looser sense of the concept. Thus, in both societies a certain connotation of prestige and privilege was attached to the concept of "household." In both societies the household was conceived as a patriarchal institution, whose male head (κύριος, *pater familias*) exercised sweeping, although not entirely unrestricted authority over the other members. These members fell into three main categories, namely, wife, children, and slaves. In each category the primary structural relationship was one of subordination to the authority of the householder. For instance, wives in both societies were subjected to a sexual double standard that demanded strict chastity of them, while allowing their husbands extensive sexual freedom. Furthermore, in both societies the household was a religious institution that maintained and handed down religious traditions of its own.

There were also some differences in the traditional households of Greece and Rome. On the one hand, Greek women had to endure more severe limitations on the social activities and freedom of movement than did their Roman counterparts, and there was a greater social disparity between husbands and wives in Greece, in part, because of a greater average age differential and in part because of differences in education. Furthermore, Greek women were more severely handicapped in the area

---

the constantly salient concern is a sense of order: everything must be in its place, and the differentiation and ranking of women and men became a potent symbol for the stability of the world order." Religious minorities were apparently particularly vulnerable to the charge of beguiling women and undermining the household. In some cases they responded by making exaggerated claims to orthopraxy in this area, as Josephus did on behalf of the Jewish people in *Ap.* 2.199ff. Balch gives a thorough treatment of this aspect of the question, pp. 115ff.

of property ownership than were Roman women. On the other hand, Roman husbands had more nearly absolute authority over their wives, at least in marriage with *manus*, than did Greek husbands. Roman householders also traditionally possessed more sweeping authority over their children and their slaves than was the case in Greece.

However, by the time of the early empire, most of the significant differences between households in the two societies had disappeared in the wake of parallel social changes. In Rome there had been a gradual decrease in the powers of the *pater familias* over his wife, his children, and his slaves. Most marriages now took place without *manus*, so that married women were able to exercise a considerable degree of independence over against their husbands. For instance, they could own and manage property, and they could, with the permission of their guardian, divorce their husbands. The evidence from the Greek marriage contracts of Hellenistic Egypt indicates that Greek wives were also experiencing new freedom and power. They too could now own and manage property and initiate divorce proceedings if they chose. Furthermore, Greek women in many places were no longer bound by such restrictive social customs. Many of them were giving dinner parties with their husbands and taking part in public affairs like their sisters in Rome.

The traditional Jewish household, like the traditional households of Greece and Rome, was patriarchal in structure. At the same time it was characterized by a number of distinctive social features. However, in Hellenistic Judaism, most of these distinctive features disappeared, so that, from the social structure alone, one would have a difficult time distinguishing pagan from Jewish households in the cities of Hellenistic-Roman Diaspora.

The class structure of society in the early empire was characterized by verticality. The upper classes comprised an extremely small group resting at the top of a steep social pyramid. The Greek and Roman households described in the literature of the period belong almost exclusively to this stratum of society. Upper class householders typically possessed roomy private homes and numerous slaves. In many cases their marriages would have been carefully arranged political alliances.

Among the great numbers of people in the lower classes, there were a few wealthy freedmen like Trimalchio, whose households would have resembled those of the acknowledged upper classes in many respects. A rather sizeable number of people probably lived in multi-room apartments like the "luxury apartments" of Ostia. A great many more, however, lived in one or two room storefront and upper story apartments. No doubt few of the families that lived in typical urban apartments could have afforded the luxury of a slave. The average size of such families was probably relatively small, perhaps four or five members, so that in many cases only the nuclear family must have been involved. Slaves and, in many cases, freedpersons, were unable to contract fully legal marriages in which rights and obligations were established by law, and often the children of such marriages were separated from parents. Yet many ordinary people placed high value on stable marriages and the love and fidelity of marriage partners. Thus epitaphs proudly record the duration of extraordinarily long marriages and commemorate the faithfulness of *univirae*.

Social tension in connection with the wife's role was a significant and widespread feature of household life in the early empire, and, in fact, had been a rather constant feature of household life since at least the middle of the Hellenistic period. In conjunction with the dramatic changes that had come about in the social and legal status of women, popular values had also undergone a process of change. The notion that women possessed intellectual and moral capacities equal to those of men could, in the first century A.D., receive a hearing in a basically conservative setting, as the example of Seneca attests. The idea that husbands and wives should be held accountable to a single standard of sexual behavior was also gaining credence. At the same time, the old values, premised upon a stricter and more consistent patriarchalism, continued to have wide approval. Predictably, this conflict in values provoked a variety of responses: for example, in Juvenal's case, bitter misogyny and nostalgia for an earlier, purer day; in Plutarch's, an attempt to subsume the new values under the old and so to preserve the essential structure of the old values by making certain minimal concessions to the times; and, in the case of Xenophon of Ephesus, easy acceptance of the new spirit of egalitarianism.

In addition the traditional patriarchal household and conventional sex roles had come to be associated on a symbolic level with the preservation of an orderly and stable society. Consequently, people whose behavior defied the traditional values in this area risked the charge of political subversion. Mark Anthony, for example, was charged with being a traitor to Rome, in part, on the basis of the accusation that he had allowed himself to be ruled by a woman. Paul considered long hair in men a contravention of the natural order. Epictetus attacked as politically subversive the Epicurean teaching which opposed marriage on the grounds that, if followed, this teaching would destroy the traditional family and render impossible the proper upbringing of children. Thus social tension in the area of the household spilled over into the larger social arena.

III

The Haustafel Tradition in the Pastorals

Given that much of the material in the Pastorals is concerned with problems of social structure and relations in household and church, should this material be understood to reflect the author's focused understanding of issues which his church faces and his response to these issues, or should this material be seen as reflecting an accumulation of traditions dealing with various social concerns, a number of which may not be particularly current? For instance, is the problem of widows one to which the author responds because it is a troublesome problem in his community, or is the material on widows accumulated tradition which is simply being preserved as part of the tradition. The question is then, not whether this material deals with real issues, but whether they were live issues in the author's situation and whether his was a deliberate response to these issues.

THE *HAUSTAFELN* AS EARLY CHRISTIAN PARAENESIS

As noted in Chapter I, the focal material of this study is presented according to the form of the early Christian *Haustafeln*. The *Haustafel* form has usually been characterized as a schema, but has recently been classified as a topos by Balch, on the basis of his identification of the topos "concerning household management" as the antecedent of the *Haustafeln*. One would expect such a schema or topos to be utilized and thus realized in different ways by different authors. The following discussion will seek to identify the basic traditional elements of the *Haustafel* schema/topos and the utilization of this schema/topos in several examples from among the *Haustafeln*. The question of what difference it makes to think of the *Haustafel* form as a schema or to think of it as a topos will be explored in the course of the discussion.

The Haustafel *Schema/Topos*

The *Haustafeln* are characterized by a number of features, some of which can be explained by reference to Balch's topos, "concerning household management." Balch's most important example of the use of this topos comes from the beginning of Aristotle's *Politics.*[1] This passage may thus serve to illustrate the key features of the topos. After an introductory discussion of the various elements which make up the πόλις, Aristotle introduces the subject of household management in the following manner: "And now that it is clear what are the component parts of the state (πόλις), we have first of all to discuss household management; for every state (πόλις) is composed of households (οἰκίων)" (*Pol.* 1253b 1ff.). A brief summary of the subject matter of this topos follows, in which the required subtopics are given, namely, the relationship of master and slave, or mastership (δεσποτική); the relationship of husband and wife, or marriage (γαμική); the relationship of father and children, or the progenitive relationship (τεκνοποιητική); and the art of getting wealth (χρηματιστική) (1253b 5-14). In the remaining portion of Book I these subtopics are discussed in detail (especially that of mastership). Here the relationships within the household are considered under the rubrics of ruling and being ruled (τὸ ἄρχειν καὶ ἄρχεσθαι) (1254a 22ff.), so that the primary question in each case becomes how is the ruler (master, husband, father)'s authority appropriately expressed here: for example, in the case of slaves, "it is clear that the authority of the master over slaves (δεσποτεία) is not the same as the authority of a magistrate in a republic (πολιτική) . . ." (1255b 17ff.). The topos "concerning household management" may thus be described as follows: it is comprised of four subtopics: master-slave relationships, husband-wife relationships, father-child relationships, and the art of acquiring wealth; furthermore, the three basic relationships are approached as relationships of ruler and ruled, or of superior and subordinate; and finally, the context of this topos is that of a larger topos which concerns the πολιτεία as a whole.[2] The topos "concerning household management" appears repeatedly in philosophical discussions of the state (πόλις, πολιτεία), with all or at least most of these features.[3]

---

[1]Balch, 49, 70.

[2]See Balch's discussion, 49f., and also his summaries, 70ff. and 112.

[3]One of Balch's clearest examples comes from Arius Didymus (83ff.).

In addition, this topos appears in apologetic literature such as the encomium on Rome which is given by Dionysius of Halicarnassus in his *Roman Antiquities* (2.24.2-27.6). Here the same basic features appear, with the exception of the theme of money-making. In this case, however, the lax customs of household management among Greeks and barbarians are contrasted with the (superior) strict customs of the Romans, in which the father's authority is almost absolute, so that the superior strength of Rome is held to be founded on her superior customs and laws with respect to the household.[4] The flexibility of the topos is shown in these two examples. In the former, the argumentation is general and theoretical; in the latter, the argumentation is apologetic in purpose and proceeds by the use of concrete historical illustration. At the same time the rather consistent moral viewpoint is also reflected: proper management of domestic affairs is a matter of the proper exercise of ruling power by the (male) head of the household over wife, children, slaves, and (other) property. Furthermore, proper household management is seen to be one's patriotic duty, in that the stability of households is believed to undergird the πολιτεία.

The early Christian *Haustafeln* provide still another context for the use of the topos "concerning household management," namely the context of ethical exhortation directed by a minority religious group toward itself. The topos is most clearly reflected in the *Haustafeln* of Colossians 3:18ff. and Ephesians 5:22ff. Here not only do the three pairs of relationships--wives-husbands, children-parents, and slave-masters--appear together, but they are also treated expressly as relationships of subordinate to superior. Thus wives are urged to subordinate themselves (ὑποτάσσεσθαι) to their husbands, while children and slaves are exhorted to obey (ὑπακούειν), respectively, their fathers and masters. Thus the traditional domestic morality represented by the household management topos is here taken over uncritically. There is no discussion of money making, however. Moreover, there is no explicit link made between the traditional subtopic of household management and the government of the larger society, although it might be argued that the analogy between the relationship of husband and wife and that of Christ and the church in Ephesians represents an adaptation of this traditional linkage to a context in which the church is the significant larger society.

---

[4]See Balch, 144ff. and LCL ed. of Dionysius, *Roman Antiquities*, 2.24.2-27.5.

The other *Haustafeln* do not reflect as fully the traditional characteristics of the topos "concerning household management." Thus the *Haustafel* which begins at 1 Peter 2:13 treats the relationship of slaves to masters and of wives and husbands to each other, on the basis of the concept of subordination, but omits the parent-child relationship. It is true, however, that the *Haustafel* is introduced by a general exhortation which appears to relate behavior within the household to behavior in the larger society in a manner reminiscent of the topos. Christians are urged to subordinate themselves to "every human institution," that is, the various representatives of governmental authority. Then the same verb (ὑποτάσσεσθαι) is used to exhort slaves to subordinate themselves to their masters, and wives, to their husbands. It thus appears that an analogy is being suggested between behavior in the household and behavior vis-a-vis the state. Pol. Phil. 4:2-6:1 preserves a *Haustafel* which only faintly reflects the household management topos. Here, of the three traditional family relationships, only that of husband and wife is addressed, although children are mentioned in the exhortation to wives. At the same time, other groups not traditionally discussed in the topos come into view: widows, deacons, young men, virgins, and presbyters. In addition, while it is interesting that the subject of money is addressed (4:1) immediately prior to the first exhortation of the *Haustafel* (4:2), the general content of the teaching on money is very different from that of the traditional topos.[5]

Thus while the topos "concerning household management" can account for a number of key recurring features which the *Haustafeln* exhibit in varying degrees, there are other recurrent features, especially syntactical features, which are not accounted for by this topos. In fact the individual exhortations of the various Christian *Haustafeln* appear to be structured according to a predictable schema which is not associated with the household management topos anywhere except in the *Haustafeln* themselves.[6]

---

[5]It is noteworthy that in the examples cited by Balch of the use of the topos in Philo, some of these same groups appear: *Spec. Leg.* 2. 225-7, *Decal.* 165ff. Cf. Stob. 4.27.23 from Hierocles, on the subject of one's duties toward one's kinsmen in various degrees, which resembles 1 Tim 5:1.

[6]Partial parallels do exist in several Hellenistic-Jewish sources, a fact which suggests the possibility that this schema may have been taken over from the Hellenistic-Jewish synagogue (see below, p. 90, n. 10). In addition, Balch cites a parallel in Epictetus 3.7.21, which does not appear to be very close to the basic form of the schema as described below,

The schema has primarily to do with the structure of the individual exhortations and secondarily with the way in which these exhortations are characteristically linked. The elements of the schema may be outlined as follows: Firstly, there is an address (usually in the plural) to a group of persons representing a certain social station (αἱ γυναῖκες, οἱ δοῦλοι, etc.). Secondly, there is an imperative, variously expressed with imperative proper, infinitive or participle, and often accompanied by an object in the appropriate case. Thirdly, there is an amplification, which is typically expressed as a prepositional phrase, although other forms are used as well, especially the form μή (οὐ) . . . ἀλλά . . . The amplification either defines the imperative more fully (typically as an adverb of manner) or provides a general motivation for it. Finally, there is a reason clause providing motivation, theological justification, etc., which is typically introduced by γάρ, ὅτι, or εἴδοτες ὅτι. The reason clause may be expanded into a paragraph. Several examples serving to illustrate the schema are presented below in Chart 1.

All four elements are to be found in approximately half of the exhortations belonging to the *Haustafeln* of Colossians, Ephesians, 1 Peter, Polycarp to the Philippians and Ignatius to Polycarp. Furthermore, the full pattern is found at least once in each of these codes, a fact which indicates broad familiarity with this pattern. Clearly, however, the essential elements of the schema are the address to a defined group and the accompanying imperative. In the codes in question, the imperative (or its equivalent) is lacking only in one instance, the address to women in Ephesians 5:22ff., and here the imperative ὑποτάσσεσθε is transparently implied. Similarly, there is no address only in 1 Peter 2:13ff., where the congregation is exhorted to be subject to "every human institution. . . ."

Secondarily, the schema is characterized by the fact that the exhortations which belong to it do not appear alone, but in series with other exhortations of the same type.[7] The link between exhortations is

---

although it is closer to that of the sections in the Pastorals where Timothy and Titus are addressed: ἄφες ταῦτ' ἄνθρωπε, ζῇς ἐν ἡγεμονούσῃ πόλει· ἄρχειν σε δεῖ, κοίνειν δικαίως, . . . A possible parallel is also suggested in Iamblichus' *Vit. Pyth.* 54-7, where Iamblichus summarizes Pythagoras' remarks to a group of women. However, no assured conclusions can be drawn from the summary about the form of these remarks (cf. Balch, 103).

[7]As noted above, the various *Haustafeln* exhibit considerable variety in the selection of social groupings to be dealt with, so that the particular

CHART 1

Elements of the *Haustafel* Exhortations

Passage	*Address*	*Imperative*	*Amplification*	*Reason*
Col 3.21	τὰ τέκνα	ὑπακούετε τοῖς γονεῦσιν	κατὰ πάντα	τοῦτο γὰρ εὐάρεστον . . .
1 Pet 2:18f.	οἱ οἰκέται	ὑποτασσόμενοι τοῖς δεσπόταις	(between verb and object) οὐ μόνον . . . ἀλλὰ καί	τοῦτο γὰρ (introducing a paragraph)
Pol. Phil. 4:3	(indirect address - teach) τὰς χήρας	σωφρονούσας (εἶναι)	περὶ τὴν τοῦ κυρίου πίστιν . . . (expanded by a virtue list)	γινωσκούσας ὅτι . . . (several clauses)

typically expressed with the connectives καί, ὁμοίως, and καί ὁμοίως. These connectives are especially likely to link together reciprocally related exhortations. Thus in Ephesians the exhortation to fathers is linked to the exhortation to children by καί (6:4) and the exhortation to masters is linked to the exhortation to slaves in the same way (6:9). Similarly, in 1 Peter, the exhortation to husbands is linked to the exhortation to wives by ὁμοίως, and in Ignatius to Polycarp, the exhortation to brothers (husbands) is linked to the exhortation to sisters (wives) by καὶ

---

set--husbands/wives, fathers/children, and masters/slaves--is not determinative for the schema. Campenhausen reflects awareness of this fact when he argues that the basic concept of the *Haustafel* is the different social "stations." The culmination of the form is reached in Polycarp to the Philippians and in the Pastorals, where these stations are no longer the natural familial ones alone, but those of church order as well. Thus Campenhausen emphasizes the utilization of the basic form for conceptualizing the social organization of the church (*Polykarp*, 33).

ὁμοίως (5:1-2). Other exhortations are also sometimes linked in this manner, especially in the later *Haustafeln*. Thus, in 1 Peter, the section dealing with slaves is connected to that dealing with women by ὁμοίως, and in Polycarp to the Philippians, the section dealing with deacons is connected to the section dealing with younger men by ὁμοίως καί. Thus there appears to be an increasing tendency to make use of such connectives.[8]

The schema has experienced development in other ways during the course of its use. First, as has often been noted,[9] the reason clauses undergo development, so that in a number of instances, they become entire paragraphs. (Cf. Ephesians on wives in 5:22f. and 1 Peter on slaves in 2:18ff.) Similarly, the amplifications tend to become lengthier. The device of οὐ (μόνον) . . . ἀλλα . . . is used this way. In Polycarp to the Philippians virtue lists typically supplement or replace the amplificatory prepositional phrases, so that a list of duties or virtues is given (Pol. Phil. 4:3ff.). In addition, in the codes found in Ignatius and Polycarp, other types of exhortations are sandwiched between the typical exhortations dealing with various groupings of people. Thus the exhortation to Polycarp on the subject of widows in Ign. Pol. 4:1 is followed by several other exhortations which have to do with Polycarp's leadership of the church, for example, "Let nothing be done without your approval, and do nothing yourself without God. . . . Let the meetings be more numerous." Similarly, in Pol. Phil. 5:1, between the section on widows and that on deacons, the congregation as a whole is urged to "walk worthily of (God's) commandment and glory." Furthermore, in Colossians, Ephesians and 1 Peter the various groups are addressed directly, while in Ignatius to Polycarp and Polycarp to the Philippians the address is only indirect, in that the congregational leadership is urged to exhort various groups in various ways (ταῖς ἀδελφαῖς προσλάλει ἀγαπᾶν τὸν κύριον. . . . Ign. Pol. 5:1). Finally, there is a tendency in Ignatius to take greater liberties with the basic structure of the schema. For example, he does not address exhortations to widows, but instead makes them the object of care: "Let not the widows be neglected." Similarly, the section on slaves is concerned first of all with behavior toward them, and only afterwards with the behavior of the slaves themselves: "Do not be haughty to slaves, either men or women; yet do not let them be puffed up . . . " (Ign. Pol. 4:3).

---

[8]Consistent with this observation is the fact that the Colossian *Haustafel* contains no connectives between exhortations.

[9]E.g., Weidinger, 51.

On the one hand, then, the *Haustafeln*, especially those of Colossians and Ephesians, have been shaped by the topos "concerning household management." This fact makes it likely that the original thrust of the *Haustafeln* was indeed toward relationships within the households of Christians. On the other hand, the *Haustafeln* have been shaped according to a schema which appears both to have originated and to have experienced development within the early church.[10] This schema may perhaps be best characterized, with the help of Campenhausen's terminology, as a station code schema.[11] It thus appears that the literary-traditional influences upon the *Haustafeln* were of two kinds: (1) influences (associated with the household management topos) which were essentially external to the early church and which exerted influence on the various *Haustafeln* independently, and (2) specific inner Christian influences (associated with the station code schema) which gave to the *Haustafel* form the status of a schema which underwent a traceable evolutionary process in the history of the early church.[12]

The *Haustafeln* thus employ the topos on household management, and in so doing, carry forward its basic ethical perspective. Yet they employ this topos in a way essentially unparalleled in pagan philosophical

---

[10]Partial parallels to this schema are present in several of the Jewish sources which are commonly cited as forerunners of the *Haustafeln*. Of these, the closest occurs in Philo, *Decal.* 165ff., where there is a suggestion that the law contains exhortations to various social groupings: "And there are many other instructions given, to the young on courtesy to the old, to the old on taking care of the young, to subjects on obeying their rulers, to rulers on promoting the welfare of their subjects. . . ." In line with Crouch's argument that the Hellenistic-Jewish synagogue knew a version of the Jewish law especially designed as a proselyte catechism (see pp. 84ff.), it might be supposed that Philo is referring to a passage in this catechism which had the form of the station code schema. It is possible, therefore, that the station code schema was taken over by the church from the synagogue. The most important point in this context, however, is not the origin, but the presence and development of the station code schema in early Christianity.

[11]Balch, it will be recalled, argues that the similarities in the various *Haustafeln* can be accounted for by the theory that they represent independent applications of the household management topos to similar problems.

[12]The position being taken here is thus a somewhat revised version of Crouch's view that the *Haustafeln* are the product of a combination of influences external and internal to the church (p. 146f).

or apologetic literature. The topos is employed in conjunction with a schema which involves ethical exhortation addressed to various specific social groupings within the church, especially social groupings present in the household. The form of the *Haustafeln* thus strongly suggests that they address real, concrete, and in some cases persistent social needs within the church.[13]

THE USE OF THE *HAUSTAFEL* TRADITION IN THE PASTORALS

The Household Management Topos in the Pastorals

Traces of the influence of the household management topos are present in the material under consideration here. The relationships of husbands and wives, parents and children, and masters and slaves (the relationships emphasized in the topos) continue to receive treatment in this material in various contexts. Furthermore, these relationships continue to be presented as relationships of superior and inferior parties. Thus in the section in 1 Timothy on the bishop and deacons, father-child relationships are touched upon in the context of an enumeration of qualifications for office: church officers must be persons who manage their own households well, which includes keeping their children "submissive and respectful" (3:4; cf. 3:12; Titus 1:6).[14] In Titus 2 it is urged that the younger women be taught to love their husbands and children (φιλάνδρους εἶναι, φιλοτέκνους) and to be submissive to their husbands (ὑποτασσομένας τοῖς ἰδίοις ἀνδράσιν). Slaves are urged in 1 Tim 6:1 to "regard their masters as worthy of all honor," and in Titus 2:9, Titus is instructed to teach slaves to "be submissive" (ὑποτάσσεσθαι) to their masters. It is also interesting that in 1 Tim 2:11-12 it is urged that women learn "in silence" (ἐν ἡσυχίᾳ) "in all submission" and that they "exist in silence" (εἶναι ἐν ἡσυχίᾳ), since a woman should not be permitted to teach or to have authority over a man (διδάσκειν

---

[13]Thus this analysis supports the basic position of Crouch (p. 144, esp.).

[14]1 Tim 3:12b reads, "let them manage their children and their households well." "Households" (οἴκων) may be a reference to household servants and slaves. This question will be discussed more fully below, chapter IV.

δὲ γυναῖκι οὐκ ἐπιτρέπω, οὐδὲ αὐθεντεῖν ἀνδρός...). Although the issue here appears to be the respective roles of men and women in worship rather than the relationship of husband and wife in the household, the household management topos held up silence as a desirable trait in women.[15]

In addition, as seen above, the household management topos characteristically included a section on money making. The exhortation of the wealthy in 1 Tim 6:17ff. may be an adaptation of this feature to the topos, although the negative evaluation of wealth (τοῖς πλουσίοις ... παραγγέλλε μὴ . . . ἠλπικέναι ἐπὶ πλούτου ἀδήλοτι...) runs directly counter to what one would expect based on, for example, Aristotle's discussion of property and wealth in *Politics* (1256a. 1ff.).

Finally, it will be recalled, the household management topos is usually employed in the context of the discussion of the larger πολιτεία. Above (p. 86) it was noted that the opening section of the 1 Peter *Haustafel* (2:13ff.), which urges subjection to governmental authority, may reflect this traditional topical connection. Sections with a similar thrust are to be found in the Pastorals in close proximity to *Haustafel* material. Thus, in 1 Tim 2:1ff. "prayer for all men, for kings and for all who are in high positions (πάντων ἐν ὑπεροχῇ ὄντων)" is urged,[16] and in Titus 3:1, Titus is directed to remind the Cretan Christians "to be submissive to rulers and authorities."

The Development of the Station Code Schema in the Pastorals

The most straightforward use of the station code schema in the Pastorals occurs in Titus 2:1-10. The outstanding features of the schema as it appears here are given below in Chart 2. As in Pol. Phil. 4:2ff. and Ign. Pol. 4:1ff., there has been a departure here from exclusive focus on relationships within the household. This shift in focus is seen both in the selection of groups to be exhorted (older men and women, younger women and men, slaves) and in the content of the exhortations. Thus the older men are envisioned, not primarily as heads of households, but as models of

---

[15]Cf. Arist. 1260a 30 "silence (σιγή) gives grace to a woman."

[16]Bartsch disputes the contention that 1 Tim 2:1ff. is mainly concerned with obedience to governing authority (pp. 35-36). The more common interpretation, adopted here, is that this exhortation is indeed parallel to those in 1 Pet 2:13ff. and Rom 13:1ff.

CHART 2

The Station Code Schema in Titus 2:1-10

Address	*Imperative*	*Amplification*	*Reason*
πρεσβύτας	νηφαλίους εἶναι	σέμνους, σώφρονας, . . .	---
ὡσαύτως			
πρεσβυτίδας	ἱεροπρεπεῖς (εἶναι)	ἐν καταστήματι (before imperative) μὴ διαβόλους, . . .	ἵνα σωφρονίζωσιν.
τὰς νεάς (embedded in previous ἵνα clause)	φιλάνδρους εἶναι	φιλοτέκνους, . . .	ἵνα μὴ ὁ λόγος τοῦ θεοῦ βλασφημῆται.
ὡσαύτως παρακάλει			
τοὺς νεωτέρους	σωφρονεῖν	---	---
(Titus)	σεαυτὸν παρεχόμενος τύπον καλῶν ἔργων	ἐν τῇ διδασκαλίᾳ ἀφθορίαν, . . .	ἵνα ὁ ἐξ ἐναντίας. . .
δούλους	ἰδίοις δεσπόταις ὑποτάσσεσθαι	ἐν πᾶσιν, εὐαρέστους εἶναι	ἵνα τὴν διδασκαλίαν κοσμῶσιν.

behavior in the community at large, so that they are called upon to be "sound in faith, love, and endurance." Similarly, older women are called upon to instruct younger women in proper behavior. The content of the instructions for younger women, however, does reveal a continuing interest in household relationships: young wives should be counseled to love their husbands (φιλάνδρους) and children (φιλοτέκνους), to become good household managers (οἰκούργους), and to subordinate themselves (ὑποτάσσεσθαι) to their husbands. Similarly, slaves are to be counseled to be subordinate to their masters.[17] The interweaving of directions to

[17] The particular groups named here recall the list mentioned by Philo in *Decal.* 165-67 (old/young, rulers/subjects, benefactors/dependents, servants/masters).

the intermediary, seen here in the special instructions to Titus (perhaps as one of the "younger men") is also a characteristic seen in Pol. Phil. 4:2ff. and Ign. Pol. 4:1ff.

The structure of the individual exhortations most closely resembles that of Pol. Phil. 4:2ff. The various groups are no longer directly addressed; instead, an intermediary (here, Titus) is instructed to deliver the exhortations. Otherwise, as in Pol. Phil. 4:2ff., the exhortations preserve the basic structure of address, imperative, amplification and reason, but with one modification: the amplification is consistently supplemented or replaced by a virtue (or vice) list.

The exhortations to older men and to older women are linked by ὡσαύτως, as are the exhortations to younger women and to younger men. This usage appears to be similar to the use of καί and ὁμοίως in other *Haustafeln* linking reciprocally related groups.

In addition, Titus 1:5-9 and 3:1ff. contain material similar to that which appears elsewhere in station codes. The first passage contains elements that reflect the structure of the station code schema, while the second does not. The structure of 1:7ff. may be represented as in Chart 3:

CHART 3

The Station Code Schema in Titus 1:7ff.

Office	*Requirement*	*Amplification*	*Reason*
(δεῖ γάρ)			
τὸν ἐπί-σκοπον	ἀνέγκλητος εἶναι	ὡς θεοῦ οἰκονό-μον, μὴ αὐθά-δη, . . . ἀλλά	ἵνα δυ-νατὸς ᾖ παρα-καλεῖν

3:1ff. contains an indirect exhortation to the church to be subject to the ruling authorities, followed by a list of other exhortations and a general theological rationale.

In 1:5ff. qualifications for church office are presented in a form very close to that of the station code schema. The passage is closely parallelled by 1 Tim 3:1ff., discussed below. As noted above (p. 92), the reference in Titus 3:1ff. (cf. 1 Tim 2:1ff., 1 Pet 2:13ff.) to governmental authorities may reflect the influence of the topos on household management.[18]

The station code schema is also to be found in 1 Tim 2:1-6:1. Here, however, development and expansion of the schema have gone so far that it is not easy to decide whether certain material should be viewed as expanding and developing the schema or simply intruding upon it. Chart 4 attempts to highlight the features of various sections within 1 Tim 2:1-6:1 which identify these passages as developments of the station code schema.

Here, as in Titus 2:1-10, Pol. Phil. 4:2ff., and Ign. Pol. 4:1ff., the social sphere envisioned includes, but also extends beyond, the boundaries of the household. The section on slaves focuses upon the slave-master relationship, a household concern. The section on widows, however, deals with both household concerns and concerns of the larger community. Thus part of the section deals with the household's responsibility toward its widows (vv. 4, 8, 16?); another part deals with the behavior and responsibilities of widows in the larger community and the qualifications by which one meets the community's definition of real widowhood (vv. 5-7, 9-15); and still another part deals with the community's responsibility toward "real" widows. Furthermore, the sections on bishop and deacons are

---

[18]Although Titus 2:1-10 appears to be a discrete section, it may not be wrong to view 1:5-3:11 as a compositional unity in the form of a station code that has been augmented with other kinds of material. Interpreters have differed widely in their attempts to divide this material into sections. In Dibelius/Conzelmann, 130, it is divided into three sections: 1:5-16; 2:1-15; 3:1-11. Spicq, 600, 615, divides the epistle into two main parts: 1:5-16; 2:1-3:11. A. T. Hanson, *The Pastoral Letters*, 105, divides it still differently: 1:5-2:10; 2:11-14; 2:15-3:11. Lock views 1:5-3:11 as a unity, p. 123.

The material which separates Tit 1:5-9 from 2:1ff. involves polemic against false teachers, whom the bishop must be able successfully to confute. Their teaching is to be contrasted with the "sound teaching" of 2:1ff. (ἡ ὑγιαίνουσα διδασκαλία). Polemic of this kind is also interposed between the exhortations of 1 Tim 2:1-6:1 (see below, p. 96), as well as in Pol. Phil. 4:1ff. Titus 3:1ff. is separated from 2:1-10 by a brief section (2:11-14) in which a theological rationale for the previous exhortations is given, and by a summary to Titus: "Declare these things; exhort and reprove (παρακάλει καὶ ἔλεγχε) with all authority (ἐπιταγῆς). Let no one disregard you." Both theological rationale and summary exhortation are used in 1 Tim 2:1-6:1 as well (see pp. 96ff. below).

CHART 4

The Station Code Schema in 1 Timothy 2-6

Passage	Address	Imperative	Amplification	Reason
2:1-7	παρακαλῶ . . .	(This section includes material associated with the codes, but not the schema.)		
2:8-15	τοὺς ἄνδρους	προσεύχεσθαι (before address)	ἐν παντὶ τόπῳ, ἐπαί-ροντας	---
	ὡσαύτως			
	γυναῖκας	κοσμεῖν ἑαυτάς	ἐν καταστολῇ κοσ-μίῳ. . . . μὴ . . . ἀλλὰ. . . . (before imperative)	᾿Αδὰμ γὰρ πρῶτος ἐπλά-σθη. . . .
3:1-13	τὸν ἐπίσκοπον	ἀναπίλημπτον εἶναι	μιᾶς γυναικὸς ἄνδρα . . . , τοῦ ἰδίου οἴκου καλῶς προϊσταμένου . . .	εἰ δέ τις τοῦ ἰδίου οἴκου προστῆναι οὐκ οἶδεν. . . .
			μὴ νεόφυτον ⟶	ἵνα μὴ εἰς κρίμα ἐμπέσῃ
			μαρτυρίαν καλὴν ἔχειν ⟶	ἵνα μὴ εἰς ὀνειδισμὸν ἐμπέσῃ
	ὡσαύτως			
	διακόνους	σέμνους (εἶναι)	μὴ διλόγους	
	ὡσαύτως			

CHART 4 (continued)

Passage	Address	Imperative	Amplification	Reason
	γυναῖκας	σεμνάς (εἶναι)	μὴ διαβόλους, . . .	---
	διάκονοι (resumed)	ἔστωσαν	μιᾶς γυναικὸς ἄν- δρες. . . .	οἱ γὰρ καλῶς διακο- νήσαντες βαθμὸν . . . περιποιοῦνται.
3:4-16	(ταῦτά σοι γράφω. . . .)			
4:1-5	(Behavior and teaching of false teachers)			
4:6-16	(Instructions to Timothy)			
5:1-2	(Timothy's duties toward various groups in the church)			
5:3-16	(Section on widows; does not follow schema)			
5:17-24	(Section on elders; miscellaneous rules and observations; does not follow schema)			
6:1-2	ὅσοι εἰσιν ὑπὸ ζυγὸν δοῦλοι	τοὺς ἰδίους δε- σπόταις πάσης τιμῆς ἀξίους ἡγείσθωσαν	---	ἵνα μὴ τὸ ὄνομα τοῦ θεοῦ . . . βλασφη- μῆται
	δὲ			
	οἱ . . . πιστοὺς ἔχοντες δεσπότας	μὴ καταφρονεί- τωσαν	ὅτι ἀδελφοί εἰσιν ἀλλὰ μᾶλλον. . . .	ὅτι πιστοὶ . . . οἱ ἀντιλαμβανόμενοι τῆς εὐεργεσίας.
6:17-19	τοῖς πλουσί- οις ἐν τῷ νῦν αἰῶνι	μὴ ὑψηλοφρονεῖν	μηδὲ ἠλπικέναι . . . ἀλλὰ. . . .	ἀποθησαυρίζοντας ἑαυτοῖς θεμέλιον καλὸν . . . εἶναι . . . .

CHART 4 (continued)

Several passages in 2:1-6:1 that are concerned with groups in the church have another form, in which the group is the recipient of someone else's action.

Passage	Group	Imperative	Amplification	(Reason)
5:1-2	πρεσβυτέρῳ	μὴ ἐπιπλήξῃς	ἀλλὰ παρακάλει ὡς πατέρα	---
	νεωτέρους	(παρακάλει)	ὡς ἀδελφούς	---
	πρεσβυτέρας	(παρακάλει)	ὡς μητέρας	---
	νεωτέρας	(παρακάλει)	ὡς ἀδελφὰς ἐν . . . ἁγνείᾳ	---
5:3	χήρας	τίμα	τὰς ὄντως χήρας	---
5:17	οἱ καλῶς προεστῶτες πρεσβύτεροι	διπλῆς τιμῆς ἀξιούσθωσαν	μάλιστα οἱ κοπιῶντες ἐν λόγῳ καὶ διδασκαλίᾳ	λέγει γὰρ βοῦν ἀλοῶντα οὐ φι-μώσεις

primarily concerned with the qualifications for community offices, yet the qualifications themselves have to do in part with household relationships (3:2, 4-5, 3:11-12; cf. Titus 1:6).

Similarly, most of the groups or stations included here have parallels in Titus 2:1ff., Pol. Phil. 4:2ff., or Ign. Pol. 4:2ff. Men and women (2:8-15) (husbands and wives) are included as groups, not only here, but also in the less diversified *Haustafeln* of Colossians, Ephesians, and 1 Peter. While the bishop (3:1-7) does not appear as a subject of any of the other *Haustafeln*, his office is closely tied to that of the elders in Titus 1:5ff., and elders comprise one of the groups in Pol. Phil. 4:1ff. The subject of deacons (3:8ff.) is also taken up in Pol. Phil. 5:2. Just as Timothy is addressed here (4:6ff., etc.) as a singular community leader, so also Titus is addressed in Titus 2:7-8, and Polycarp in Ign. Pol. 4:1. The categories of old and young men and women (5:1-2) appear also in Titus 2:1-10, while "young men" and "virgins" appear as categories in Pol. Phil. 5:3. The subject of widows (5:3-16) is treated in both Pol. Phil. (4:3) and in Ign. Pol. (4:1). Elders (5:17ff.) are also treated as a group in Pol. Phil. 6:1 (cf. Titus 1:6ff.), although the subject matter is not the same. The category of slaves (6:1-2) appears in almost all of the *Haustafeln*. The exhortation for the wealthy has no parallel in the other *Haustafeln*, although the *Haustafel* of Pol. Phil. 4:2ff. is introduced with a brief reference to the futility and danger of the love of money (4:1).

The tendency in Polycarp to the Philippians and Ignatius to Polycarp toward free adaptation of the schema is evident in even greater degree in 1 Timothy. The code opens with a section (2:1-7) in which "prayer for all people" and for rulers is urged. Although this section may reflect the influence of the topos on household management it does not reflect use of the station code schema. In 2:8-15 the typical structural characteristics of the reciprocal exhortations to husbands and wives are present, except that the order is reversed: τους ἄνδρας . . . . ὡσαύτως . . . γυναῖκας. . . . The content, however, departs markedly from the usual content of exhortations to husbands and wives in the *Haustafeln*. The exhortation to men does not concern their role as husbands, but has to do with their conduct in worship (βούλομαι οὖν προσεύχεσθαι τοὺς ἄνδρας. . . .). Similarly, the exhortation to women has to do primarily with their dress and behavior in worship.[19]

---

[19]On the proper context of the exhortations in this passage see Dibelius/Conzelmann, 45; Barrett, 53ff.; Jeremias, 17.

The schema has also undergone modification in the sections on bishop and deacons. In Polycarp to the Philippians the corresponding sections contain genuine exhortations regarding the conduct and responsibilities of church officers. Thus the exhortation to elders (6:1) deals primarily with the way in which oversight of the congregation is to be carried out: "And let the presbyters also be compassionate, merciful to all, bringing back those that have wandered, caring for all the weak. . . ." By contrast, in 1 Timothy in the section on the bishop (3:1-7) it is no longer principally a question of exhorting office-holders, but of establishing the qualifications which one must have in order to be eligible for office. The ethical imperative of the station code schema has been replaced by δεῖ εἶναι (3:2), what "one must be" in order to qualify for office; furthermore, the virtue list of the amplification has to do more with prerequisites than with duties of office. Thus the bishop "must be," among other things, a good teacher (διδακτικόν), a successful household manager (τοῦ ἰδίου οἴκου καλῶς προϊστάμενον), and no newcomer to the faith (μὴ νεόφυτον).[20]

In similar fashion, the section on deacons is concerned primarily with qualifications of office and only secondarily with exhortation of office holders. The familiar structure of the husband/wives exhortation is again used here: διακόνους. . . . γυναῖκας ὡσαύτως. . . . The function of the section on wives (γυναῖκας), however, is not primarily to exhort deacons' wives, but to describe the kind of wife that a deacon should have, that is, the qualifications for the office of deacon include having a dutiful and faithful (πιστὰς ἐν πᾶσιν) wife. This interpretation is supported by the fact that immediately following the reference to wives (3:11), the list of qualifications for deacons continues (3:12). The schema thus plays a role in the shaping of this material, but it has been adapted thoroughly, apparently for the specific purpose of establishing qualifications for office.[21]

The discussion of opponents in 4:1-5 (cf. 6:3ff.) does not reflect the influence of the station code schema. It is interesting, however, that the *Haustafel* of Pol. Phil. 4:2ff. is followed by a reference in 6:3 to "false brethren" (ψευδαδελφῶν) who "deceive empty-minded men." Similarly,

---

[20]Cf. Leaney, 55; A. T. Hanson, *The Pastoral Letters*, 39; Spicq, 426. In Dibelius/Conzelmann they are seen rather as duties (p. 50).

[21]The majority of interpreters understand 3:11 as referring to deaconnesses. See Lock, 41; Spicq, 456f.; Jeremias, 20f.; and Leaney, 58. 3:14-15, which is not a traditional part of the schema, will be examined below.

the instructions in 4:6ff. to Timothy as a singular figure would not be associated with the station code schema except for their location in the text. As noted above, these instructions also have parallels in the *Haustafeln* of Titus and Ignatius to Polycarp. Thus, in Titus 2:7, Titus is exhorted to become a model of behavior for the younger men, and in Ign. Pol. 4:1, Polycarp is urged to become the personal protector of widows. It appears, then, that at some point in the development of the station code schema, exhortation addressed to a particular leading individual in the community became a regular feature of the schema.

The exhortation in 5:1-2 recalls the *Haustafel* of Titus 2:1-10 without actually reproducing it, since the same groups (old men, young men, old women and young women) are mentioned. As the exhortation stands, however, the imperatives are addressed to Timothy himself; and therefore they actually continue the section begun in 4:5. Thus the only feature of the station code schema that occurs here is that of the stations themselves.

The section on widows (5:3-16) contains more than one kind of material. On the one hand, it contains exhortations having to do with the community's (including Timothy's) responsibility toward widows (6:3, 4, 18). This material is roughly paralleled in the section on widows in Ignatius to Polycarp, in which it is urged, "Let not the widows be neglected" (4:1). On the other hand, the section in 1 Timothy contains both prerequisites of "real" widowhood (for example, to be enrolled, widows must be at least sixty years old, v. 9) and ethical exhortations and practical advice for young widows (for example, "so I would have younger widows marry. . . ." v. 14). This material is partially paralleled by the exhortation to widows in Pol. Phil. 5:3. On the whole 5:3-16 reflects the structure of the station code schema only faintly. Rather this material gives the appearance of having taken shape in response to the various dimensions of the problem of widowhood as the early church encountered this problem. This question will be explored more thoroughly below.

The section on elders (5:17ff.), which, again, deals with behavior toward elders rather than elders' behavior, deals with very different concerns than the section on qualifications of the bishop (elders) in 1 Tim 3:1ff. and Titus. 1:5ff.[22]

---

[22]Following Dibelius/Conzelmann, 77-79; Barrett, 78. The problems of interpreting vv. 21-25 and relating this section to the preceding verses are reserved for the following chapter.

The section on slaves (6:1-2) once again returns to the basic schema, yet with different wording than in the exhortations to slaves in other *Haustafeln*: ὅσοι εἰσὶν ὑπὸ ζυγὸν δοῦλοι instead of οἱ δοῦλοι; πάσης τιμῆς ἀξίους ἡγείσθωσαν, instead of ὑποτάσσεσθε. Furthermore, this section contains a second exhortation which is addressed to a subcategory of slaves, namely, slaves whose masters are believers (6:2). This second exhortation also follows the basic form of the station code schema.

Finally, the exhortation to the wealthy (6:17-19) follows the schema closely, even though it is not usually considered a part of the *Haustafel* of 1 Timothy. This judgment appears to have been made, not because of the form of the exhortation, but because this particular station is not mentioned in the other *Haustafeln*, although in Polycarp to the Philippians, the *Haustafel* is introduced by a discussion of wealth.

Even where the author makes no innovations in the schema itself, the content of the material reflects, to a great extent, his use of common, traditional notions rather than fixed traditions, although he employs the latter as well at times. His method can be illustrated by reference to two sets of parallel passages in 1 Timothy and Titus.

The first set of passages are the exhortations to slaves found in 1 Tim 6:1 and Titus 2:9-10. As Chart 2 and Chart 3 show, the two passages exhibit the basic features of the station code schema. Furthermore, they express essentially the same thought: slaves should be obedient to their masters in order to be a credit to Christian teaching. However, the choice of words and concepts to express this thought is quite different in the two passages. Thus, in 1 Tim 6:1, the author is content to say that slaves consider their masters "worthy of all honor," (πάσης τιμῆς ἀξίους) while in Titus he expands on the obedience of slaves with reference to the more specific matters of not being refractory and not pilfering (μὴ ἀντιλέγοντας, μὴ νοσφιζομένους). In addition, the passage in 1 Timothy contains an additional exhortation that is directed toward slaves with Christian masters, where an entirely different rationale for obedience is given. It thus appears that what stands behind these two passages is neither a written source nor a fixed tradition, but the traditional station code schema and the traditional notion of the behavior expected of a slave. This notion is expressed in a somewhat different way and developed in a somewhat different direction in the two passages.

CHART 5

Parallels in 1 Tim 3:1ff. and Titus 1:6ff.

1 Tim 3:1ff.	Titus 1:6ff.
εἴ τις	εἰ τίς ἐστιν
ἐπισκόπης ὀρέγεται, καλοῦ ἔργου ἐπιθυμεῖ. δεῖ οὖν τὸν ἐπίσκοπον ἀνεπίλημπτον	ἀνέγκλητος,
εἶναι, μιᾶς γυναικὸς ἄνδρα,	μιᾶς γυναικὸς ἀνήρ,
νηφάλιον, σώφρονα, κόσμιον, φιλόξενον, διδακτικόν, μὴ πάροινον, μὴ πλήκτην, ἀλλὰ ἐπιεικῆ, ἄμαχον, ἀφιλάργυρον, τοῦ ἰδίου οἴκου καλῶς προϊστάμενον, τέκνα ἔχοντα	τέκνα ἔχων
ἐν ὑποταγῇ μετὰ πάσης σεμνότητος·	πιστά, μὴ ἐν κατηγορίᾳ ἀσωτίας ἢ ἀνυπότακτα.
(εἰ δέ τις τοῦ ἰδίου οἴκου προστῆναι οὐκ οἶδεν, πῶς ἐκκλησίας θεοῦ ἐπιμελήσεται;)	

1 Tim 3:2ff.	Titus 1:7ff.
δεῖ οὖν τὸν ἐπίσκοπον ἀνεπίλημπτον εἶναι,	δεῖ γὰρ τὸν ἐπίσκοπον ἀνέγκλητον εἶναι ὡς θεοῦ οἰκονόμον,
μιᾶς γυμαικὸς ἄνδρα, νηφάλιον, σώφρονα, κοσμίον, φιλόξενον, διδακτικόν,	
μὴ πάροινον, μὴ πλήκτην, ἀλλὰ ἐπιεικῆ, ἄμαχον, ἀφιλάργυρον,	μὴ αὐθάδη, μὴ ὀργίλον, μὴ πάροινον, μὴ πλήκτην, [μὴ ὀργίλον]
τοῦ ἰδίου οἴκου καλῶς προϊστάμενον, τέκνα ἔχοντα ἐν ὑποταγῇ μετὰ πάσης σεμνότητος. (εἰ . . . ἐπιμελήσεται;) μὴ νεόφυτον, ἵνα μὴ τυφωθεὶς εἰς κρίμα ἐμπέσῃ τοῦ διαβόλου. δεῖ δὲ καὶ μαρτυρίαν καλὴν ἔχειν ἀπὸ τῶν ἔξωθεν, ἵνα μὴ εἰς ὀνειδισμὸν ἐμπέσῃ καὶ παγίδα τοῦ διαβόλου.	
[φιλόξενον] [σώφρονα]	ἀλλὰ φιλόξενον, φιλάγαθον, σώφρονα, δίκαιον, ὅσιον, ἐγκρατῆ, ἀντεχόμενον τοῦ κατὰ τὴν διδαχὴν πιστοῦ λόγου, ἵνα δυνατὸς ᾖ καὶ παρακαλεῖν ἐν τῇ διδασκαλίᾳ τῇ ὑγιαινούσῃ καὶ τοὺς ἀντιλέγοντας ἐλέγχειν.

The second set of parallel passages is to be found in 1 Tim 3:1ff. and Titus 1:6ff., the sections dealing with the bishop (elders).[23] These passages are, for convenience sake, reproduced in Chart 5 in such a fashion that their similarities and differences may be observed.[24]

The basic picture of the bishop's (elders') qualifications is very similar in the two passages. However, with several exceptions, the vocabulary and the sentence structure is not the same. Thus the possibility that the writer has copied himself appears very remote. The greatest similarities are at the following points:

1. The list of qualifications for the bishop's office is introduced in the two passages with almost identical wording:

δεῖ οὖν τὸν ἐπίσκοπον ἀνεπίλημπτον εἶναι . . . (1 Tim 3:2)
δεῖ γὰρ τὸν ἐπίσκοπον ἀνέγκλητον εἶναι . . . (Titus 1:7)

The close correspondence here suggests the existence of a fixed element of tradition. The two clauses have the same grammatical structure. Differences occur only in the introductory conjunctions (οὖν and γάρ) and in the predicate adjectives ἀνεπίλημπτον and ἀνέγκλητον, which may both be translated "unblamable."[25]

2. The list of qualifications for bishop in 1 Timothy and that for elders in Titus begin with the same two items:

ἀνεπίλημπτον εἶναι, μιᾶς γυναικὸς ἄνδρα . . . (1 Tim 3:2)
ἀνέγκλητος, μιᾶς γυναικὸς ἀνήρ . . . (Titus 1:6)

This correspondence suggests that these two qualifications for office have become traditionally linked, although this linkage is not present in Titus 1:7, where the qualifications for bishop begin.

3. The list of qualifications for bishop in 1 Timothy and that for elders in Titus both include the requirement of having obedient children:

---

[23]The abrupt introduction of the office of bishop in Titus 1:7 has given rise to the hypothesis that 1:7-9 (and 1 Tim 3:1-13) is an interpolation. For a discussion, see Dibelius/Conzelmann, 56, and Bartsch, 83ff., where the hypothesis is rejected. In Dibelius/Conzelmann, 6, it is suggested that in vv. 7-9 the author quotes a primitive church order. A question is thus raised with regard to the relation of bishop and presbyters in the Pastorals. This question will be addressed in the next chapter.

[24]Cf. Dibelius/Conzelmann, 133, where the parallels between the two passages are laid out in different fashion.

[25]This concept seems to be a summary for all the bishop's qualifications. Thus Lock, 34, 36; Jeremias, 19.

τέκνα ἔχοντα ἐν ὑποταγῇ . . . (1 Tim 3:4)
τέκνα ἔχων μὴ ἐν κατηγορίᾳ ἀσωτίας ἢ
ἀνυπότακτα . . . (Titus 1:6)

The similarity of structure here again suggests that a relatively fixed tradition is being reproduced.

4. Both lists of qualifications for bishop contain the pair of items μὴ πάροινον, μὴ πλήκτην. In addition, φιλόξενον (1 Tim 3:2, Titus 1:8) and σώφρονα (1 Tim 3:2, Titus 1:8) appear in both lists, although in different order. ἀφιλάργυρον in 1 Tim 3:3 parallels μὴ αἰσχρωκερδῆ in Titus 1:7 in meaning, although the vocabulary is different. ἄμαχον in 1 Tim 3:3 and μὴ ὀργίλον in Titus 1:7 convey the same idea. These items appear thus to represent relatively fixed traditional elements in the lists.

A detailed comparison of the two passages thus reveals that they reproduce certain fixed elements. At the same time, this comparison indicates that fixed elements play a limited role in both passages. Elsewhere, the author appears mainly to be drawing upon his own insights in order to fill out the meaning of the basic qualification, εἶναι ἀνεπίλημπτον. Thus, for example, in both passages, in different ways, the notion is conveyed that the bishop should be a prudent, circumspect, wise individual.[26] In addition, in each passage he adds what appears to be special concerns: in Titus 1:9, he adds that the bishop must be firmly anchored in sound doctrine (ἀντεχόμενον τοῦ κατὰ τὴν διδαχὴν πιστοῦ λόγου), so as to be able to confute those who are contradicting it. This qualification serves as a smooth transition to the next section of the epistle, which describes these opponents.[27]

Similarly, in 1 Timothy 3, the author takes time to reflect on the connection between skill in household management and skill in ruling the church (3:4-5); he warns against making a neophyte a bishop (3:6), and he stresses that a bishop must be someone who possesses a good reputation with outsiders.[28]

The general picture, then, is this: the author has a basic notion of what sort of person should fill the office of bishop (elder). This notion appears to be determined in part by certain relatively fixed traditional

---

[26] See Dibelius/Conzelmann on the virtues of a good general, pp. 50-51; also Lock, 35; Spicq, 476. Cf. 1 Tim 3:2-3; Titus 1:7-8.

[27] The list of qualifications thus is integrated into its context in the epistle, unlike, e.g., the *Haustafel* of Colossians.

[28] The latter appears to be an extension of the basic qualification of εἶναι ἀνεπίλημπτον.

elements which appear together in Titus 1:6. The bishop (elder) must be blameless, be the husband of one wife, and have obedient children. In addition, the author shares the broadly traditional idea that a bishop should be prudent, wise, and sober. His rendering of the qualifications for bishop (elder) in the two passages are shaped by these factors as well as by special concerns which he promotes in each instance.[29]

The above analysis indicates that, at least in these two test cases, the author of the Pastorals has not simply reproduced wholesale already fixed traditions. Rather, within the general framework of the station code schema, he has employed certain fixed traditions and traditional ideas as he has addressed himself to the respective topics. In each instance the final written product possesses its own peculiar emphases and reflects its own peculiar combination of traditional and non-traditional elements. Since these are the only two sets of parallel exhortations in the *Haustafel* material in the Pastorals, the rest of this material cannot be tested in the same way. However, unless evidence to the contrary is found in individual instances, one is justified in assuming that the author of the Pastorals approached the composition of the rest of the station exhortations in a similar manner.

Assessment

The station code schema has influenced the shape of the material in 1 Tim 2:1ff. and Titus 2:1-10, 1:5ff.; 3:1ff., although this influence is considerably greater at certain points than at others. At the same time the schema has been freely adapted, modified, and even ignored as concrete problems of the church have been addressed.

Perhaps the most important result of the above analysis is the following: Campenhausen's contention that 1 Tim 2:1-6:1 should be understood as the most fully developed example of the station code has been confirmed. There is a clear line of development from the codes of Colossians and Ephesians, which deal exclusively with the household relationships of the household management topos, to the codes of Ignatius to Polycarp and Polycarp to the Philippians, where exhortations to other groups, including church officers are included, then to the code of

---

[29]N. J. McEleney, "The Vice Lists of the Pastoral Epistles," *CBQ* 36 (1974) 203-19, has shown that the vice lists of the Pastorals reflect subtle shaping in the service of particular concerns.

1 Timothy, where the sections on church officers have become, in part, lists of qualifications for office. That the code of 1 Tim 2:1ff. belongs to the same development as those in Ignatius to Polycarp and Polycarp to the Philippians is confirmed by the fact that all three codes exhibit the basic structure of the station code schema, as described above. Furthermore, it has been shown that these three codes (as well as Titus 2:1ff., 1:5ff., 3:1ff.) exhibit the same developments of the station code schema.

Therefore, even though 1 Tim 2:1ff. (cf. Titus 1:5ff.) deals with matters of church order in a fuller sense than other extant examples of the station code, it is unnecessary to hypothesize an extensive church order source behind the station code of the Pastorals.[30] Similarly, it would seem somewhat beside the point to divide this material into a *Haustafel* and a *Gemeindeordnung* as do Dibelius/Conzelmann and Karris.[31] Rather, 1 Tim 2:1ff. should be viewed as a development and adaptation of the station code schema in the attempt to regulate the behavior and relations of various groups, official and unofficial, in the Christian community. The station code material in Titus provides a similar, but less fully developed example of such an attempt.

Thus the author of the Pastorals has made use of a traditional schema with a clear history of development in the service of his own composition and for his own ends. In light of this understanding of the author's compositional process, one may ask whether any guiding concept underlies his actualization of the schema in the station code material of the Pastorals. The contention is that 1 Tim 3:14-15 provides evidence of such a guiding concept.

1 Tim 3:14-16 and the Station Codes of the Pastorals

1 Tim 3:14-16, which begins, "I am writing these things to you . . . in order that . . . ," has naturally enough been understood by a number of interpreters as the author's statement of purpose (either for 1 Timothy or for the Pastorals taken together).[32] If indeed the author of the Pastorals is to be viewed as essentially a composer with his own particular interests and viewpoint rather than as a collector of traditions, then one would

---

[30]Bartsch does so in *Die Anfänge urchristlicher Rechtsbildungen.* See the discussion in chapter I, p. 15.

[31]See above, chapter I, p. 16 and Dibelius/Conzelmann, 5-6; Karris, *Function*, 103-4.

[32]See the discussion in chapter I, pp. 13ff.

expect a statement which begins in this way to articulate his purpose and point of view. The task of interpretation thus becomes to discover what purpose is articulated and what point of view is reflected.

A number of problems confront the interpreter at this point. First, there is no clear delimitation of the material to which the statement of purpose in 3:15 applies. The author designates the material to which he refers simply as "these things" (ταῦτα). ταῦτα here could conceivably refer only to the material in the immediately preceding chapters, or it could refer to the whole of 1 Timothy, or perhaps even, in a sense, to the Pastorals together. Thus, any judgment about the intended scope of the purpose statement in 3:14 will have to be inferred from the content of the statement itself.

It is noteworthy that the interactional element between the author and the reader receives special emphasis here: "I am writing to you" (σοι γράφω); "hoping to come to you" (ἐλπίζων ἐλθεῖν πρὸς σὲ); "if I am hindered" (ἐὰν βραδύνω); "that you may know" (ἵνα εἰδῇς). Highlighting of the interactional element appears in fact to belong to the author's technique of organizing and presenting paraenetic material. Thus, such highlighting occurs in 1 Tim 1:3: "I urged you. . . ." (παρεκάλεσά σε), where warning against false teachers and their teachings is introduced. 1 Tim 1:8ff., which serves as a summary and transition between the pseudo-autobiographical section which precedes it and the expanded station code which begins in 2:1, contains similar highlighting: "This charge I commit to you, Timothy, my son. . . ." (παρατίθεμαί σοι, τέκνον Τιμόθεε).[33] Likewise, Titus 3:8b, which summarizes the preceding hortatory material, highlights the interaction between author and addressee in the process of expounding the purpose of the exhortation: "I want you to. . . ." (βούλομαί σε . . . ἵνα. . . .).[34] Thus, in light of these passages, one would expect 1 Tim 3:14ff. to contain a summary that in some way comments upon adjacent paraenetic material.

That the primary concern in 3:14ff. is with behavior is directly stated: "I am writing . . . in order that you may know how one ought to behave (ἀναστρέφεσθαι). . . ." A check of the use of ἀναστρέφεσθαι in Christian literature from roughly the same period indicates

---

[33]See Dibelius/Conzelmann, 32, on the summaries; also A. T. Hanson, *Pastoral Letters*, 121, and Barrett, 144.

[34]Cf. 1 Tim 6:14; Titus 1:5. In 2 Timothy highlighting of the interactional element is present almost everywhere. Here, however, this highlighting appears to have a different function.

that this verb was consistently used to reflect the way in which individuals or groups habitually live: their habits and customs, their way of life. In Ign. Mag. 9:1, it is used to describe the Jews, who, prior to Christian conversion, "walked (ἀναστραφέντες) in ancient customs. . . ." In 1 Clem 21:8, it is urged that children "share in the instruction (παιδεία) which is in Christ, which among other things, gives salvation to all who live (ἀναστρεφομένους) holily in it." Thus ἀναστρέφεσθαι here refers to the way of life which is inculcated through Christian training. In Herm.m. 11:12, where the characteristics of a false prophet are being discussed, it is noted that such a person "lives (ἀναστρεφόμενος) in great luxury and in many other deceits. . . ." Here, too, ἀναστρέφεσθαι refers to the habitual behavior that characterizes one's way of life.[35]

The behavior with which the author is concerned in 1 Tim 3:14ff., is behavior ἐν οἴκῳ θεοῦ. As it was noted in chapter I, οἶκος θεοῦ here has sometimes been understood as the "house of God" in the sense of an architectural structure. This interpretation receives some support from the fact that in v. 15 this οἶκος is described in unambiguously architectural imagery as the pillar and bulwark (στύλος, ἑδραίωμα) of the truth. This understanding of οἶκος allows the interpretation that the author is primarily concerned here with the way in which Christians conduct themselves in the place of worship.[36]

This interpretation, however, appears unlikely. In the first place, it requires a different meaning for ἀναστρέφεσθαι than the meaning which this verb has consistently in the contemporary Christian literature. On the basis of the usage described above, one would not expect ἀναστρέφεσθαι to refer to the social conventions which one follows in the specific context, for example, of the marketplace, the court, or the worship assembly. Rather, one would expect it to refer to the way in which one conducts one's life, for example, as a Jew or a Christian, or a pagen, as a good or an evil person. Thus here the reference would be not to the way a Christian acts in church, but the way one lives as a Christian. If οἶκος in 3:15 describes the church as a social entity, then the latter meaning follows easily; the author is concerned with the way one ought to conduct one's life in the Christian community, the οἶκος θεοῦ.

---

[35]Cf. Eph 2:3, 1 Pet 1:17, 2 Pet 2:18.

[36]This position is clearly articulated by P. Dornier, *Les Épîtres pastorales* (Paris: J. Gabalda, 1969) 66.

In the second place, οἶκος in the Pastorals consistently means "household" in the sense of a social entity rather than "house" in the sense of a physical structure. Thus one qualification for the office of bishop is that he rule (προϊστάναι) his οἶκος well, a task which includes having obedient children (3:4). The same requirement applies to deacons (3:12).[37] Similarly, in Titus 1:11, false teachers are accused of upsetting οἶκοι and leading astray weak women in them.

Thus the οἶκος θεοῦ in 3:15 is the "household of God," and the issue with which the author is concerned is the way of life which Christians follow as a part of this "household." The further description of this οἶκος as the ἐκκλησία θεοῦ ζῶντος and the στύλος καὶ ἑδραίωμα τῆς ἀληθείας emphasizes its greatness and therefore also the importance of the way in which its members conduct their lives.

The final problem in 3:14ff. involves the relation of 3:16 to the rest of the passage. A number of interpreters have argued that the Christological hymn in 3:16 is in fact the goal toward which the author has been moving and that vv. 14-15 merely preface this doctrinal statement.[38] The contention here is that, on the contrary, the author expresses his central concern in the purpose statement of 3:14-15 and that the hymn in 3:16 performs a supplementary function.

The author does in fact use traditional doctrinal formulations in this way rather consistently. Thus the exhortation to pray for all men in 1 Tim 2:1-2 is given theological undergirding by the introduction in vv. 3b-6 of doctrinal material which has to do with the role of Christ as redeemer for all. In 1 Tim 6:14ff., the exhortation to keep the commandment unstained is reinforced by traditional doctrinal material which deals with the appearance of Christ "at the proper time," and with the majesty of God. Similarly, in 2 Tim 2:11-13 a traditional formulation concerning Christ's faithfulness climaxes a section in which Christians are urged to be steadfast in the midst of suffering.[39] In 1 Tim 3:16, the Christ-hymn brings to a climax the author's description of the greatness

---

[37]There is a question, especially in the case of 3:12, whether οἶκος refers to the household in the sense of everyone who lives under the same roof, or only to the household in the sense of the servants. This question will be explored in the following chapter.

[38]Dibelius/Conzelmann, ad loc.; Spicq, ad loc.; Jeremias, ad loc.

[39]Cf. Titus 2:1-4; 3:4-8; for an example of a similar use of a secular "doctrine," see Titus 1:11.

of the church: καὶ ὁμολογουμένως μέγα ἐστὶν τὸ τῆς εὐσεβείας μυστήριον.[40] Here the "truth" with which the church has been entrusted is given concrete expression, so that its majesty may speak for itself. The function of the Christ-hymn is therefore to drive home the conviction that the way one conducts oneself as a member of the Christian community is a matter of the highest significance.

Thus the ἵνα clause in 3:14 expresses the author's central thought in this passage: He is writing "these things" (ταῦτα) in order to address the question of how one should conduct one's life as a member of the household of God. It is impossible to determine with certainty exact boundaries for "these things." However, the kind of material which the author has in mind is clear enough, namely, material which deals with this question of proper behavior in the Christian community, described here as the household of God. The station codes of 1 Tim 2:1-6:1 and Titus 2:1-10, 1:5-9, and 3:1ff., which have been analyzed from another perspective in this chapter, are comprised of precisely this kind of material. Thus these codes may legitimately be approached with the following question: what concept of the Christian community as the household of God emerges from this material? From this initial question others arise: (1) What does the author's concept of the household of God, together with the way in which he presents this concept, indicate about (a) his perception of the community's social structure (including the social strata) and (b) his perception of where there is social tension in the community and what the nature of the tension is; (2) As these questions are answered, (a) what, if any, indications are given of the community's actual social structure (and social strata) in distinction from the author's perceptions, and (b) what, if any, indications are given of the nature of the actual social tensions in distinction from the author's perceptions?

---

[40]Cf. Dibelius/Conzelmann, 58, on μυστήριον as the content of the gospel.

EXCURSUS: PARAENETIC DISCOURSE

The preceding chapter was occupied with analysis of material usually characterized as paraenesis. In this connection the following excursus is offered on the characteristics of paraenetic discourse. Paraenesis has been described above as moral exhortation which is both general and traditional in character. This description conceals two related issues which have troubled New Testament scholarship since Dibelius. These two issues involve, respectively, what is meant by the assertion that paraenesis is traditional and what is meant by the assertion that paraenesis is general.

Dibelius understood paraenesis as discourse characterized by aggregations of traditional ethical exhortations. He understood it to be so general in character that it could often be applied in pagan, Jewish, or Christian settings with equal validity. Paraenesis, therefore, could not be expected to reflect a coherent theological viewpoint or to reveal specific ethical crises among an author's intended readers. Thus Dibelius discounted, for example, the notions that Pauline paraenesis had been shaped by Paul's theological reflection and that the paraenesis of James revealed specific ethical crises among the author's addressees.[1]

In Dibelius' understanding, then, the characterization of paraenesis as "traditional" appears to indicate that it is made up largely of aggregations of fixed traditions; and the characterization of paraenesis as "general" precludes the possibility that paraenetic discourse could reflect a coherent (especially, theologically coherent) viewpoint. In what follows, issue will be taken with this understanding through a re-examination of the ways in which the concepts "traditional" and "general" apply to paraenesis.

Paraenetic discourse is found in such diverse literature as Isocrates' moral essays, Seneca's *Epistulae Moralis*, the Synoptic Gospels, and the letters of Paul. A number of investigators in recent years have given attention to the characteristics of paraenetic discourse as it occurs in a variety of literary works from the Greco-Roman period. The following

---

[1]See M. Dibelius, *James: A Commentary on the Epistle of James* (rev. H. Greeven; trans. M. A. Williams; Hermeneia; Philadelphia: Fortress, 1976) 3, 21-22 and *From Tradition to Gospel*, 239ff.

discussion represents an attempt, not to summarize this research, but to draw on it in order to bring to light in what ways one may expect paraenesis to be general and in what ways, traditional.

The Traditional Nature of Paraenesis

Paraenetic discourse can express traditional character in a variety of ways. The most obvious way is by direct appropriation of fixed traditions and by direct quotation of literary authorities. In the literature of the early church, the Old Testament is frequently quoted. In the paraenesis of Romans 12, for example, verses 19 and 20 contain quotations from Deuteronomy 32:3 (other sources are quoted as well, however) and Proverbs 25:21-22. The Ephesian *Haustafel* (5:22-6:9) appears to be an unacknowledged quotation, with some modifications, of the *Haustafel* in Col 3:18-4:1. Relatively fixed traditions also are incorporated into paraenesis. The Philippians Hymn (2:6-11), for example, generally acknowledged to be a fragment of early Christian liturgy, is incorporated into what is usually identified as the paraenetic section of Philippians (1:27ff.).[2]

Another way in which paraenetic discourse expresses traditional character is through the use of traditional schemata.[3] It appears that such a schema accounts for the basic structure of the station codes or *Haustafeln* and the vice and virtue lists, which are characterized by the straightforward listing of a number of commonly recognized vices or virtues, perhaps, but not necessarily, drawn from a master list.[4]

---

[2]See R. W. Funk, "Apostolic Parousia: Form and Significance," *Christian History and Interpretation* (ed. W. R. Farmer, et al.; Cambridge: Cambridge University Press, 1967) 249-68; for discussion of this section of Philippians, see especially p. 262.

[3]By "schema" is meant the arrangement of certain key recurring linguistic features, e.g., specific vocabulary, key motifs, and/or grammatical forms, according to a certain pattern.

[4]A. Seeberg, *Der Katechismus der Urchristenheit* (Leipzig, 1903; reprint ed., Theologische Bücherei 26, Munich, 1966), argued that these lists were drawn from an early Christian catechism. Subsequently, other researchers have suggested that early Christian writers drew upon a master list of vices and virtues, or alternatively, that commonly known vices and virtues were drawn upon without reference to any such list. For a summary of research on this material, see the introduction to Seeberg, *Katechismus*, by F. Hahn, in the 1966 edition, pp. 27-28.

In addition, a number of investigators have directed attention to the presence in paraenetic discourse of another traditional form, which has been designated as the "topos." D. G. Bradley describes the topos as a self-contained piece of general moral exhortation that is traditional in nature and that is only loosely related to its literary context.[5] It is commonly introduced by περί plus an indication of the subject matter of the topos. It thus is a preformulated essay in miniature that can be inserted when the writer wishes to give general ethical advice pertaining to a given subject such as friendship, sexual morality, or money. Bradley notes the presence of topoi in the writings of such pagan authors as Isocrates as well as in Jewish intertestamental literature. It is not entirely clear, in Bradley's description, whether one should expect a topos to consist of an extended quotation from another source, or whether it will normally be the author's own preformulated composition. From his examples, however, it appears that the latter is what he has in mind, and that what is traditional about topos is not so much the formulations as the ideas that it contains. Thus Bradley finds numerous examples of topoi in the ethical writings of Isocrates, who describes his own method in paraenetic discourse as follows:

> But the truth is that in discourses of this sort we should not seek novelties, for in these discourses it is not possible (οὐκ ἔξεστιν) to say what is paradoxical or incredible or outside the circle of accepted belief; but rather we should regard that man as most accomplished in this field who can collect the greatest number of ideas scattered among the thoughts of all the rest and present them in the best form (φράσαι κάλλιστα περὶ αὐτῶν). (Nicocles 41)

From this description, then, it appears that at least with this author, it is the ideas, not their specific formulations, which are traditional. Furthermore, in the paraenesis of Paul, the main object of Bradley's inquiry, it is clearly the case that Paul has formulated his own topoi. Thus, according to Bradley, the paraenesis in Romans 12ff. consists of a

---

[5]Bradley, in "The Topos as a Form in the Pauline Paraenesis," *JBL* 72 (1953) 238-46, uses this word in a somewhat different way than does Balch. Balch's topos is not originally paraenetic at all, but appears in the context of political-philosophical discourse. Furthermore, Balch's topoi characteristically appear as parts of larger topoi, e.g., the topos on household management as a part of the topos on the πολιτεία.

series of topoi which Paul has composed as a general response to problems and questions which have repeatedly come to light in his churches.[6]

Paraenesis may thus be traditional in a number of ways: it may repeat fixed traditions or quote traditionally authoritative sources; its structure and content may reflect traditional schemata; it may, as appears to be the case with Bradley's topoi, simply make use of traditional ideas. Thus one can predict that paraenetic discourse will often be characterized by traditional ethical exhortation. One cannot, however, predict exactly what the relation to tradition will be for any given piece of paraenesis. This relation can only be determined by detailed examination in each instance.

The General Nature of Paraenesis and the Issue of Coherence

Dibelius argued, not only that paraenesis was traditional in its form and content, but also that it was composed in such a way that it could have extremely general applicability, that is, applicability in a wide variety of circumstances. Thus, paraenesis could not be expected to embody the developed, coherent viewpoint of a particular author. Subsequently, heated debate has taken place among New Testament scholars over the validity of Dibelius' insights as applied to the paraenetic sections of Paul's letters, in particular, the paraenetic section of Romans.

Bradley, essentially reflecting the viewpoint of Dibelius, analyzes the paraenetic section of Romans (and 1 Thessalonians) as a series of paraenetic topoi strung together by catchwords. In particular, he finds that Romans 13 consists of four consecutive topoi, each essentially self-contained and unrelated to the others. Here Paul was simply rounding out his letter to the Romans by including general advice, which, no doubt, was similar to moral advice commonly given to churches by Paul as well as by other Christian missionaries. Thus the paraenetic section of Romans, as viewed by Bradley, is not closely related in theme or viewpoint to the rest of the letter, nor does it reveal anything specific about the situation in Rome, nor does it reflect any sort of coherent theological ethic, much less Paul's own.[7]

---

[6]Bradley, "Topos," esp. 240-41, 246. At this point Bradley's concept of the "topos" is close to that of Balch.

[7]Bradley, "Topos."

V. P. Furnish, in *Theology and Ethics in Paul,* contends against this assessment of Pauline paraenesis in general and of the paraenetic section of Romans in particular. According to Furnish, Paul "has not been simply a collector and curator of miscellaneous moral advice; the impress of his own interests, perspectives, and objectives has been left upon them to a greater extent than Dibelius, for example, was inclined to acknowledge."[8] From this perspective Furnish takes issue with Bradley's division of Romans 12-15 into a series of unrelated topoi. Chapter 12, for example, contains, not a string of unrelated topoi, connected only by catchwords, but a series of exhortations which are all governed by the theme of love. Thus, while Bradley finds that 12:13b "practice hospitality," (τὴν φιλοξενίαν διώκοντες) and 12:14, "bless those that persecute you," (εὐλογεῖτε τοὺς διώκοντας) are related only by the catchword διώκω, Furnish contends that these exhortations are related thematically by the fact that they both seek to explicate the meaning of love within the Christian community. The repetition of διώκω functions not merely as a catchword, but as a play on words which suggests that "love has responsibilities also for those who 'pursue' the 'pursuers of love.' "[9] Furthermore, thematic coherence can be found, not only within the paraenetic section of Romans, but also between the paraenetic section and the rest of the letter. Taking an approach earlier championed by Bultmann, Furnish argues that the Pauline paraenesis is an essential part of Paul's proclamation of the gospel, and that, in fact, the function of paraenesis in Paul's letters is to concretize the meaning of the gospel for the present existence of believers. Thus the paraenetic section of Romans presents concrete, practical implications of the transformation which takes place "in Christ" from the ἀδόκιμος νοῦς (1:28) to the ἀνακαίνωσις τοῦ νοός (12:12).[10] In Furnish's view, then, Paul has

---

[8] *Theology and Ethics in Paul* (Nashville: Abingdon, 1968) 81.

[9] Ibid., 99-100. Furnish is here citing Bradley's dissertation, "The Origins of the Hortatory Materials in the Letters of Paul" (Unpublished dissertation; Yale, 1947) 141ff.

[10] Furnish, *Theology and Ethics*, 103. Furnish makes other connections as well between Romans 12:1-2 and previous portions of the letter, especially chapters 1 and 6. Part (but only part) of Furnish's argument for the close relation between Pauline proclamation and paraenesis is concerned with Paul's use of παρακαλεῖν and παράκλησις. Here following W. Schrage, *Die konkreten Einzelgebote in der paulinischen Paränese* (Gütersloh: Gütersloher Verlagshaus (Gerd Mohn), 1961), and H. Schlier, "Vom Wesen der apostolischen Ermahnung nach Röm. 12:1-2," *Die*

placed his own stamp on the paraenesis of Romans 12-15 both by the way in which he has selected and arranged traditional material (as in chapter 12) and by the way in which he has integrated this presentation with his basic theological perspective.

Karris, who is in general agreement with Furnish that the paraenetic section of Romans has the stamp of Paul's own perspective, turns his attention to the background of this section in Paul's experience with his churches.[11] He finds that Paul has previously addressed most of the subjects taken up in Rom 12-15:13, with the notable exception of 13:1-7, during the course of dealing with problems in his churches. For example, the subject of spiritual gifts and the unity of the church, which is addressed in 12:3-8, has been previously confronted in similar language (using the metaphor of the body of Christ) in 1 Corinthians 12; and the problem of dietary practices, addressed in 14:1-15:13, has already been

---

Zeit der Kirche (2d ed.; Freiburg: Herder, 1956) 74ff., Furnish argues that in Paul's usage, "paraklesis . . . itself embraces the twin aspects of Paul's preaching: the gift of God's love in Christ and the consequent demand of God upon men" (p. 109). C. J. Bjerkelund, writing at approximately the same time as Furnish, showed convincingly that παρακαλῶ as used by Paul and other letter writers of the period will not bear such heavy theological weight by itself. Bjerkelund, however, did not dispute the basic insights of Bultmann with respect to the function of Pauline paraenesis: *Parakalō: Form, Function und Sinn der parakalō-Sätze in den paulinischen Briefen* (Oslo: Universitetsforleget, 1967). See especially pp. 112ff. and 188ff. Bultmann addressed the general problem under the categories of the relationship between indicative and imperative in "Das Problem der Ethik bei Paulus," *ZNW* 23 (1924) 123-40.

Bjerkelund rejects any attempt to understand Rom 12:1-2 as establishing the theological context of the following chapters, on the ground that the function of such *parakalō-Sätze* in Paul as well as elsewhere was the much simpler one of establishing an atmosphere of fraternal interchange, viz., the sender explicitly recognizes the dignity and autonomy of the addressees, even as he makes a formal request of them. Thus, Bjerkelund argues, the function of such passages in letters should be viewed as diplomatic rather than theological (pp. 156ff.). Nevertheless, while Bjerkelund's case for the diplomatic function of *parakalō-Sätze* such as the one in Rom 12:1-2 is convincing, there is no compelling reason why this passage cannot have more than one function. Thus, it does not appear that Bjerkelund's study refutes Furnish's basic perspective on the passage.

[11]Bradley, "Topos," had earlier suggested, but not emphasized or explored in detail, the relationship between the "topoi" of Romans 12-15 and Paul's previous experience as a Christian missionary.

taken up in 1 Corinthians 8-10, although the vocabulary and the organization of the two passages differ. Thus Karris is able to show that, although the paraenesis of Romans 12-15 probably does not reflect subjects which were of peculiar concern to the Roman church, it does reflect subjects which were generally current in Paul's churches. Furthermore, this material is properly understood not as traditional paraenesis reflecting no particular perspective, but as precisely the tempered judgment of Paul on a series of questions which he encountered repeatedly in his churches. Therefore, this material reflects not only problems which were current in the Hellenistic church of this particular time, but also the peculiar perspective of one Christian missionary on these problems.[12]

Greater clarity still needs to be gained on the ways in which the paraenetic material of Romans coheres both in itself and within the structure of the letter as a whole. However, the work that has been done since Bradley strongly indicates that it is a mistake to view the paraenetic section of Romans as a miscellaneous collection of moral advice. That Paul himself has composed the "topoi" of this section on the basis of his experience in the church is clear. That there are thematic links within the material is also clear. That the thematic links suggested by Furnish between 12-15 and the rest of the letter are indeed significant links seems probable. Thus the investigator of paraenesis is warned against concluding that paraenetic discourse has no logic or coherence, when it does

---

[12]Karris, "Rom. 14:1-15:13 and the Occasion of Romans," *CBQ* 35 (1973) 155-78, esp. 165-67 and 174ff. Karl P. Donfried has argued, against Karris, that Paul was in fact addressing a specific situation in Rome. "False Presuppositions in the Study of Romans," *CBQ* 36 (1974) 332-44, esp. pp. 339-41. The significant issue for the present study, however, is not whether a specific situation in Rome is addressed, but whether the paraenesis represents the coherent perspective of Paul. On this issue, Karris and Donfried agree. W. Wuellner comes to similar conclusions about the "logical and purposeful thought sequence" of this paraenetic section, both in itself and within the argumentative structure of the letter, when he analyzes the structure of Romans according to the categories of rhetorical argumentation. "Paul's Rhetoric of Argumentation in Romans: An Alternative to the Donfried-Karris Debate over Romans," *CBQ* 38 (1976) 330-51; quotation from p. 347. None of the above scholars wish to deny or minimize the presence of traditional material in Romans 12-15. Thus the brief article of Charles Talbert, "Tradition and Redaction in Romans 12:9-21," *NTS* 16 (1969/70) 83-94, is cited approvingly by the participants in this discussion. Talbert argues that vv. 14-21 consist of Paul's redaction of a semitic code on the theme of returning good for evil.

not happen to exhibit the kind of logical coherence found in certain other types of discourse.

Hildegard Cancik has demonstrated the importance of heeding this warning in the case of Seneca's *Epistulae Moralis*.[13] Prior to the Cancik study, the prevailing view in scholarship on Seneca portrayed him as a mere collector of the thoughts of others, who had brought together traditional philosophical ideas without integrating them logically. Cancik argues that this view results on the one hand from an attempt to impose arbitrary and rigid standards of "compositional logic" on Seneca's work, and on the other from a failure to be attentive to the compositional logic which emerges when one studies the *Epistulae* on their own terms. Cancik's study thus explores the structure or compositional logic actually present in the *Epistulae*.[14]

Cancik investigates the compositional principles employed in the *Epistulae Moralis* at every level: principles which relate one book of letters to another, principles which are at work between letters, and principles which operate within individual letters. The part of the investigation which is of special interest here is that which concerns the compositional principles at work in individual letters. The letters are of three types: paraenetic, theoretical, and mixed letters. Correspondingly, there are two basic types of argumentation in the letters, theoretical and paraenetic. The former is characterized by the indicative mood, while the latter is characterized by the imperative mood.[15]

Cancik pays particular attention to the forms of argumentation according to which paraenetic discourse is structured in Seneca's letters. A number of elements commonly characterize paraenetic discourse or "prescriptive speech" in the *Epistulae*. The most basic element is that of the imperative itself, for example, "Despise death" (*Ep*. 78.5). The simple imperative, however, is usually supplemented by other elements which have the function of lending force to the imperative. Thus the imperatives such as "despise death" are generally undergirded by value statements such as "There is no sorrow when we escape this fear" (78.5). Furthermore, several kinds of moral examples are employed by Seneca to lend weight to imperatives: the exemplum, or example, which refers to a historical person; the typical example, which is constructed by the author

---

[13]H. Cancik, *Untersuchungen zu Seneca Epistulae morales* (Hildesheim, 1967).

[14]For a summary and evaluation of previous research, see Cancik, 1-7.

[15]Ibid., 7, 14-16.

and refers to a type of person rather than to a particular individual, for example, an athlete or a king; and the comparison, which involves comparison of the human and the non-human, for example, human desire and a raging fire. These types of moral examples are often supplemented by the use of another type, the application, which directly portrays the reader(s) himself as a negative or positive example. The application often leads up to a direct imperative, which Cancik calls the "adhortation," or summons to action. In Seneca, then, paraenetic discourse is not bare exhortation, but moral argumentation.[16]

Seneca's method of moral argumentation is illustrated in *Ep.* 74, which combines theoretical and paraenetic elements, that is, it is a letter of the mixed type. The thesis of the letter, given in 74:1, is that "the chief means of attaining the happy life (consists) in the belief that the only good lies in that which is honorable." 74.1-9, the initial paraenetic section of the letter, develops this thesis by means of moral argumentation. Vv. 2-6 contain negative typical examples (for example, "men who are completely upset by failure to win an election," 74.3) and negative comparisons (for example, "men . . . whose sufferings resemble shipwreck," 74.4). V. 7 contains an allegory in which fortune is pictured as a noblewoman tossing gifts into a frenzied mob. Vv. 8-9a provide the application, in which the reader is brought into the midst of the mob: "Similarly with the gifts which Fortune tosses down to us; wretches that we are, we become excited, torn asunder. . . ." Finally, in v. 9b, Seneca brings the argument to a head with the following imperative or adhortation which continues to draw upon the allegory of Fortune: "Let us therefore withdraw from a game like this, and give way to the greedy rabble. . . ."

Vv. 10-15 comprise a theoretical section in which after a restatement of the original thesis, a logical argument is given for why virtue should be considered the only good. The chief argument runs as follows: many of the external things which pass for human goods, such as wealth, banquets, and sexual pleasure, are things which do not pertain to God. But it is incredible that there are goods which God does not possess. Therefore, none of these external things can truly be called goods.

V. 16 begins a new paraenetic section. Building on the argument of the previous section, it offers this thesis: "Let us limit the Supreme Good

---

[16]Ibid., 22ff., 32ff. Seneca is consciously using examples to lend weight to his exhortations: "Life should be provided with conspicuous illustrations" (83:17). The "seeing" (= example) together with the "hearing" (= precept) of good men leads to moral training (94:39-40). See Cancik, 25.

to the soul. . . ." Examples of the fleeting nature of external goods in vv. 16-19a lead up to a moral syllogism in v. 19b, which comprises the climax of this section. The syllogism has the following structure: Premise 1: "We should fortify ourselves against such calamities" (the loss of external goods). Premise 2: "No wall can be erected against Fortune. . . ." Conclusion: "Let us strengthen our inner defenses." It can be seen that this moral syllogism consists of a value statement (Premise 1), a statement of fact (Premise 2), and a concluding imperative. This section is then brought to completion by an explanation of how the imperative can be carried out, that is, what one's inner defenses are and how they can be strengthened (vv. 20-21).

The concluding section of the letter, 22-34, answers one further objection to the major thesis. This objection runs as follows:

> Men say to us: "You are mistaken if you maintain that nothing is good except that which is honourable; a defence like this will not make you safe from Fortune and free from her assaults. For you maintain that dutiful children, and a well-governed country, and good parents, are to be reckoned as goods; but you cannot see these dear objects in danger and be yourself at ease."

Seneca informs his readers that he will make two replies, the first of which will be the traditional Stoic answer to this objection and the second of which will be an answer which he himself has formulated (v. 23). The first answer, which is given in vv. 23b-29, is theoretical in nature. It employs, for example, the argument that a good can be lost only by transforming it into something which is bad. Thus the loss of good health implies the presence of bad health. However, the death of a dutiful son does not imply his replacement by a son who is not dutiful. Therefore, the death of a dutiful son is not really to be considered as the loss of a good. Seneca's own argument, which begins in v. 30, offers the thesis that the wise man neither grieves in the loss of others, nor fears his own death. This is advanced by means of several key value statements: (1) "It is ever a dishonour for a man to be troubled and fretted, to be numbed when there is any call for activity" (v.30). (2) "For anyone would admit that it is a mark of folly to do in a slothful and rebellious spirit whatever one has to do, or to direct the body in one direction and the mind in another, and thus to be torn between utterly conflicting emotions" (v. 32). (3) "But what is greater madness than to be tortured by the future and not to save your strength for the actual suffering, but to invite and bring on wretchedness?" (v. 34). Thus while the traditional answer to the objection raised in v. 23 reflects the theoretical mode of argumentation, Seneca's own answer, with its use of key value statements, tends toward the paraenetic mode of argumentation, even though no imperatives are used.[17]

Cancik concludes that the primary intention of the letter is a paraenetic one, namely, to urge the reader to adopt a certain practical stance, in this case a manner of life in which virtue (that which is honorable) is regarded as the only good. The theoretical sections of the letter are thus to be regarded as standing in the service of the paraenetic sections, rather than vice versa. Furthermore, Cancik finds that this is a typical pattern in Seneca's work. In fact Seneca repeatedly distinguished the traditional theoretical mode of argumentation among the Stoics from his own method (paraenetic) as he has done in 74.23, sometimes even arguing openly for the superiority of his own method (e.g., *Ep.* 82.19ff.). It appears, then, that at least in Seneca's letters, paraenetic discourse is characterized by a deliberately chosen and carefully crafted form of moral argumentation. Furthermore, Seneca's use of this form of argumentation reflects his basic philosophical commitment to the importance of practice. Thus theory and practice as exemplified in the theoretical and paraenetic sections of the *Epistulae* constitute a logical unity which reflects Seneca's own approach to the philosophical-ethical problems which he treats.[18]

The question arises whether the paraenetic discourse of Seneca is an exception to the rule that paraenesis consists of loosely connected, essentially undeveloped exhortations, rather than connected and developed moral argumentation. Isocrates' moral essay, "To Demonicus," may serve as a test case, both because it makes explicit claim to being paraenesis (1.5) and because New Testament scholarship has used this essay as a source of paraenetic topoi capable of illuminating the nature of paraenesis in the New Testament (see p. 115 above).

One quickly sees, when one reads the sections of "To Demonicus" quoted by Bradley, that he has correctly described them as a loosely connected series of briefly developed exhortations on a variety of ethical issues (vv. 22ff.). Thus this material does not resemble the moral argumentation of Seneca. However, if one turns to the opening section of the essay (vv. 1-12), one finds a different kind of discourse that invites application of the analytical categories of moral argumentation developed by Cancik. Thus the essay begins with the thesis that "much disparity exists

---

[17]Ibid., 27ff. The basic analysis is Cancik's, although at a number of points I have given fuller content summaries of *Ep.* 74 and included fuller quotations than Cancik does, in the effort to show how her analysis works.

[18]Ibid., 36ff.

between the principles of good men and the notions of the base," and, most of all, they have "parted company in the quality of their friendships." Typical examples of the conduct of the good and the base in matters of friendship are given in v. 1b. The good remain loyal to their friends even through long separations. These typical examples are followed in vv. 2-3a by an exemplum of true friendship, in which Isocrates himself serves as the model: because of his friendship for Demonicus' (apparently deceased) father, Hipponicus, Isocrates has determined to compose this essay as a gift for the son. Thus, in this very act, Isocrates exemplifies the steadfast loyalty of a true friend.[19]

Vv. 3b-5a then describe the nature and purpose of the essay: "I am going to counsel you on the objects to which young men should aspire and from what actions they should abstain, and with what sort of men they should associate and how they should regulate their own lives" (v. 5). This amounts to a restatement of the thesis given in v. 1. The importance of such moral education consists in the fact that "only those who have travelled this road in life have been able in the true sense to attain to virtue--that possession which is the grandest and the most enduring in the world" (v. 5b). The value statement contained in the latter half of this sentence then is supported by a series of comparisons in vv. 6-7a, in which virtue is seen to be preferable to such goods as beauty, riches, and high birth. Then, in v. 7b, the focus shifts to the qualities which virtue exhibits. In v. 8 the example of Heracles and Theseus are briefly cited, after which, in vv. 9-11a, Hipponicus, Demonicus' father, is portrayed as the exemplum of virtue. The importance of friendship as a theme in the essay is underlined by the emphasis given to Hipponicus' devotion to his friends (v. 10). This exemplum is then followed by an application, the force of which is to urge Demonicus to pattern his own life on his father's (vv. 11b-12a).[20]

Finally, v. 12b makes the transition to the series of exhortations that constitute most of the remainder of the essay by connecting Demonicus' progress toward virtue with the practices which Isocrates is about to urge on him: "Wherefore I shall endeavor to set before you concisely by what practices I think you can make the most progress

---

[19]It is interesting that Seneca also on occasion portrays himself as an *exemplum*. Cf. *Ep.* 78.1ff.

[20]Isocrates is explicit with regard to his method here: "I have produced a sample of the nature of Hipponicus, after whom you should pattern your life as after an example, regarding his conduct as your law, and striving to imitate and emulate your father's virtue. . . ." (v. 11b).

toward virtue and win the highest repute in the eyes of all other men." The first part of Isocrates' essay makes use of a method of argumentation that is not at all unlike the method which Seneca used in the paraenetic sections of his letters. Thus, even though portions of "To Demonicus" conform to Bradley's picture of paraenetic discourse,[21] other portions of the same essay, which Isocrates describes as a paraenetic essay, exhibit strikingly different compositional characteristics. The matter may be put in more general terms: the above analysis has shown that paraenesis may take the form of developed moral argumentation as well as that of loosely connected and undeveloped or only briefly developed exhortations. It is even possible for paraenesis of different types, exhibiting different degrees of inner development and coherence, to exist together within the same composition. This observation is significant here because, presumably, the more developed the argumentation, the more likely it is to be shaped by and to reflect the particular perspective of the author.

In fact, returning briefly to Pauline paraenesis, one finds that here also paraenetic discourse displays no single pattern of development and coherence, but a variety of patterns. For example, while the paraenetic section of Romans constitutes a distinct block of material made up of a series of paraenetic topoi, the division between paraenesis and letter body is not so clear in Philippians. Robert Funk observes that, while 1:27 has commonly been identified as the beginning of the paraenetic section of Philippians, the immediately following verses return to the subject of the body, before the resumption of paraenesis in 2:1ff. It may be added that both Paul's self-description in 1:12ff. and the Christ-hymn in 2:6ff. recall Cancik's paraenetic exempla. On the one hand, Paul's self-description appears to function as an exemplum of suffering: "For it has been granted to you that for the sake of Christ you should not only believe in him but also suffer for his sake, engaged in the same conflict which you saw and now hear to be mine." (1:29-30) On the other hand, the Christ-hymn appears to function as an exemplum of humility: "Have this mind among yourselves, which you have in Christ Jesus. . . ." (2:5) In other words, Paul's self-description, which belongs to what is normally identified as the letter body, and the Christ-hymn, which belongs to what is normally identified as the paraenetic section, appear to have complementary paraenetic functions. These observations suggest that Funk's reference to

---

[21]There is some indication that even the series of exhortations in vv. 13f. reflect the thematic emphasis on friendship which exists in the opening section. The exhortations return repeatedly to various aspects of this theme. Cf. vv. 22, 24-26, 29, 30, 31, 32, 34, 41, 44, 45.

"the tightly conceived unity of theological body and paraenesis" in this letter is a point well taken.[22]

In this same vein Furnish notes that various characteristic elements of the Pauline letter which are not normally associated with paraenesis can have a paraenetic function. Thus, in Philemon, the commendation of Philemon's "love" and "partnership of faith" in the thanksgiving section (vv. 4ff.) becomes the basis upon which Paul later appeals to him to follow the desired course of action (vv. 9, 17, 20). One could say that in the thanksgiving Paul composes an exemplum, using Philemon as his subject, which then functions as the model according to which he exhorts Philemon to act.[23] Further evidence of a similar nature could be brought. However, the above examples should suffice to suggest the variety of forms which Pauline paraenesis takes.

Assessment

From the above sampling of paraenetic discourse, it can be concluded that paraenesis is often traditional and that often it is a challenging task to discern in it a coherence of presentation and/or perspective. A given paraenetic text may, however, express its relation to tradition in a variety of ways. Furthermore, both the degree and the means of coherence may vary from one instance to the next. Thus the question of how and to what extent a given paraenetic text reflects a coherent perspective can be answered only by examination of that particular text. For example, in the case of the paraenesis of the Pastorals, one ought not to prejudge the issue of what role tradition plays in this material and to what extent a coherent perspective emerges from it. One additional observation may be added here. In the course of the preceding discussion judgments on the coherence of paraenetic texts did not prove to be dependent on judgments with regard to whether the texts were responses to specific situations or not. Seneca's paraenetic argumentation, in fact, was seen to be coherent in presentation and perspective and yet at the same time not to be addressed to any specific situation. Thus the issues of coherence and generality should be kept as distinct issues.

---

[22]Funk, "Apostolic Parousia," 261-62; quotation from p. 262.

[23]Furnish, *Theology and Ethics*, 94-95. For this interpretation Furnish draws on the observation of Paul Schubert, *Form and Function of the Pauline Thanksgiving* (Berlin: A. Töpelmann, 1939) 89, that " 'all Pauline thanksgivings have either explicitly or implicitly paraenetic function.' "

IV

The Household and the Household of God in the Church of the Pastorals

It has now been established that the author of the Pastorals characterizes the church as the household of God in 1 Tim 3:14 and that he writes with the explicitly stated intention of describing the way that church members ought habitually to behave as members of this great household. It has further been established that much of the material in 1 Timothy and Titus reflects the influence of the station code schema, which first appears in the *Haustafeln*, which represent a paraenetic adaptation of the traditional topos on household management. Thus the author of the Pastorals, who conceives of the church as the household of God, presents material concerned with behavior in the church according to a schema that is closely associated with the early church's ethical codes for household life.

The task of the present chapter is to examine this material (and some additional related material) for what can be learned about the households of the church of the Pastorals and about the church itself as a social entity capable of being understood on the model of the household. The presumption, based on the findings of chapter III, will be that the author writes purposefully and coherently in addressing the general situation of the church of the Pastorals. Only specific evidence to the contrary in particular passages will result in a different approach to the material in question.

As the investigation proceeds, a consistent attempt will be made to distinguish that which represents the author's own notions and attitudes from that which represents actual conditions in the church of the Pastorals. In this connection four categories of material will be distinguished: material indicating (1) that which the author assumes to be true and accepts without question; (2) that which the author opposes vigorously; (3) that which the author advances as his own view without explanation or defense; and (4) that which the author advances, explains and/or defends as his own view. The first three categories will be used to identify actual conditions in the church of the Pastorals, while the second and the fourth will be used to identify the author's peculiar viewpoint.[1] The second and third categories should be useful in locating the author's place in the social structure of the church as well as in identifying the perspective from which he views social groups and addresses social tensions in the church. The material gathered in chapter II will serve as a basis for relating what is discovered about the church of the Pastorals to features of the larger society.

THE HOUSEHOLD

The author of the Pastorals never addresses the subject of the household life of church members as a topic in its own right. Rather, whenever he introduces the topic of household life, he does so in the course of discussing one aspect or another of life in the household of God. Thus to treat the household as a separate topic is to depart from the way in which he conceptualizes the Christian community. Nevertheless, such a separate treatment is offered here in the belief that it will prove helpful in penetrating the author's conceptualizations to discover the social realities.

The Householder

The only discussion of householders in the Pastorals comes in sections in which qualifications for office in the church are given. Thus direct information is available only about householders among the leadership of the church. Three passages come into consideration here, namely, 1 Tim 3:2ff., 1 Tim 3:8ff., and Titus 1:6.

1 Tim 3:2ff., which deals with the office of bishop, contains several pertinent items, beginning with the qualification that the bishop be "the husband of one wife" (μιᾶς γυναικὸς ἀνήρ). This qualification appears in 3:2 as the second item in a list that extends through v. 6. The same qualification is applied to deacons in 1 Tim 3:12 and to elders in Titus 1:6, and in 1 Tim 5:9 it is demanded that widows be "the wife of one husband" (ἑνὸς ἀνδρὸς γυνή) in order to be enrolled.

---

[1]Cf. the guidelines laid down by Theissen for the sociological evaluation of ethical norms and symbols in "Die soziologische Auswertung religiöser Überlieferungen," *Kairos* 17 (1975) 290f.

The meaning of these two similarly structured expressions has been widely debated. Four main possibilities exist. Firstly, it is possible that the former is directed against the practice of polygyny, while the latter has some other meaning.[2] Monogamy was the only recognized form of marriage in both Greek and Roman societies, but Jewish law continued to consider polygyny as a legitimate alternative to monogamy.[3] Thus it is at least theoretically possible that some Christians of Jewish background were polygynists. However, as noted in chapter II, Jews in the Hellenistic world appear for the most part to have adopted the marriage customs of the society in which they lived. It is therefore unlikely that it would have been necessary to discourage candidates for office in the church in the Hellenistic cities of Asia Minor from this practice. Furthermore, no possibility of a correspondence in meaning between μιᾶς γυναικὸς ἀνήρ and ἑνὸς ἀνδρὸς γυνή exists if the former has the practice of polygyny in view, since polyandry was unknown in the culture.

Another possibility is that both expressions refer to sexual fidelity within a monogamous marriage.[4] This interpretation has the advantage of being equally applicable to both expressions, but it has the disadvantage of depending upon a less than obvious rendering of the Greek. Unambiguous expressions such as μὴ μοιχός, "not an adulterer," were readily available[5] and one wonders why, if this was the intended meaning, they were not used.

A third possibility is that a prohibition of remarriage after divorce was in view.[6] Remarriage after divorce was condemned as adultery in the synoptic tradition and in Hermas (Mark 10:11 and pars.; Herm. m. 4.1.6). In addition, Paul, citing the authority of the Lord, charged women who separated from their husbands not to marry anyone else (1 Cor 7:11). Thus the presence in the Pastorals of a requirement that church officers meet such a standard would reflect the ethical atmosphere in the early church generally. This interpretation also would have the advantage of explaining μιᾶς γυναικὸς ἀνήρ and ἑνὸς ἀνδρὸς γυνή as parallel concepts. Furthermore, it would explain the fact that in 1 Tim 5:14 the author advises younger widows to marry again. The main

---

[2]See Lock, ad loc., and Str.-B. III, 648.

[3]See Chapter II, p. 45.

[4]Barrett, ad loc., and P. Trummer, "Einehe nach den Pastoralbriefen," *Bib* 51 (1970) 471-84, are among the proponents of this view.

[5]See *BAG*, "μοιχός," for examples.

[6]Advocates of this view include Jeremias, ad loc., and W. A. Schulze, "Ein Bischof sei eines Weibes Mann," *KD* 4 (1958) 300.

difficulty with this interpretation is that, as with the second possibility, one wonders at the choice of words, if this is really what was meant. It has been pointed out that the *univira* or μονανδρός of the burial inscriptions was honored especially in reaction to the frequency of divorce in the period.[7] Nevertheless, these terms essentially designate women married only once, and they do not distinguish between widows and divorcees.[8] Thus the average Greek speaker of the period would not have gained any clue from the expressions μιᾶς γυναικὸς ἀνήρ and ἑνὸς ἀνδρὸς γυνή that a distinction was being made between divorced persons who remarried and widowed persons who did so.

These considerations lead to the fourth possibility, namely that the intention is to require that church officers and enrolled widows should have been married only once.[9] Like the second and third possibilities, this one applies the same explanation to both expressions. In addition, it has the advantage of being based on a comparatively straightforward understanding of the Greek, namely, that "husband of one wife" and "wife of one husband" mean "once-married." Furthermore, a prohibition of second marriages for church officers and widows would be in accord with ethical trends in the second century church. The question of whether it is a sin to marry again after the death of one's spouse is answered in the negative in Herm. m. 4.4.1f., but with the additional comment that to remain single in such a case brings honor to the Lord. This advice echoes the earlier response of Paul to this question in 1 Cor 7:39f. Later in the century Athenagoras maintains that a second marriage, whether it follows divorce or the death of one's spouse, is "gilded adultery" (εὐπρεπὴς . . . μοιχεία, *Leg.* 33.4-5). Then, early in the third century, Tertullian declares that, while a second marriage is not a sin, it is the practice of the church to prohibit men and women who have been married twice from becoming church officers and official widows, respectively (*Ad ux.* 1.7).[10]

---

[7]See Dibelius/Conzelmann, 52.

[8]See the discussion in Chapter II, 62ff., and also Lightman and Zeisel, "Univira," esp. 22ff.

[9]Advocates of this view include Spicq, ad loc.; H. Baltensweiler, *Die Ehe im Neuen Testament* (Zurich: Zwingli Verlag, 1967) 239-40; J. Leipholdt, *Die Frau in der antiken Welt und im Urchristentum* (2d ed.; Leipzig: Koehler und Amelang, 1955) 224; and H. Preisker, *Christentum und Ehe in den ersten drei Jahrhunderten* (Berlin: Trowitzsch und Sohn, 1927) 149.

[10]It should be noted that this treatise was among Tertullian's pre-Montanist works. The usage of the term *univira* and μονανδρός in pagan burial inscriptions has sometimes been cited as supporting evidence

Two difficulties also arise in connection with this interpretation. Firstly, a requirement of celibacy for widows and widowers tends toward sexual asceticism, and thus would be somewhat surprising in view of the generally anti-ascetic stance in the Pastorals. Secondly, if one accepts this interpretation, then one must draw the puzzling conclusion that in 1 Tim 5:14, the author urges younger widows to act in a way that will disqualify them from becoming enrolled.

Nevertheless, the fourth possibility represents the most likely interpretation. It involves a simpler explanation of the Greek expressions than do the second and third possibilities; and it suits the social and ethical context of urban Hellenistic Christianity far better than the first. The first possibility appears to be by far the least likely for the same reason.

If this conclusion is correct, then the author of the Pastorals may be seen to be influenced to some extent by the same ascetic tendencies which characterize his opponents.[11] It may also be seen that he holds husbands and wives to a single sexual standard, an ethical stance which reflects the broad movement in his day toward improvement of the wife's position in marriage.[12] His egalitarian approach here represents a striking contrast to the position he usually takes on husband-wife relationships, as will become increasingly clear below. Furthermore, since he presents μιᾶς γυναικὸς ἀνήρ and ἑνὸς ἀνδρὸς γυνή in the lists of qualifications, without special explanation or defense, it is highly probable that he expects his audience both to be familiar with the terminology and, for the most part at least, to agree with his position. Thus it is most likely that he is reflecting the generally, although not universally, accepted view in his church.

---

for this interpretation as well. However, this argument is based on an interpretation of the data that receives a decisive refutation in the article of Lightman and Zeisel, 25-27. They show that prior to the specifically Christian usage, "*univira*" invariably designated a woman who had pre-deceased her husband. Thus the issue of remarriage for widows could hardly have been in view. Lightman and Zeisel thus reaffirm the interpretation of J. B. Frey and call into question that of H. J. Leon. See chapter II, 62f.

[11]See pp. 175ff. below on the adherents of the false teaching.

[12]This observation would hold true for the second and third possibilities as well. Cf. Baltensweiler, 240. This single sexual standard was broadly characteristic of the church from its beginnings. Cf. Matt 15:18-20; 1 Cor 6:12-20; F. Hauck and S. Schulz, "πορνή," in *TDNT* V.

The second item of interest occurs in 3:4, where the reader learns that, in addition to being μιᾶς γυναικὸς ἀνήρ, the bishop must be τοῦ ἰδίου οἴκου καλῶς προϊστάμενον, τέκνα ἔχοντα ἐν ὑποταγῇ μετὰ πάσης σεμνότητος. This item stands out because of its length in comparison with the previous items in the list. προϊστάναι, which refers in general to the activity of governing,[13] is also used in 3:5 and in 5:17 to describe what the bishop and elders do.[14] The issue here is not whether the prospective bishop governs his household, but how successfully he does so, as v. 5 makes clear (εἰ δέ τις τοῦ ἰδίου οἴκου προστῆναι οὐκ οἶδεν. . . .). Thus the author assumes the supreme authority of the householder in the affairs of the household without stopping to argue for this view. In particular, the way in which the bishop governs his children receives attention. He must keep them "in subjection" (ἐν ὑποταγῇ), that is, it is his responsibility to see that their behavior properly reflects their station in the household.[15] It is not entirely clear whether μετὰ. . .σεμνότητος refers to the father or the children. σεμνότης sometimes appears to mean "respectfulness," in which case the phrase here would specify the attitude of the children ἐν ὑποταγῇ. More often, σεμνότης means "dignity." If this is the case here, then the phrase refers to the father's deportment in governing his children.[16] Since the latter meaning of the word is the more common, the second alternative is the more likely. The requirement would thus be that the bishop be a man who governs his household well, and who in particular, is able to keep his children properly subordinate, while maintaining the dignity appropriate to his own position.

The section on deacons in 1 Tim 3:8ff. contains some additional information on the subject of householders. If, as is argued in chapter III, 3:11 refers to deacons' wives, then deacons are being made specifically accountable for the behavior of their wives here, just as the bishop is

---

[13]See BAG, s.v.

[14]See the discussion below, p. 152, in the section on the leadership of the church.

[15]See G. Delling, "τάσσω," in *TDNT*, VIII, esp. pp. 31-32 on τάγμα and pp. 39ff. on ὑποτάσσω and its cognates; and the discussion of 1 Tim 2:11 below, pp. 169f.

[16]On σεμνότης, see BAG, s.v. The meaning "respectfulness" or "reverence" suits the context well in 1 Tim 2:2 and in 1 Clem. 41:1, e.g., but not in most other references given in BAG. Most commentators prefer "dignity," e.g., Kelly, ad loc., Dornier, ad loc., Barrett, ad loc., Holtz, ad loc.

made accountable for that of his children in 3:4. The dignified and upright women of 3:11 would, in any case, have been a credit to their husbands' reputations.[17]

An interesting variation on the qualification in 3:4 is contained in 3:12, which requires that deacons be men who govern their children and their own households well (τέκνων καλῶς προϊστάμενοι καὶ τῶν ἰδίων οἴκων). The phrasing here indicates more clearly than that in 3:4 that the author is thinking of households that include not only wives and children, but also slaves. Otherwise, the addition of καὶ τῶν ἰδίων οἴκων would be totally superfluous.[18] Thus here the author betrays his assumption that prospective church officers will be householders with sufficient means to own household slaves. This fact in itself locates these householders in the higher social strata of the Asian cities.[19] It is most important to recognize that relatively high social standing does not appear here as a requirement which the author is intent on imposing on would-be office holders, but as a casual assumption that he makes about them. Thus it is not the author's special program or prejudices that are reflected here, but the actual situation in the churches. He apparently accepts this situation without question and pursues his own aims within it.

Finally, in Titus 1:6, a variation on the requirement of having properly subordinate children is given. Here elders are required to have τέκνα . . . πιστά, μὴ ἐν κατηγορίᾳ ἀσωτίας ἢ ἀνυπότακτα. The τέκνα πιστά here are probably "believing children," that is,

---

[17]The majority of interpreters prefer to take this verse as referring to deaconesses, e.g., Spicq, ad loc., Barrett, ad loc., Brox, ad loc., on the grounds that (1) the subject matter in 3:1-13 is offices in the church and (2) that one would expect the definite article before γυναῖκας if the reference was to deacons' wives. Neither of these arguments is decisive, however. In the interpretation given above, 3:11 still involves a requirement for the office of deacon, namely, that deacons should have properly upright wives; and the absence of the definite article may simply reflect the influence of the station code schema as the author knows it. Cf. 2:9. No other indication of an office of deaconess is found in the Pastorals. (See the discussion below, pp. 161ff.) Furthermore there is no equivocal evidence of the existence of deaconesses in the church before the middle of the third century, despite the reference to Phoebe as a διάκονος in Romans 16:1 and the reference in Pliny, *Ep.* 10:96 to "ministrae." (See Leipholdt, 201ff.)

[18]Cf. Theissen, "Soziale Schichtung," 248.

[19]See chapter II, 54ff.

children who are Christians. Such children would have adopted their father's religion as children in classical antiquity were expected to do.[20] The fact that the fathers are held accountable suggests that they were expected to supervise the religious training of their children, as was the practice in Judaism. ἀσωτία, literally, "the inability to save," is the vice not of a child but of a young adult. Its cognate ἀσώτως is the adverb used to characterize the lifestyle of the prodigal son in Luke 15:13. Thus prospective elders are apparently being held accountable for the behavior even of their adult children.[21]

In this material, then, one finds an emphasis on propriety and proper order in the household. The householder, who is incidentally assumed to be well-to-do enough to have household servants, governs his household and must account for the behavior of its subordinate members, especially his children. While it is nowhere stated that he "governs" his wife, this idea is clearly implied. Only the insistence of a single sexual standard for husbands and wives bears any hint of an egalitarian approach to household management. Householders who fulfill the obligations of their position poorly are unworthy to hold office in the church. Most important, the author does not present such notions as if they were new or controversial. Rather he presents them as familiar ideas which he expects to be received with general assent.

Women in the Household

The author presents his views on the matronly duties of women in straightforward and terse fashion in Titus 2:4-5 and 1 Tim 5:14. 1 Tim 5:10 and 2 Tim 1:5 provide supplementary material on the subject. In Titus 2:4 the older women are given the responsibility of instructing[22] the younger women in their proper role. It is assumed without further ado that the younger women are married. As married women they are to be φιλάνδρους and φιλοτέκνους. These virtues appear in the inscriptions as well as in the literature of the period as virtues of the ideal matron, the loving wife and mother. For example, in a Pergamene inscription from the reign of Hadrian a husband pays tribute to his deceased

---

[20]See Spicq, ad loc. and chapter II above, p. 28.

[21]Cf. Lock, ad loc.; Holtz, ad loc.

[22]The verb used in σωφρονίζειν, which means to advise, admonish or instruct. Synonyms include παιδεύειν and νουθετεῖν. See Dibelius/Conzelmann, ad loc.; Spicq, ad loc. Note also the discussion below of σωφροσύνη.

wife as τῇ γλυκυτάτῃ γυναικὶ φιλάνδρῳ καὶ φιλοτέκνῳ. . . .[23] This description recalls the picture given in Attalid propaganda of Apollonis and Stratonice.[24]

The younger women are also to be σώφρονας and ἁγνάς. σωφροσύνη, one of the cardinal Greek virtues, involves the self-control and self-discipline to conduct one's life within the established order in a way appropriate to one's place within that order.[25] When it is applied to women, it is often linked with αἰδώς, "modesty," and connotes self-control in sexual matters.[26] ἁγνεία, "purity," also refers to sexual continence.[27] Thus together these two terms emphasize uprightness and self-control in the area of sexual morality. In v. 5 οἰκουργούς probably means "busy with household duties." A cognate form, οἰκουργεῖν,[28] which occurs in 1 Clem. 1:1, means "to keep house." Baltensweiler takes ἀγαθάς with οἰκουργούς and suggests the translation "capable in household management."[29] At any rate the idea is that the proper sphere of activity for young women is the household. The final item in the list, ὑποτασσομένας τοῖς ἰδίοις ἀνδράσιν, repeats the familiar notion found in the *Haustafeln* and in treatments of the topic of household management generally that wives should be subject to their husbands, who rule the household.

The resulting picture of the matron looks very much like that seen in the Egyptian marriage contracts and in Plutarch's "Advice to the Bride and Groom." She is expected to be a loving wife and mother, chaste in her attitudes and behavior. She is expected to live within the sphere of the household insofar as possible, and to accept her subordinate role as the wife of the householder.

---

[23]*Ins. Per.* II 604ff. See Dibelius/Conzelmann, ad loc.; Baltensweiler, 241. Cf. 4 Macc 15:4.

[24]See chapter II, 65ff.

[25]Thus the antonym of σωφροσύνη is ὕβρις. See U. Luck, "σώφρων," *TDNT* VII, 1100.

[26]See Baltensweiler, 241. σωφροσύνη and αἰδώς are found in close connection in 1 Tim 2:9. Another example is found in Plutarch's "Advice to the Bride and Groom," where it is observed that "the virtuous woman" (ἡ σώφρων) puts on "modesty" (τὴν αἰδῶ) instead of her undergarment in the marital bed (*Mor.* 139C).

[27]See Guthrie, ad loc.; Baltensweiler, 242.

[28]The Koine text contains the textual variant οἰκουρούς, a more common word which would be translated "staying at home."

[29]P. 242. Cf. Dibelius/Conzelmann, ad loc.; A. T. Hanson, *The Pastoral Letters*, ad loc.

This picture is reinforced in 1 Tim 5:14, where the author gives advice to younger widows. This advice should be viewed in the context of his condemnation of the behavior of young widows in the community in v. 13. Unmarried, they have been going about from house to house "saying what they should not" (λαλοῦσαι τὰ μὴ δέοντα). He therefore (οὖν) wants them to marry (γαμεῖν), to bear children (τεκνογονεῖν),[30] and to "rule the household (οἰκοδεσποτεῖν)." The author is not inviting such women to become οἰκοδεσπόται, like, for example, the well-to-do householder of Luke 12:39, but οἰκοδέσποιναι, that is, wives of οἰκοδεσπόται and mistresses of the household. The οἰκοδέσποινα holds a place of honor as the wife of the master but is still definitely subordinate to him. She is in other words the traditional matron of a well-to-do household.[31] It is the possibility of attaining such a traditionally respected and secure position that the author apparently wants to suggest to young widows.

In 1 Tim 5:10 and 2 Tim 1:5 it is hinted that mothers have a role in the training of their children. In 1 Tim 5:10, in addition to the requirement that a widow be a ἑνὸς ἀνδρὸς γυνή, there is the requirement that she shall have raised children (τεκνοτροφεῖν). τεκνοτροφεῖν normally implies the activity of nurturing in a broad sense,[32] although it sometimes means no more than making the decision not to expose one's children.[33] This decision was not, however, the mother's to make. It thus appears that the reference is to a mother's role in the care and training of her children.[34] In 2 Tim 1:5, the line of faith is traced from Lois and

---

[30]Cf. 1 Tim 2:15, where the woman's salvation is said to come about through child-bearing (τεκνογονία).

[31]Plutarch makes clear the subordinate role of the οἰκοδέσποινα when he describes her as always allowing her husband to take the lead in their love-making (*Mor.* 140C). In a marble inscription from Apameia in Phrygia a husband praises his deceased wife for the virtues of φιλανδρία and οἰκοδεσποσύνη. *MAMA* VI, 194. Cf. *MAMA* VIII, 193, a decorated inscription dedicated to Zoe who is described as ἡ σεμνὴ οἰκοδέσποινα. For further discussion, see Spicq, ad loc.; Rengstorf, *Mann und Frau im Urchristentum* (Köln: Westdeutsche Verlag, 1954) 41.

[32]See BAG, s.v.; Rengstorf, *Mann und Frau, 40.*

[33]As in Epictetus 1.23.3.

[34]J. N. D. Kelly, *A Commentary on the Pastoral Epistles* (HNTC; New York: Harper & Row, 1963) ad loc.; G. Holtz, *Die Pastoralbriefe* (Theol. Hk. NT 13, 1965) ad loc.; and Spicq, among others, suggest that the care of orphans by widows in the community is also in view. Cf. Herm. m. 8.10.

Eunice, Timothy's grandmother and mother, to Timothy himself. While there is no mention of the nurturing process here, the reader is invited to conclude that Lois and Eunice have nurtured Timothy in faith.[35] It thus appears that, although fathers were regarded as having the main responsibility for the education of their children as in the traditional Jewish family, mothers were accorded some part in the process, as in Greek and Roman households.

The Pastorals contain indications of other roles that women played in households as well. 1 Tim 5:11ff. suggests that a considerable number of younger widows in the church were remaining unmarried. Whether they tended to head their own households or what other living arrangements they made cannot be determined. That the author perceived them as not properly domestic is clear from his portrayal of them as "going from house to house" (περιερχόμεναι τὰς οἰκίας), unlike their married sisters who are occupied with their own households (οἰκουργούς [Titus 2:4]).

1 Tim 5:4 and 5:8 present a picture of women in still different household situations. V. 4 urges that the children and grandchildren of widows shoulder the responsibilities of supporting them. Despite the fact that the widows in question belong to τὸν ἴδιον οἶκον, it is not clear whether they are envisioned as actually living with their children and/or grandchildren, since οἶκος appears to be used here in the sense of "family line" rather than "household."[36] V. 8 appears to repeat the instruction of v. 4, this time raising the negative possibility that some people may not take proper responsibility for "their own" (τῶν ἰδίων) widows. The negative formulation, together with the emphatic condemnation of any such person as "worse than an unbeliever" (ἀπίστου χείρων) strongly suggests that the author was addressing a real problem in the church of the Pastorals.

---

[35]Lock observes that the faith mentioned here is not specifically designated as Christian (ad loc.). Unless one assumes that the author was interested in a strict chronology here, however, there is no reason to assume that he was thinking of Judaism.

[36]See BAG, "οἶκος," 3, and the discussion of v. 8 below. It should be noted that the interpretation given here assumes that τέκνα and ἔκγονα are the subjects of μανθανέτωσαν. The understood subject could also be χῆραι, in which case the author would be urging widows to care for their own households. Either choice involves a rather awkward construction, but the resulting sense of the former appears better in the context.

There is a special interpretative problem here in connection with the meaning of ἰδίων καὶ μάλιστα οἰκείων. Both ἴδιος and οἰκεῖος are capable of a wide range of meanings, depending on the context. ἴδιοι can refer to comrades in battle (2 Macc 12:22), one's family (Sir 11:34) and fellow Christians (Acts 4:23), among other groups. The context defines the group envisioned. οἰκεῖος in its basic meaning designates a member of a household, whether a family member, slave or other servant. However, it can also be used to refer to blood relatives, as in Barnabas 3:3.[37] O. Michel translates the phrase in question in v. 8 as "his own and especially those of his own house," a translation which conveys the vagueness of the original.[38] Spicq understands οἱ ἴδιοι here as including slaves and freedpersons of the household, and οἰκεῖοι as referring only to blood relatives. Kelly understands the distinction to be between one's relatives in general and the members of one's immediate family. This interpretation has to commend it a passage in the Testament of Reuben in which οἰκεῖοι is set alongside γένος as a closer degree of kinship (3:5). The solutions of both Spicq and Kelly would considerably broaden the circle of a householder's responsibility in comparison with v. 4. A third possibility is that the distinction in view has to do with family members who live in the household and those who do not. Thus ἴδιοι here would include widows living apart from their relatives, while οἰκεῖοι would designate widows living with them. This solution encounters the difficulty of explaining why the duty of caring for widows who live in one's household should be especially emphasized in distinction from widows in one's family who live outside the household. It would seem that the latter would be in greatest danger of neglect.[39] On balance, it seems most likely that the distinction is between degrees of relationship. One's greatest responsibility would thus be toward one's closest kin.

In any event, a situation is envisioned in which a woman has been left without adequate financial resources at her husband's death. Since by this time Greek law made provision for ownership of property and inheritance by women, the problem should not be viewed as a legal one. Rather such women must have come from families that possessed only modest means and married men in the same circumstances, so that support from inheritance, dowry or other property holdings would have never been a serious possibility.

---

[37]See BAG, s.v.; Spicq, ad loc.

[38]"οἰκεῖος," *TDNT* V.

[39]The third solution is set forth by Dornier, ad loc., among others.

1 Tim 5:16 apparently speaks about women from a higher social stratum. Here the author directs attention to the πιστή[40] who "has" (ἔχει) widows. Although one cannot be certain what was involved in "having" widows, the portrayal of Tabitha in Acts 9:36ff. probably reflects the type of circumstances that are presupposed. Tabitha, a woman noted for works of charity, has died. Widows gather at Tabitha's deathbed mourning and displaying clothes which she made, probably for them. When Tabitha is revived the widows are singled out as a group to be notified. It thus appears that Tabitha has been their special benefactor.[41] The πισταί of the church of the Pastorals are, in all probability, women like Tabitha, who have taken poor widows under their protection. Whether or not the πισταί were themselves widows is unclear. At any rate, the author urges them to take full responsibility for the support of widows in their care so that the church will not have to shoulder this burden. He thus regards them as women of means who have the power to take actions that can affect the financial health of the church.

The Pastorals thus present a picture of women in a variety of domestic situations. Some are the wives of prosperous householders. Others are probably married to men of much more modest means. Still others are widows, whose living arrangements and relations with their families are not clear. Some widows probably live with their children and/or grandchildren, while others perhaps find shelter in the home of a πιστή. In the author's view, the οἰκοδέσποινα who displays the proper matronly virtues has reached the pinnacle of achievements possible for a woman; but widows are a social burden.[42] He is suspicious of younger widows who do not remarry, yet at the same time has high regard for the ἑνὸς ἀνδρὸς γυνή, apparently, especially if she is an older woman. In all these respects he appears to reflect common attitudes in the church for which he writes.

---

[40]The reading πιστὸς ἢ πιστή represents an attempt to improve upon the text.

[41]See E. Haenchen, *The Acts of the Apostles: A Commentary* (trans. B. Noble & G. Shinn; Philadelphia: Westminster Press, 1971). The presence of well-to-do women in the first Christian communities has often been noted, e.g., by Meeks, "Image," 197f.; Judge, "Early Christians." Cf. the story of Lydia, Acts 16:13ff.; Paul's description of Phoebe as his προστάτις, i.e., his patroness, in Romans 16:2.

[42]See also the discussion below of widows as a group in the church, pp. 161ff.

Children

Children are given no duties in the Pastorals. They are important only as the object of discipline and nurture, as noted above. When they reached adulthood, they have the responsibility of caring for their parents and/or grandparents (1 Tim 5:4).

Slaves

In their content the exhortations to slaves in the Pastorals (Titus 2:9f.; 1 Tim 6:1f.) are similar to those in the other station codes or *Haustafeln* in two principal respects. Firstly, they urge slaves to give faithful, obedient service to their masters. In Titus 2:9 the slaves are urged to "be subject in everything" (ὑποτάσσεσθαι ἐν πᾶσιν) to their masters, while in 1 Tim 6:1, they are exhorted to view their masters as "worthy of all honor" (πάσης τιμῆς ἀξίους). The exhortations are comparable, for example, to those in Col 3:22 (ὑπακούετε κατὰ πάντα) and 1 Pet 2:18 (ὑποτασσόμενοι ἐν παντὶ φόβῳ). Secondly, they interpret such service as Christian service. In 1 Tim 6:1, it is maintained that slaves should be good servants, "in order that the name of God and the teaching (ἡ διδασκαλία) not be blasphemed (μὴ βλασφημῆται)." In Titus 2:10, the same rationale is given, except that this time it is stated positively rather than negatively: ". . . in order that they may adorn (κοσμῶσιν) . . . the teaching of God our Savior." Thus obedient servanthood is portrayed here as Christian witness. Other codes take different approaches. Thus in Col 3:23-24, slaves are told, "Whatever your task, work heartily (ἐκ ψυχῆς ἐργάζεσθε) as serving the Lord . . . ; you are serving the Lord Christ (τῷ κυρίῳ Χριστῷ δουλεύετε)." A still different rationale is given in Ign. Pol. 4:3, where slaves are "to endure slavery (πλέον δουλευέτωσαν) to the glory of God." Yet despite the varying approaches, the thrust in each case is the same, namely, to portray the slave's service as Christian service.[43]

The slave exhortations of the Pastorals also contain a number of special features. First, while most of the other codes that have exhortations to slaves also contain reciprocal exhortations to masters, no such reciprocal exhortations are to be found in the Pastorals. In fact, of the

---

[43]Cf. Bartsch, 147, for another listing of similarities among the slave regulations. Bartsch attempts to locate many common features and in the process includes in his list features that appear in only a few of the codes.

other codes containing exhortations to slaves, reference to the duties of masters is missing only in 1 Peter. H. Gülzow argues that the failure of 1 Peter and the Pastorals to contain exhortations to masters indicates the worsening of the slaves' position in the communities involved as compared with their position in the communities of, for example, Colossians and Ephesians.[44] At the very least, the absence of exhortations to masters in the Pastorals suggests the author's lack of interest in viewing matters from the standpoint of the slave. This impression is strengthened and clarified by other special features of the exhortations to slaves.[45]

A second special feature occurs in Titus 2:9f., where Titus is urged to warn slaves not to be backtalkers (μὴ ἀντιλέγοντας), or pilferers (μὴ νοσφιζομένους). What is particularly interesting about these admonitions is the attitude toward slaves that they reveal. The slave exhortations of Colossians and Ephesians urge slaves toward development of noble character. Thus the slaves of Ephesians are to serve "in singleness of heart" (ἐν ἁπλότητι καρδίας) and not as "men-pleasers" (ἀνθρωπάρεσκοι), but as "slaves of Christ" (δοῦλοι Χριστοῦ) (Eph 6:5f.). The slaves of Titus 2 are, by contrast, warned against petty vices attributed to slaves according to the popular stereotype.[46] These warnings convey a sense of great social distance from slaves and underlying contempt for them as a class.

Thirdly, following the general exhortation in 1 Tim 6:1 is a special exhortation addressed to slaves with Christian masters.[47] This special exhortation, unparalleled in other station codes, confirms what was intimated in 1 Tim 3:12, namely, that there were slave owners among the Christians addressed by the author. In addition, since slaves of Christians are addressed as a sub-group among slaves in the church, there is also an

---

[44] *Christentum und Sklaverei*, 74.

[45] Holtz, assuming authenticity, suggests that the absence of exhortations to masters in Titus is evidence that there were no slave holders among the Christians on Crete (p. 222). This suggestion would not, however, answer the question of why there are no such exhortations in 1 Timothy, where in 6:2 the presence of Christian slave-owners is assumed.

[46] On νοσφίζομαι see Spicq, ad loc.; Aboth 2:8; 2 Macc 4:32.

[47] Lock and Guthrie suggest that 6:1 refers to slaves of pagan masters alone, arguing that the expression ὑπὸ ζυγὸν δοῦλοι describes the harshness of life under a pagan master. However, the yoke was a common symbol of slavery. Cf. Gülzow, 74.

indication here that a considerable number of slaves who had pagan masters were also members of the church.[48]

The particular problem which comes to light in connection with the slaves of Christian masters is also unique to this exhortation. These slaves are warned not to be guilty of disrespect for their masters (δεσπότας μὴ καταφρονείτωσαν)[49] on the grounds that their masters are brothers (ὅτι ἀδελφοί εἰσιν).[50] The negative formulation suggests that the author perceived such attitudes as a real problem in the Christian community. Such attitudes would have been grounded in thinking similar to that evidenced in the tradition preserved in Gal 3:28, that is, in an outlook that minimized the importance of worldly social distinctions within the Christian community.[51]

The next clause, which gives the positive exhortation, has caused considerable uncertainty and confusion among interpreters. Slaves of Christian masters are to serve diligently, ὅτι πιστοί εἰσιν καὶ ἀγαπητοὶ οἱ τῆς εὐεργεσίας ἀντιλαμβανόμενοι. There is, again, general agreement that the ὅτι clause here, like the preceding one, refers to the masters. This time, however, it presents the grounds for the author's position. The masters are described as πιστοί and ἀγαπητοί. There has been some debate over whether the author is suggesting that the masters are beloved by their slaves or by God.[52] Neither of these alternatives quite captures the author's point. Slaves

---

[48]Gülzow, 115, argues that slaves in the first Christian communities almost always came into the church as a part of Christian households. Beginning with 1 Clement, there is evidence that more slaves outside Christian households were joining the church.

[49]On καταφρονεῖν, see Kelly's discussion, ad loc. He defines it as "to treat without full consideration due to the other person's station."

[50]There is general agreement that the ὅτι clause here gives the reason for καταφρονεῖν, not for μὴ καταφρονεῖν, and that it is the slaves who are thinking of their masters as ἀδελφοί. See, e.g., Dibelius/Conzelmann, Kelly, Spicq, ad loc.

[51]See Meeks, "Image," 181. Meeks argues that in Gal 3:28 Paul is quoting a baptismal formula to his readers. Thus the notion that the distinction between slave and free and male and female are abolished in Christ would not have been Paul's idiosyncratic notion, but a widely accepted idea in his churches. R. Gayer, *Die Stellung des Sklaven in den paulinischen Gemeinden und bei Paulus* (Bern: Herbert Lang, 1976) 135ff., comes to similar conclusions.

[52]E.g., Lock takes the former, Dibelius/Conzelmann the latter position.

have apparently been making use of the fact that Christians commonly call themselves ἀδελφοί, in order to justify insubordination against their masters. The author counters this argument by making his own appeal to other widely used designations for Christians, namely, πιστοί and ἀγαπητοί. In other words, he urges slaves not to lose respect for their masters on the grounds that the latter are "brethren," but to serve them even more diligently, because they are "faithful" and "beloved." It is the last phrase, οἱ τῆς εὐεργεσίας ἀντιλαμβανόμενοι, that has caused the greatest problems. The following translations represent the basic alternatives:

1. "(masters), who receive the benefit of your (the slaves') service." (*NEB*)
2. "(masters), who devote themselves to good works." (Dibelius/Conzelmann)

The *NEB* reading understands εὐεργεσία here as the good service that slaves render to their masters. If this is its meaning, then, in the context, ἀντιλαμβάνεσθαι must mean something like "benefit from," or "enjoy," as an expansion of "perceive," which is one of the basic meanings of the verb. In this way the entire clause can be translated, "because they (the masters) who enjoy your good service are 'faithful' and 'beloved.' "[53] However, there is a major difficulty in understanding εὐ-εργεσία as the "good service" of the slaves, because it usually refers to the beneficence of a superior in relation to an inferior. Thus Hellenistic kings, in taking the title "Euergetes," were claiming to be benefactors of their subjects. Spicq, taking note of this fact, concludes that the author is making a subtle suggestion that slaves, by their good service, actually reverse the accepted order of superior and subordinate, becoming benefactors by their service.[54] However, the author of the Pastorals nowhere else shows any inclination toward the ironic perspective on prevailing social values that is implied in Spicq's explanation.

The translation of Dibelius/Conzelmann, by contrast, reflects the usual meaning of εὐεργεσία, and also that of ἀντιλαμβάνειν, which in the active or middle voice generally means "take part in" or "devote oneself to," when the object of the action is inanimate as in 1 Tim 6:2.[55] The major problem with this translation involves the resulting

[53]Cf. Barrett, Dornier, Spicq, ad loc.

[54]Spicq, ad loc. Seneca makes use of such a concept in *Ben.* 3. 18-20.

[55]BAG, s.v.

sense of the clause. The author would be arguing that masters should be served diligently, "because they are 'faithful' and 'beloved,' (people) who devote themselves to works of beneficence." However, that all Christian masters are devoted to beneficent works is a questionable assumption that surely would not have strengthened the author's case from the slave's perspective.

Nevertheless, this probably was the author's argument. Its weakness from the standpoint of the slaves is explained by the fact that the author is speaking totally from the perspective of the slave owners. The problem that concerns him here is not the behavior of the masters, but that of the slaves. Of course in other places (1 Tim 3:1ff., 3:8ff., etc.) he is concerned with the behavior of Christians who are slave owners and there he shows his awareness of the human failings to which they are subject; but in the present context he can afford to portray Christian masters as model Christians. Thus the great social distance that existed between the author and slaves in the church is again emphasized.[56]

The fourth special feature of the slave exhortations in the Pastorals has to do with their approach to characterizing the slave's service as Christian service. Slaves are to be obedient, "in order that they may adorn the teaching of God our Savior in everything," (Titus 2:10) or alternatively, "in order that the name of God and the teaching may not be blasphemed" (1 Tim 6:1). Gülzow argues that, just as so-called foreign religions were reputed to have a bad effect on women, so also they were supposed to contribute to the unruliness of slaves.[57] Thus, slaves, especially those with pagan masters, risked damaging the public image of the church, if they expressed their Christian freedom by attempting to loosen or break the yoke of slavery. Conversely, by obeying their masters, they could "adorn the teaching," that is, they could enhance the reputation of the church and its teaching.[58]

One finds, then, that the slaves of the church of the Pastorals belonged both to pagan and to Christian households. There was a tendency among the slaves of Christian masters to overstep the traditional boundaries of slave-master relationships on the grounds that Christians

---

[56]Cf. the second-class citizenship of slaves in the church in Hippolytus, *Apostolic Tradition*, 16:4-5, where the slave of a Christian needs his master's permission and character attestation in order to be admitted to the church.

[57]*Christentum*, 74.

[58]On the concept of "the teaching" in the Pastorals, see the discussion below, p. 158.

were "brothers." The author of the Pastorals views the slaves among the membership of the church from the perspective of the slave owner. He is concerned that Christian slaves in general not damage the church's public image by insubordination. Of course, insubordination among slaves would damage the church's image primarily, if not exclusively, among the slave-owning class.

Summary and Assessment

The author of the Pastorals presents an ideal of domestic life that reflects the prevailing view in his church. According to this ideal, the model domestic situation is a prosperous household managed skillfully and prudently by the householder. The householder exercises authority over his wife, children and slaves and ultimately must account for their behavior. The subordinate members of the household recognize their proper roles and behave in such a way as to reflect credit upon the household. Young men in the community look to the day when they will become successful householders in their own right. Young women are encouraged to aspire to become οἰκοδέσποιναι, the respected matrons of established households. One recognizes in the ideal household of this community the traditional patriarchal household of Hellenistic-Roman society and of the *Haustafeln,* and one concludes that the prevailing social values of the church of the Pastorals in this area directly and uncritically reflect the dominant social values of the larger society.

In one respect the prevailing domestic ideal in the church of the Pastorals does depart from that of the larger society, namely, in its strict sexual ethic, which, departing from the traditional model of the patriarchal household, holds up a single standard of behavior for husbands and wives. This sexual ethic also has a certain ascetic element that runs counter to traditional values. Thus, whereas the traditional ethic stresses the value of having and raising children in order to strengthen the πόλις and assure its future,[59] in the Pastorals women and men who have chosen not to remarry after the death of their spouses hold a special place of honor. While the egalitarian tendencies here reflect a trend in the larger society, the ascetic tendencies reflect a special development in the second century church.

The actual domestic situations in the Christian community present a more varied picture. Some Christian households no doubt approximated

---

[59]See chapter II, p. 78.

the prevailing ideal. Otherwise the qualifications for church officers in 1 Tim 3:2ff., 3:8ff. and Titus 1:6ff. could not have been seriously offered. However, many Christians lived in quite different circumstances. There were prosperous households in which πισταί exercised considerable independence of action. Such prominent women, who must have been either widows or the wives of well-to-do pagans, occupied important roles in the churches from the beginning, as, for example, the stories of Lydia and Tabitha in Acts illustrate. The πισταί probably took in poor Christian widows to live in their households. In addition there were families of very modest means, some of whom may have suffered severe economic strain in the attempt to care for widowed relatives. In some cases widows must have lived with relatives. In other cases they probably lived alone. Finally, the church included not only the slaves of prosperous Christian householders, but also slaves living in pagan households. The latter, it appears, were considered to be something of a public relations problem for the church.

Social tensions arising from value conflicts existed in connection both with the role of slaves and the role of women in Christian households. On the one hand, there was a conflict of values involving slaves who thought of their Christian masters as ἀδελφοί, and in so doing overstepped the boundaries of their subordinate station in the household, according to the prevailing domestic ideal in the church. This value conflict apparently belonged in a special way to the Christian community and was not characteristic of society in general. On the other hand, social tension in connection with the role of women in the household was characteristic of the whole society. However, this tension came to expression in a special form in the households of the church of the Pastorals in connection with the peculiar Christian attitude toward widowhood. While every young woman was encouraged to want to become an οἰκοδέσποινα, she also learned that the highest standard of behavior demanded that she should not remarry if her husband should die before her. For an older woman who had already fulfilled the role of the οἰκοδέσποινα in raising a family, and who then became a widow, no contradiction in values was felt. However, the young widow was regarded as a threat to the households of the community and was urged to relinquish the ideal of celibate widowhood in order to realize her as yet unfulfilled role as an οἰκοδέσποινα.

Perhaps the most significant result so far is the identification of the prevailing domestic ideal in the church of the Pastorals. It is an ideal which valued prosperity and propriety as they were valued in the larger society. It is not clear as yet to what extent these social values characterized the social and religious life of the church as a whole. This issue will be explored in the next section.

THE HOUSEHOLD OF GOD

The investigation now returns to the social structure of the church. The author of the Pastorals conceptualizes the church as the household of God. He thus conceptualizes the social structure of the church on the model of the household.

The Leadership of the Church

In this section passages dealing with the offices of bishop, deacon and elder and passages which picture Timothy and Titus in leadership roles will be investigated. Study of these passages often focuses on the question of the church's official structure according to the Pastorals, for example, the background, character, and relationships of the respective offices. The present investigation, by contrast, is interested in what these passages reveal about the social characteristics of the leadership, for example, the social strata from which they come, the social rewards of office, and social control of access to office. Of course the two sets of questions cannot be entirely separated. Thus the official structure will come into consideration to some extent as well.

Offices and Official Structure

In the view of most interpreters the Pastorals assume an official structure which includes the offices of bishop, elder, and deacon.[60] However, attempts to delineate a hierarchical structure of office and to describe relationships between offices have met with, at best, limited success, because the Pastorals nowhere describe the relationships between the offices nor do they expressly set forth a hierarchy of office.

The most prominent problem that has occupied scholars in connection with the office of bishop is whether or not the Pastorals assume the institution of a monarchical episcopate. On the one hand, in both passages where ἐπίσκοπος occurs (1 Tim 3:2; Titus 1:7), it occurs in the

---

[60]Jeremias, ad loc., and Holtz, 124-25, are among a minority that view πρεσβύτερος in the Pastorals as simply an age designation.

singular, while in the passages dealing with deacons (1 Tim 3:8ff.) and elders (1 Tim 5:15ff.; Titus 1:6), these officials are spoken of in the plural. In addition, the Pastorals are addressed to single individuals, Timothy and Titus, who are portrayed as church leaders. It is possible that they are intended as prototypes of the monarchical bishop.[61] On the other hand, in Titus 1:5ff., ἐπίσκοπος appears to be used interchangeably with πρεσβύτερος. Titus is instructed to appoint πρεσβύτεροι from among the men who meet a list of specified qualifications. The list begins, εἴ τίς ἐστιν ἀνέγκλητος. . . . This list is apparently supplemented in 1:7ff., which begins, δεῖ γὰρ τὸν ἐπίσκοπον ἀνέγκλητον εἶναι. . . .

None of this evidence is unequivocal. Thus, with respect to the occurrence of ἐπίσκοπος in the singular in 1 Tim 3:2 and Titus 1:7, it has been pointed out that this usage need not imply the monarchical episcopate, but may be a generic usage.[62] With respect to the argument that Timothy and Titus serve as implied models of the monarchical bishop, convincing evidence has been brought to bear by P. Burke to show that they do not serve as models of a particular office in the church of the author's time.[63] Rather they are portrayed, as in Acts and in Paul's letters, as Paul's assistants who visit churches as his personal representatives, commissioned with specific instructions. Thus in 1 Tim 1:3, Paul urges Timothy to remain in Ephesus in order to charge certain persons to lay aside false teachings, and in Titus 1:5 Titus is left in Crete in order to attend to unfinished business, including the appointing of elders in every town. They are not pictured as remaining in these positions indefinitely, but are envisioned as returning to Paul after a brief interval (2 Tim 4:9; Titus 3:12). W. Stenger comes to similar conclusions, using the Pauline topos of the apostolic parousia to explicate the function of Timothy and

---

[61]Cf. E. Käsemann, "Ministry and Community in the New Testament," in *Essays on New Testament Themes* (trans. J. W. Montague; London: SCM, 1964) 87; H. von Campenhausen, *Ecclesiastical Authority and Spiritual Power*, 107-8. The author would thus be addressing monarchical bishops in the church as if he were Paul addressing Timothy and Titus. However, H. Schlier, "Die Ordnung der Kirche nach den Pastoralbriefen," in *Die Zeit der Kirche* (4th ed.; Freiburg: Herder, 1966) 137, assuming Pauline authorship, also views Timothy and Titus as models of church officials--in this case, the metropolitan. Cf. Spicq, 59ff.

[62]Cf. P. Burke, "The Monarchical Episcopate at the End of the First Century," *JES* 8 (1970) 514; Dibelius/Conzelmann, ad loc.

[63]Ibid., 513-14.

Titus in the Pastorals.[64] In his letters Paul endeavors to make himself present to his congregations in three ways: (1) through the letters themselves; (2) through the apostolic delegates who deliver the letters and reinforce their content; and (3) through the promise of his personal presence in the near future. All these elements are also present in the Pastorals. The apostolic delegates play the same role that they play in Paul's letters, except that now that role receives greater emphasis. Their function is to represent Paul to the churches in his physical absence. Thus the letters do not intend to picture Timothy and Titus as models of a particular office. Rather they are vehicles of Paul's presence and power, and, as such, of the apostolic gospel/teaching.[65]

Similarly, the contention that the offices of elder and bishop are equated in Titus 1:5ff. is also problematic. γάρ in 1:7 indicates that the reader should expect a further elaboration of the subject matter of the preceding material, namely, qualifications for the office of elder. However, the term ἐπίσκοπος appears where the reader expects to find πρεσβύτερος. The identification of the two terms is thus made on this basis. Yet the text itself makes no such equation explicit. Another suggestion is that the bishops are a smaller group within the elders, the former having special leadership responsibilities, and that it is being urged that all elders meet the standards required of bishops.[66] In fact, the relation between the two sections is so puzzling that it has been suggested that 1:7-9 is an interpolation, the intention of which is to make the text seem to reflect the monarchical episcopate.[67] This text, then, cannot be used with assurance as an argument either for or against the presence of the concept of the monarchical episcopate in the Pastorals.

The Pastorals assume the existence of a council of elders (πρεσβυτέριον) in the congregation (1 Tim 4:14). However, it is not clear what their leadership role was. It is possible that the author envisions

---

[64]"Timotheus und Titus als literarischen Gestalten. Beobachtungen zur Form und Funktion der Pastoralbriefe," *Kairos* 16 (1974) 252-67.

[65]Stenger, especially pp. 257-58; 259ff.; 265-66. This is not to say that Timothy and Titus are never pictured functioning as officials of the church in the author's day.

[66]Cf. Dibelius/Conzelmann, ad loc., and the discussion of 1 Tim 5:17 below.

[67]This evidence is now almost universally rejected. There is no textual evidence for it and it would suggest that 1 Tim 3:1ff. is also a late interpolation, an extremely unlikely theory. For a discussion, see Kelly, ad loc.; Bartsch, 83-84; Dibelius/Conzelmann, ad loc.

congregations with a single bishop presiding over a council of elders. It is also possible that "elder" and "bishop" designate the same office and that congregations are governed by elder councils. 1 Tim 5:17 provides additional data to complicate the picture still more. Here mention is made of "the elders who govern well" (οἱ καλῶς προεστῶτες πρεσβύτεροι), as well as of those among this group who teach and preach (οἱ κοπιῶντες ἐν λόγῳ καὶ διδασκαλίᾳ). It is possible to derive from these two brief phrases as many as four categories of elders: (1) elders who govern well, (2) elders who govern poorly, (3) elders who govern well and who include preaching and teaching among their activities, and (4) elders who do not govern. Thus it is possible that among the elders was a smaller group with particular leadership responsibilities that included in some cases preaching and teaching. These "governing elders" would perhaps be the equivalent of bishops.[68] However, it is not necessary to understand οἱ καλῶς προεστῶτες πρεσβύτεροι as implying that some elders are προεστῶτες πρεσβύτεροι (= ἐπίσκοποι), while others are not.[69]

It is generally assumed on the basis of other evidence from the early church[70] that the deacon's office was subordinate to that of the bishop. In the Pastorals, however, no mention is made of the deacons' relationship to bishops or elders, and no clear evidence of the functions of deacons is present.[71] It thus appears that the Pastorals' author is not interested in describing and defending a particular ecclesiastical structure.[72]

---

[68]Cf. Barrett, ad loc.; Kelly, ad loc.; Dibelius/Conzelmann, ad loc.; N. Brox, *Die Pastoralbriefe* (Regensburg: Verlag Friedrich Pustet, 1969) ad loc.

[69]Thus Lock, ad loc.; Campenhausen, *Ecclesiastical Authority*, 113.

[70]Among the earliest clear evidence is that of the letters of Ignatius, in which the bishop is the supreme officer of the church.

[71]Interpreters have sometimes attempted to derive deacons' duties from the ethical list in 1 Tim 3:8ff. Thus from μὴ διλόγους, μὴ αἰσχροκερδεῖς, Brox and Kelly, ad loc., suggest that deacons were responsible for administering charity. Holtz, ad loc., suggests that the office of deacon may have been the most important office connected with the liturgy, based on the association with Jesus' role as servant at the last supper (pp. 82, 86). On the whole these suggestions are only speculations.

[72]On this question see the excellent article of G. Lohfink, "Normitivität der Amstvorstellungen in den Pastoralbriefen," *TQ* 157 (1977) 93-106. Campenhausen, *Ecclesiastical Office*, argues that government by

General Features of the Leadership

Although the Pastorals offer no clear picture of the official ecclesiastical structure which they presuppose, they nevertheless contain a considerable amount of other kinds of information about the leadership of the churches addressed and about the author's attitude toward this leadership. The passage on the bishop in 1 Tim 3:1ff. opens with a "faithful saying" which has been often regarded as a rather peculiar example of its class:[73] "If someone aspires to the office of bishop (ἐπισκοπή) he desires a good work (καλοῦ ἔργου)." καλὸν ἔργον has a connotation of a charitable deed performed on behalf of someone less fortunate than oneself.[74] To hold the office of bishop, then, is to involve oneself in such a benevolent undertaking. It has been suggested that the saying originated in a secular context as encouragement for potential municipal office seekers at a time when the popularity of municipal office was waning because of the increasingly heavy financial burdens that were involved.[75] Whether or not this is in fact the case, the saying would fit very well into that context, because it reflects the general concept of public office that one commonly finds in the Hellenistic municipalities, namely, that office holding is a public service to be undertaken by the (comparatively) well-to-do.[76] This saying also indicates that office in the church has become something to which one aspires, as one aspires to office in the secular world.[77]

---

elders and government by bishops and deacons originally represented two distinct forms of ecclesiastical organization that only gradually merged. The Pastorals would reflect the period in which the two systems were merging. See especially pp. 68, 77-78, 107. Cf. Brox, 151; Dibelius/Conzelmann, 47.

[73]Thus the textual variant ἀνθρώπινος ὁ λόγος is explained. πιστὸς ὁ λόγος has sometimes been taken as referring to v. 15 of the previous chapter. For a discussion, see Lock, ad loc.

[74]Jeremias has gathered the pertinent material to demonstrate this point in his commentary on the Pastorals, pp. 33-34. He identifies a cluster of words and expressions that refer to "das Liebeswerk," including ἐπαρκεῖν, ἀγαθοεργεῖν and ἀγαθὰ ἔργα. Cf. 1 Tim 2:10, 5:10, 16; 6:18; Titus 3:14; Matt 25:35; Jas 2:15.

[75]See chapter II, 51; Cf. Spicq, ad loc.; Barrett, ad loc.

[76]See chapter II, 50ff.

[77]See Brox, ad loc.

Among the list of qualifications that follow, most are general virtues of the kind found in a wide variety of ethical lists.[78] Several of the qualifications do, however, apply more specifically to the office of bishop. In 3:2 one of the qualifications is that the bishop be διδακτικός, "skillful in teaching." The importance of teaching as a function of the church's leadership is emphasized repeatedly in the Pastorals, as will be seen below. In 3:4ff. it is emphasized that the bishop must be a man who governs (προϊστάναι) his own household well, since he is to be charged with governing (ἐπιμελεῖσθαι) the church. It was shown above, pp. 133f., that this passage in conjunction with 3:12 probably is envisioning rather prosperous households that included slaves. It is significant here that the author stresses, not the mere fact of the social position and status of the householder, but how well the candidate for office handles this position. Relatively high social standing is thus not the author's qualification for office, but his assumption about office holders. Thus one concludes that office holders in the church of the Pastorals must routinely have come from this level of society.

As noted in chapter II, the analogy between government of a household and government of the larger society was a traditional one in the Hellenistic-Roman world. Two implications of the analogy as it is drawn here are of particular interest. The first has to do with the range of authority implied in the analogy. Both προϊστάναι and ἐπιμελεῖσθαι can refer to authority of various kinds and at different levels, including the wide ranging authority that one associates with a householder in Hellenistic-Roman society.[79] One would thus suppose that, on this analogy, the office holder in question would be invested with such wide ranging authority not limited to one area such as worship, teaching or discipline. This supposition will be tested below. The second implication has to do with the householder's position as an individual invested with supreme authority in the household. The analogy would be particularly apt if the office of bishop is envisioned as the supreme office of the church and an office that is held by a single individual. In this

---

[78]The similarity of this list to secular lists describing, e.g., the good general or the good physician has often been noted. The appendix of Dibelius/Conzelmann includes such a list describing the good general from Onosander's *Strategikos*, pp. 158ff.

[79]BAG, s.v.; Dibelius/Conzelmann, ad loc. Both can also refer to service that one performs for another, as in Titus 3:8. But the emphasis here is on keeping proper order, as keeping one's children ἐν ὑποταγῇ. See Spicq, 445f. for secular examples of this use of ἐπιμελεῖσθαι, as in the case of the master of *ephebes*.

connection it is interesting that although deacons are required to govern their households well (3:12), no explicit analogy is made here between their position in the household and in the church. Similar expectations are present in the case of elders in Titus 1:6, but, again, no analogy to their position in the church is drawn. By contrast, in Titus 1:7 an analogy is again drawn from the household to the bishop's position as a church officer, except that here he is envisioned as the chief household servant, the οἰκονόμος, again, a position of pre-eminence held by one individual.[80] These observations do not prove the existence of the concept of the monarchical bishop in the Pastorals, but they do bring to light an additional supporting argument in favor of this view.

In 3:6 it is urged that the bishop be "no new convert" (μὴ νεόφυτος). The danger, as the author sees it, is that a new convert in the position of bishop may become "puffed up" (τυφωθεὶς) and "fall into" (ἐμπέσῃ) the judgment of the devil. False teachers are described as "puffed up" in 1 Tim 6:4 (τετύφωται) and 2 Tim 3:4 (τετυφόμενοι). Thus the author may fear the susceptibility of a new convert in a leadership position to false teaching. Nothing specific can be gleaned from the expression ἐμπεσεῖν εἰς κρίμα τοῦ διαβόλου. Similar expressions indicating unspecified dire consequences are to be found in 1 Tim 3:7 and 6:9. At any rate, the author is expressing the skepticism of an established leader at the induction of "new" people into the ranks of the leadership. This is an attitude reminiscent of that found in the municipal councils of the period.[81]

Finally, in 3:7 the author stresses the importance of the bishop's reputation with outsiders. One concludes that a bishop is viewed by the author as being in a position to improve or damage the church's standing in the eyes of the general public, based on his personal standing. The author did not stop to argue or to expand at length on any of these points. He probably therefore expected that his list of qualifications would meet with a large measure of agreement among his readers.

Titus 1:5-9 contains many similarities to the passage just discussed, but also a few differences that shed additional light on features of the leadership in the Pastorals. In 1:5 the reader learns that Titus has been commissioned to appoint (καθίσταναι) elders. Lock points out that the meaning of καθίσταναι does not necessarily rule out participation in

---

[80]In Luke 16:1ff. the οἰκονόμος is a free servant in charge of his master's accounts. For a discussion see "οἰκονόμος," *TDNT* V, 149ff.; Kelly, Dornier, ad loc.

[81]See chapter II, 51.

the selection process by the local congregations;[82] however, it usually indicates the action of a superior in selecting persons to fill offices under his authority.[83] In the present case the author portrays Titus acting as Paul's representative in selecting officers for the churches under Paul's authority.[84] While no more conclusions can be drawn from this portrayal about the process by which the leadership of the churches was regularly selected in the author's day, it does at least indicate that he assumed a selection process that operated from the top downward in the initial stages of the organization of a church.[85]

It is also interesting here that the elders are described as being appointed "in each city" (κατὰ πόλιν). Thus, in the author's conception, local congregations were in the beginning governed as city-wide entities. There are no indications in the Pastorals that the situation was different in the author's day, although there is a reasonably good possibility that, at least in the larger cities, Christians would normally have assembled for worship and instruction in several smaller groups.[86]

The requirement in 1:6 on the subject of the church officer's control of his children was discussed above, p. 132. It will be recalled that ἀσωτία is a stereotypical vice of young men rather than of children. It thus appears that the elders are envisioned as older men who have adult children. The image of the οἰκονόμος in 1:7 was also discussed above, p. 153.

---

[82]Ad loc. Cf. Barrett, ad loc. Thus in Acts 6:3 the apostles "appoint" leaders chosen by the Hellenists.

[83]Cf. Gen 41:41 (LXX), Pharaoh's appointment of Joseph; Matt 24:45, the master's appointment of a servant to be in charge of his household.

[84]In 1 Clement a similar process is envisioned in chaps. 42-43, except that here bishops and deacons are appointed by "the apostles."

[85]Käsemann sees in this text an indication that in the author's day the presbytery system of government was being instituted in the churches as a response to the gnostic threat. ("Ministry and Community," 86f.) However, the activity of Titus in this regard is probably better explained by reference to the fictitious situation of the letter, in which Titus is portrayed as a missionary to newly formed churches. This fictitious situation sets the stage for the introduction of the list of qualifications for church officers in 1:6-9. Furthermore, as noted above, pp. 149f., the Pastorals themselves do not appear to be concerned with introducing or promoting this system of government. Rather, assuming such a system, they emphasize the importance of the character and commitments of the people who fill leadership positions.

[86]See the discussion of 1 Tim 2:8, below, 166ff.

In 1:9 the teaching function of the bishop is highlighted. While in 1 Tim 3:2 the bishop's skill as a teacher is the focus (διδακτικός), here it is the content of the teaching which he follows that is emphasized. Thus it is of crucial importance that he be grounded in "the teaching" (τὴν διδαχήν), in order to be able to do the work of exhortation (παρακαλεῖν) in the sound teaching (τῇ διδασκαλίᾳ τῇ ὑγιαινούσῃ), and to confute (ἐλέγχειν) those who contradict it (τοὺς ἀντιλέγοντας). The bishop is thus viewed as a champion and a promulgator of the apostolic teaching.[87]

The section on 1 Tim 3:8ff. on qualifications for deacons contains several features that are of interest here. 3:9 indicates that deacons, like the bishop in Titus 1:9, are to be grounded thoroughly in the apostolic faith (ἔχοντες τὸ μυστήριον τῆς πίστεως ἐν καθαρεῖ συνειδήσει).[88] 3:10 specifies that deacons be tested (δοκιμαζέσθωσαν) and found blameless (ἀνέγκλητοι) before they be allowed to serve. Exactly what kind of testing the author had in mind is not clear.[89] The fact of the testing, however, highlights the official nature of the deacon's position. As noted above, pp. 133f., 3:12 reveals the author's assumption that deacons come from the class of well-to-do householders. In 3:13 the author observes that the deacon who serves well will obtain a καλὸν βαθμόν, that is, a "noble rank" or "high standing."[90] It has been suggested that the author is intimating that a deacon who serves well may expect to advance to the higher rank of bishop.[91] The more straightforward explanation, accepted by most commentators, is that the deacon who serves well achieves high standing for himself in the Christian community. Spicq interprets this as expressing the paradoxical notion that the διάκονος, the lowly servant, gains high status through his service.[92] This would thus be a variation on the dominical saying, "Whoever would be great among you must be your servant" (Mark 10:43 and pars.).

---

[87]On the concept of "the teaching" (διδαχή; διδασκαλία) see p. 158 below. On ἐλέγχειν see Barrett, ad loc.

[88]For τὸ μυστήριον as the content of the faith, see Kelly, ad loc.; Brox, ad loc.; Cf. 3:16. For the opinion that μυστήριον refers to the cult, see Hanson, Holtz, ad loc.

[89]For various suggestions, see Guthrie, Kelly, Barrett, Dibelius/ Conzelmann, ad loc. No doubt the testing concerns their faith (3:9) and character (ἀνέγκλητοι).

[90]Lock, ad loc., notes that βαθμός is used to designate ranks in the military.

[91]Cf. Barrett, ad loc.

[92]Ad loc.

No such sense of paradox is evident, however, in the present passage. Rather the same outlook is revealed here as in 3:1,[93] namely, an outlook in which office is viewed as community service undertaken by the well-to-do, whose prestige is thereby enhanced.

In 1 Tim 5:17-18 elders are described as engaging in the same activities ascribed to the bishop in 3:1ff. and Titus 1:7ff., namely governing (προεστῶτες) and preaching and teaching (κοπιῶντες ἐν λόγῳ καὶ διδασκαλίᾳ). The point of this passage, as v. 18 makes clear, is that elders who govern well and especially those who teach are worthy of the community's financial support. The exact meaning of διπλῆ τιμή in v. 17 is, however, in doubt. Some interpreters understand it to be a technical term designating an exact amount which is precisely double that of compensation received by another group.[94] Others understand it as a less precise expression that means something like "especially generous support."[95] At any rate, the important point to be recognized here is that the author is calling for the financial support of regular church officers in language reminiscent of that used from the earliest period in connection with support of travelling apostles and prophets.[96] Again, one cannot be certain to what extent the church of the Pastorals engaged in this practice. The author may have anticipated some resistance, since he bolsters his exhortation with a scriptural quotation also used by Paul (Deut 25:4; 1 Cor 9:9ff.) in a similar situation, and another saying found in the synoptic tradition (Matt 10:10 and pars.). Nevertheless, there is no indication that he is introducing this as an entirely new practice.

5:19 lays down a rule for judicial process when an accusation is brought against an elder. 5:20 envisions either guilty elders being convicted in the presence of the presbytery or sinners in general being convicted in the presence of the congregation.[97] In any case vv. 19-20 indicate that the church leadership did exercise a judicial function in addition to other functions.

---

[93]Spicq, ad loc. also notes this connection.

[94]E.g., elders who govern but do not teach (Dibelius/Conzelmann, ad loc.) or widows (Schweizer, 6h).

[95]E.g., Lock, Kelly, Brox, ad loc.

[96]See 1 Cor 9:9; Did. 13:1ff.

[97]5:17-25 consists of a series of brief exhortations that for the most part follow one on another without connectives. Thus attempts to relate one exhortation to another in this section are guesswork. This section resembles in style the section in Isocrates, "To Demonicus," often cited to illustrate the disconnectedness of paraenetic discourse (29ff.).

In 5:22 Timothy is cautioned not to lay hands (χεῖρας ἐπιτιθέναι) on anyone in haste. In Judaism laying on of hands was traditionally understood to convey the Holy Spirit.[98] It was performed in connection with a variety of cultic acts in the early church, including baptism, the restoration of sinners to fellowship in the church, and ordination, as in 1 Tim 4:14. If ordination of elders is in view,[99] then this exhortation reflects the same attitude as the caution against choosing a new convert as bishop in 1 Tim 3:6.

Timothy and Titus

It was noted above that Timothy and Titus are portrayed in the Pastorals as Paul's special assistants rather than as prototypes of the monarchical bishop. Thus their portrayal in the Pastorals does not provide direct information about the characteristics of any particular office in the church. Yet they are definitely pictured as having a leadership role in the church.

In 1 Tim 4:14 Timothy is described as possessing a charisma which he has received through prophecy (διὰ προφητείας)[100] with the laying on of hands of the presbytery, that is, ordination. In 2 Tim 1:6 he is again described as having a charisma which he has received through the laying on of (Paul's) hands.[101] Charisma and prophecy are features usually associated with charismatic leadership rather than with office. Thus, if the description of Timothy's ordination reflects the practice in the church of the Pastorals in ordaining officers, then the official leadership of the

---

[98]See Kelly, ad loc.; Dibelius/Conzelmann, excursus, pp. 70f.; Käsemann, "Ministry and Community," 86f.

[99]Proponents of this view include Dornier, Lock, Kelly, Dibelius/Conzelmann, ad loc. Hanson, *The Pastoral Letters*, ad loc., is among the dissenters. As noted above, the immediate context is of no help in deciding this question. Since laying on of hands is associated with ordination in 1 Tim 4:14 and also apparently in 2 Tim 1:6, it seems likely that ordination is also in view here. Under the circumstances, however, any conclusions drawn about the meaning of this passage must remain highly tentative.

[100]Or "on account of prophecies."

[101]Cf. 1 Tim 1:18. The discrepancy between 1 Tim 4:14 and 2 Tim 1:6 on the question of who ordained Timothy is not of primary concern here. For a discussion, see Kelly, 107f.; D. Daube, *The New Testament and Rabbinic Judaism* (London: University of London, Athlone Press, 1956) 44ff.

church has accomplished a synthesis of charisma and office that, no doubt, will have weakened the position of charismatic leaders outside the official structure.[102]

The importance of the teaching function of the leadership, emphasized in the section on the bishop in Titus 1:9, is highlighted to an even greater degree in various exhortations to Timothy and Titus. 1 Tim 4:13, in which reading aloud of scripture (ἡ ἀνάγνωσις), exhortation (ἡ παράκλησις), and teaching (ἡ διδασκαλία) are linked, suggests that the regular setting for teaching activity was the worship assembly of the church. The content of the teaching which they are urged to impart most often emerges as practical and ethical instruction of the type that dominates the Pastorals themselves, much of this instruction having to do with behavior and relationships in the household of God. Thus in Titus 2:1, Titus is urged to teach "that which befits sound teaching" (ἃ πρέπει τῇ ὑγιαινούσῃ διδασκαλίᾳ). In this case the content of the teaching turns out to be the station code of 2:2-10. Similarly, the exhortation "teach and urge these things" (ταῦτα δίδασκε καὶ παρακάλει), in 1 Tim 6:2b follows the instructions regarding various groups in the church in 5:3-6:2a.[103] In this connection Timothy and Titus are also expected to be moral examples for the community (1 Tim 4:11; Titus 2:7). Furthermore, they have the responsibility of being the first line of defense against false teaching (1 Tim 1:3f., 6:20; Titus 3:9f.).[104] Thus the transmission and defense of the teaching, especially its ethical and practical aspects, is presented as their central task.

However, the wide ranging pastoral authority attributed to Timothy should also be noted. In 1 Tim 5:1-2, Timothy is pictured as exhorting the members of different age groups in the church as if they were members of his family.[105] The point of the passage is that in exercising his authority, he should be careful to treat the members of these different groups in a way appropriate to their station. The author's assumption is thus that Timothy has pastoral authority over every member of the church regardless of his or her social station, in the way that a householder has authority over the members of his family.

---

[102]See Schlier, 135; Käsemann, "Ministry and Community," 87. Cf. Acts 13:2.

[103]K. H. Rengstorf notes the ethical and practical emphasis in the concept of "teaching" in the Pastorals in his article " διδάσκω," *TDNT* II, especially p. 147. Cf. 1 Tim 4:11; 2 Tim 2:2; Tit 1:11. Cf. Lohfink, 97f.

[104]Cf. Campenhausen, *Ecclesiastical Authority*, 109ff.

[105]For parallels in the secular literature, see Dibelius/Conzelmann, ad loc.

Summary

The leadership of the church of the Pastorals was official in character. Prospective leaders were expected to meet certain qualifications (1 Tim 3:1ff., 3:8ff., Titus 1:6ff.). They were tested before being admitted to office (1 Tim 3:10). Some of them, at least, received financial support from the Christian community.

Not everyone in the church had realistic prospects of entering the leadership circle. Access to leadership positions appears to have been controlled to a great extent by the already established leadership. This is the author's assumption in the case of the churches which he portrays as being organized on Crete. If 1 Tim 5:22 concerns the ordination of elders, then this passage too indicates that one was admitted to the ranks of the leadership by the leadership itself. The assumption in the Pastorals is that the official leaders came from among the well-to-do householders of the church (1 Tim 3:12). Thus, in all probability poor men and unmarried men must usually have been excluded. Elders are presumed to be old enough to have adult children. Thus young men would ordinarily have been excluded from this group. No women, whatever their age or socioeconomic status, had any part in the official leadership, although the church probably recognized a minor role for widows and possibly deaconesses as official workers.[106] The author of the Pastorals is concerned that the leaders conduct their lives in morally exemplary fashion. He also urges that they not be new converts (1 Tim 3:6). In both respects he probably reflects the prevailing attitudes among the leadership, since he expends no great effort to explain or defend his position.

It thus appears that the governing group in the church of the Pastorals was something of an aristocracy in relation to the general membership. In this respect this church exhibits the same social structure which Judge and Theissen have found in the first generation Pauline churches, where the leading figures in the churches appear to have been well-to-do householders who brought their dependents into the church with them. Of course in Paul's churches this leadership is still largely if not entirely

---

[106]See p. 133, n. 17 above and the section on widows in the community below, pp. 161ff.

unofficial,[107] and church order is an order according to charismata in the congregation.[108]

The officers of the church of the Pastorals, or perhaps a small group among them, had broad ranging authority that extended to all areas of the life of the Christian community. Such authority appears to have been associated in particular with the bishop(s), whose governing of the church was viewed as analogous to the householder's governing of his household (1 Tim 3:4-5). Timothy's authority is pictured in similar terms in 1 Tim 5:1-2. This broad range of authority is reflected in the variety of leadership functions that come into play in the Pastorals. Church officers had pastoral responsibility for the membership (1 Tim 5:1-2), they exercised disciplinary authority in the community (1 Tim 5:19-20), and they represented the church to the outside world (1 Tim 3:7). Their most important functions involved the preservation, transmission and defense of the teaching, which, if the content of the Pastorals themselves is any indication, consisted in large part of rules for the ordering of the social life of the church. This strong emphasis on the official leadership as the first line of defense against opposition to the teaching leads one to suspect that the teaching was in fact encountering significant opposition in the church. This suspicion will be tested below.

Finally, there is evidence here that, as in the domestic ideal which prevailed in the church, so also in the prevailing concept of the leader's role, the social values of the larger society held sway. The author appears to speak for his church in regarding office in the church as socially prestigious in the same way that citizens of Greek cities and members of associations regarded office holding (1 Tim 3:1, 13). One undertook office as a socially prominent member of one's community in order to fulfill one's civic duties. The social rewards were increased recognition and further enhanced social standing. Thus, although the leaders of the church may not have been on the same social level as the members of their municipal aristocracy, they shared the same aristocratic social aspirations within a smaller sphere. As we turn to an examination of the subordinate groups in the church, the consequences of these social values should become increasingly apparent.

---

[107]See chapter I, pp. 5f. On the beginnings of office in the Pauline churches, see Campenhausen, *Ecclesiastical Authority*, 68f., where, in particular, Phil 1:1 is discussed.

[108]See Campenhausen, *Ecclesiastical Authority*, 55ff. and Käsemann, "Ministry and Community."

Widows (1 Tim 5:3-16)

Most of the particular interpretive problems connected with this passage are related to the problem of the structure of the passage as a whole. In one view the passage is made up of a series of loosely connected sections. Vv. 3-8 are seen as comprising a section which addresses the question of care for widows. V. 9 begins a new section which deals with requirements for the office of widows. There is no connection between the two sections except for the catchword "widows" (χήρας). V. 16 constitutes a third distinct section.[109] In the other view vv. 3-16 form a unified whole, in which the central problem is to determine as exactly as possible who qualifies as a "real widow" (ὄντως χήρα). In this view no distinction is being made between real widows and official widows.[110]

The first view is supported by the fact that there are no connectives between vv. 8-9 and vv. 15-16, while elsewhere in the section connectives are consistently employed. According to this view, all truly needy widows (ὄντως χῆραι) would be entitled to the support (τιμή)[111] of the community, regardless of their age or past behavior. In order to become enrolled as an official widow, however, one would have to meet the stringent requirements outlined in vv. 9f. Thus younger widows who remarried according to the author's advice in v. 14 would be excluding themselves from becoming official widows, but not from receiving the support of the church in the event that their second husbands also died. A similar distinction between support of widows and enrollment of them in an order of widows is made in the Syrian *Didascalia*, which urges that young widows be helped financially even though they should not be appointed to the widow's order (chap. 14).[112]

The second view finds support in the following considerations. 5:3 initiates the instructions concerning widows with the imperative, χήρας τίμα τὰς ὄντως χήρας. The dual thrust of this imperative is at

---

[109]See Dornier, Jeremias, ad loc.; H. Preisker, *Christentum*, 149. Cf. the similar views of G. Delling, *Stellung*, 133; Bartsch, 137-38.

[110]See A. Sand, "Witwenstand und Ämterstructuren in den urchristlichen Gemeinden," *Bibleb* 12 (1971) 186-97; J. Müller-Bardorff, "Zur Exegese von I Tim. 5:3-16," in *Gott und die Götter. Festgabe für Erich Fascher* (Berlin: Evang. Verlagsanstalt, 1958) 113-33; Dibelius/Conzelmann, ad loc.

[111]See discussion below, pp. 162f. and cf. 5:17-18.

[112]See especially Dornier, Spicq, ad loc.

once apparent. On the one hand it requires the support of widows. On the other hand it restricts support to those who are "real widows" (ὄντως χῆραι). Care and protection of widows and orphans had long been recognized as an ethical obligation in Judaism and the same view had been adopted by the church from the beginning.[113] Restrictions on such care are, however, a non-traditional feature.[114] Thus the remainder of vv. 3-16 can be read as an explication of the phrase "real widows." In vv. 4, 8 the "real widow" is distinguished from those who have families to support them, and in vv. 11ff., she is distinguished from younger widows. The worldly (σπαταλῶσα ζῶσα) is also excluded (v. 6). In vv. 5 and 9f., the "real widow" is described in positive terms.[115] The consistent effect of the instructions is to reduce the circle of widows for whom the church has responsibility. V. 16 represents a variation on the thought expressed in v. 3: The church should be spared the care of widows who have other resources, "in order that it may be able to care for (ἵνα . . . ἐπαρκέσῃ) the real widows."[116]

A decision between these two views will be temporarily avoided, pending investigation of a related question, namely, whether there is evidence in this passage for an office of widows and, if so, what kind of office. A number of features of the passage come into consideration in this connection. It has been argued that τίμα in v. 3 means "pay," and thus that the subject is payment of widows as officers of the church. In 5:17 τιμή refers to the compensation of elders, as v. 18 indicates. Thus, it is reasoned, since 5:3ff. stands in such close connection, τίμα here must have a similar meaning.[117] This view is supported by the fact that in later church orders, τιμᾶν is a technical term for "pay."[118]

However, good reasons exist for rejecting this view. As Sand shows, τιμή and its cognates are used in the Pastorals in a variety of contexts, in none of which, with the exception of 1 Tim 5:3 and 5:17, the reference can possibly be to a payment of any kind.[119] The most striking example comes from 1 Tim 6:1f., which like 5:3ff. is adjacent to the passage concerning elders in 5:17ff. Here slaves are exhorted to consider

---

[113]See, e.g., Jer 7:6; Prov 23:10; Deut 24:19ff.; Mark 12:40 and pars.; Acts 6:1ff.; Pol. Phil. 6:1.

[114]Cf. Müller-Bardorff, 114; G. Stählin, "χήρα," *TDNT* IX, 455.

[115]Cf. Sand, 195; Müller-Bardorff, 115f.

[116]Müller-Bardorff, 116.

[117]Müller-Bardorff, 115.

[118]Bartsch, 118.

[119]P. 194; Cf. Lock, Barrett, ad loc.

their masters "worthy of all τιμή," which can only mean "worthy of all honor," and not "worthy of all payment." Thus the meaning of τίμα in 5:3 must be determined by reference to its immediate context in vv. 3-16. That some sort of practical support is involved is evident from vv. 4, 8, and 16, but the author does not appear to be thinking of this support as compensation for officers of the church, but rather as practical help for needy women. Thus, vv. 4 and 8 urge the support of widows by their relatives, and v. 16 calls for their support (ἐπαρκείτω) by πισταί, so that the church will be better able to support (ἐπαρκέσῃ) "real widows." "Support" (ἐπαρκεῖν) here does not suggest official compensation, but help or aid.[120] In all probability, then, τίμα in v. 3 refers not to official compensation but to practical and material aid, and "real widows" here designates not a group of official widows, but widows who are alone (cf. v. 5) with no relatives or benefactors to support them.

Nevertheless, there is still the possibility that vv. 9ff., if they represent a separate section, have to do with a group of official widows. V. 9 refers to the enrollment of widows (χήρα καταλεγέσθω) who meet certain qualifications, while v. 11 calls for the rejection (παραιτοῦ) of younger widows. The reference is not necessarily to an office of widows since καταλέγειν need not refer to anything more than the activity of writing down a list.[121] Nevertheless, that the church keeps a list of widows, and that only widows who possess certain qualifications are eligible to be placed on this list is clear.[122]

The list of requirements for enrollment on the list of widows resembles those for the offices of bishop, deacon, and elder (1 Tim 3:1-13; Titus 1:6ff.) with the exception of the age requirement, that enrolled widows be at least sixty years old. Thus, while the men who hold these offices are expected to be μιᾶς γυναικὸς ἄνδρες, enrolled widows must be ἑνὸς ἀνδρὸς γυναί. In addition, the virtues of hospitality (cf. 1 Tim 5:10, ἐξενοδόχησεν; 1 Tim 3:2, Titus 1:8, φιλόξενον) and proper care of children (cf. 1 Tim 5:10, ἐτεκνοτρόφησεν; 1 Tim 3:4, Titus 1:6) are demanded of widows as well as of men who are church

---

[120]See BAG, s.v.; Jos.

[121]Sand, 195. This verb is often used to refer to the enlistment of soldiers, as in Jos. *Ap.* 1.131. See BAG, s.v. G. Stählin, "χήρα," *TDNT* IX, 456, understands καταλέγεσθαι as "to be adopted into the fellowship by election." παραιτέομαι would have the corresponding meaning "vote down." While this appears to be a possible interpretation, the context in 5:9ff. does not provide means by which to confirm or disprove it.

[122]Sand, ibid.

officers.[123] This parallelism, then, suggests that enrolled widows too are church offices.

That enrolled widows fill an office in the church is also suggested by the language of v. 12. Here younger widows who desire to marry are seen as having set aside (ἠθέτησαν) τὴν πρώτην πίστιν. It is possible that τὴν πρώτην πίστιν refers to the widow's initial inward commitment to a life of celibacy and singleminded devotion to God (v. 5) and Christ (v. 11).[124] However, ἀθετεῖν usually denotes the nullifying of a will, vow, covenant, or the like, that is, a concrete and public agreement or promise.[125] Since πίστις can mean "oath,"[126] it would appear likely that v. 12 refers to an initial oath of celibacy taken by widows on the occasion of their enrollment. Thus once again the evidence favors the view that an office of widows is presupposed.

If the church had official widows, then presumably they were given duties. Yet 5:3ff. offers little evidence of anything of the sort. In 5:5 the "real widow" is portrayed as praying night and day. It has thus been suggested that widows had a special duty to pray for the community.[127] However, in this case this duty would apply to all "real widows" and not just the enrolled widows of v. 9f. V. 10 mentions such activities as raising children, washing the feet of the saints, and supporting the afflicted; but these are qualifications referring to the widow's former life, not duties of her present position.[128] Finally, v. 13 mentions younger widows who run from house to house. The possibility has been raised on the basis of this verse that widows functioned as pastoral visitors. However, this is pure conjecture. False teachers are similarly described as entering houses (2 Tim 3:6) and disrupting households (Titus 1:11). A more likely explanation for the author's reference to the household visits of younger widows is that he perceives them, like the false teachers, as in some sense a threat to the households of the Christian community.[129] Thus one can

---

[123] Cf. Müller-Bardorff, 120f.; P. Trummer, "Einehe," 473ff.

[124] As Sand argues, 196.

[125] See BAG, s.v. Cf. 1 Macc 11:36; Gal 3:15.

[126] Müller-Bardorff, 120; Brox, ad loc. Cf. 3 Macc 3:10; Jos. *Ant.* 12.382.

[127] Müller-Bardorff, 126; Bartsch, 136.

[128] Kelly suggests, ad loc., that the qualifications indicate the kind of duties which widows would be expected to perform; i.e., what they once performed voluntarily they would continue to perform as the duties of office.

[129] See above on women in the household, p. 134; below, on the false

find no clear indication of duties performed by enrolled widows. Nevertheless, this is not a particularly strong argument against the existence of an office of widows here. The Pastorals offer no real information about the duties of deacons either, although they certainly presuppose the deacon's office.

The bulk of the evidence supports the view that vv. 9ff. speak about an office of widows. At the same time, the "real widows" of vv. 3-8 and 16 can hardly be identical with the "enrolled widows" of vv. 9ff., if the latter represent an office. Rather the "real widows" are poor widows who must rely on the church for support, because they are not supported by family or by πισταί. Thus one arrives at the conclusion that vv. 9ff. comprise a distinct section within the passage and that this section addresses itself to a separate issue.

Vv. 3-8 and 16, then, are concerned with the problem of the church's social responsibility for widows. The church of the Pastorals has accepted the notion that it has a duty to care for needy widows. In this respect it reflects the outlook both of the early church generally and of Judaism, from which the church derived this outlook. In the author's view, however, this duty has become a heavy burden. He attempts to lighten the burden by defining as narrowly as possible the group that is entitled to the church's support.

Vv. 9ff., by contrast, deal with the distinct problem of official widows. The question of compensation is not addressed in this section, nor is there discussion of the duties of official widows. Rather the issue is the moral and emotional fitness of candidates for the office. The author argues that only elderly women should hold this office, while vv. 11-12 indicate that the church has not always followed this practice. Official widows should have led exemplary lives, having been married only once and having been industrious in all kinds of good works. The author is so troubled about the presence of younger women among the official widows that he urges the former to remarry, and thus in the process to disqualify themselves from ever attaining the office. Younger women have powerful sex drives (v. 11) that should be channeled into marriage (v. 14). When they remain unmarried, they display an appalling lack of domesticity, "running from house to house," and "saying what they should not" (v. 13). Some, in fact, have "strayed after Satan" (ἐξετράπησαν ὀπίσω τοῦ Σατανᾶ) (v. 15). Similar expressions in other passages in the Pastorals refer to Christians who have gone over to the false

---

teachers, pp. 175f. Kelly, Dibelius/Conzelmann, Barrett take the view rejected here.

teaching.[130] It may be, therefore, that the author views younger widows as particularly vulnerable to false teachers. On the whole, then, younger widows emerge, in the author's description, as rather dangerous and unpredictable beings who should be controlled in marriage, rather than given official status in the church. The description thus suggests that these women were the focus of real social tensions involving a conflict of values over the role of women in the household and the community.

When one views the whole of 5:3-16 together, one finds that to a certain extent it does reflect a unified perspective after all. Throughout the author views widows, official or otherwise, as a problem with which the church is forced to deal. He would like to reduce the number of widows who are dependent upon the church for support. He would also like to restrict severely entrance into the ranks of the official widows. It thus appears that he wants to minimize both the involvement of the church in the lives of widows and the involvement of widows in the official structure of the church. At the same time he gives assent both to the church's traditional practice of helping needy widows and to the continued existence of an office of widows.

Men and Women in Worship (1 Tim 2:8-15)

It was seen in chapter III that this section takes the pairing ἄνδρες . . . γυναῖκες, a standard feature in the station codes, and develops it in a new context, namely, the context of the church's worship. In 2:8 it is urged that the men pray "in every place (ἐν παντὶ τόπῳ), with holy hands (ὁσίους χεῖρους) raised,"[131] "without strife and quarreling (ὀργῆς καὶ διαλογίσμου)." The point of the exhortation is that the men should take care not to defile the worship of the church by bringing quarrels into the assembly. A similar notion is expressed in Did. 14:2, where, in the context of instructions concerning the Eucharist, the congregation is warned, "let none who has a quarrel (ἀμφιβολίαν) with his fellow join in your meeting (συνελθέτω ὑμῖν) until they be reconciled, that your sacrifice be not defiled."[132]

---

[130]As Bartsch notes, 134. Cf. 1 Tim 1:6; 6:20; 2 Tim 4:4.

[131]This was a common posture for prayer in antiquity among Romans, Greeks, and Jews. See Lock, Kelly, ad loc., Deissman, *Light from the Ancient East*, 421,

[132]Cf. E. Kähler, *Die Frau in den paulinischen Briefen* (Zurich: Gotthelf Verlag, 1960) 149; Lock; Dibelius/Conzelmann; Spicq, ad loc.

However, it is the phrase "in every place" that is of particular interest here. Since the context is the worship of the congregation, "every place" means every place where the church gathers for worship. On the assumption that this phrase is not superfluous in its present context,[133] two possible interpretations lie at hand: (1) The author, assuming that a number of local congregations will read this letter, is emphasizing that the church in every locality, is expected to conduct its worship in this way, and that, thus, a universal rule of worship is being presented. (2) The author has in mind the specific situation of the church in Ephesus, which he envisions as worshiping in a number of different locations in smaller groups rather than as a single body in one location. The second possibility is particularly intriguing. Until long beyond the latest possible period in which the Pastorals may have been written, the Christians were worshiping in private houses.[134] It appears that large rooms in the οἶκοι or *domi* of well-to-do members were often used for this purpose.[135] Even so, the number of people who could gather in such rooms at one time must have been severely limited, so that it would be hard to imagine a congregation of more than several hundred persons able to assemble for worship as a single body.[136] In fact there is considerable evidence to suggest that the Christians of second century Rome were

---

[133]Bartsch argues that this phrase became a watchword in the primitive church's proclamation of the possibility of pure worship in every place, not simply in one holy place, i.e., the Temple. Cf. Mal 1:11, 14; Did. 14:3; Acts 21:28; 1 Cor 1:2; 2 Cor 2:14; 1 Thess 1:8. Thus the presence of this phrase in 1 Tim 2:8 would indicate the presence of a preformulated rule expressing the mission orientation of the first century church order which, Bartsch hypothesizes, lies behind the Pastorals (pp. 47f., 56f.). In its present context the phrase would serve no real purpose (p. 13). However, in the present study the assumption, supported by the findings in chapter III, is that the author is ordinarily a purposeful writer, whose choice of words should be explained, if possible, by reference to meanings which he intends.

[134]See W. Rordorff, "Was wissen wir über die christliche Gottesdiensträume?" *ZNW* 55 (1964) 111; J. M. Petersen, "House-Churches in Rome," *VC* 23 (1969) 266.

[135]Rordorff, 112ff.; Petersen, 270.

[136]Rordorff mentions a passage in the *Recognitions of Clement* in which Peter is portrayed as teaching in a room that could hold five hundred people. This may be a greatly exaggerated figure. If not, it certainly represents the upper limit of the numbers one might expect to contain in the great hall of a private house.

worshiping in numerous relatively small bodies in private homes.[137] Thus it is not unreasonable to suppose that during this period Christians in a large city such as Ephesus would have faced a similar situation on a somewhat smaller scale. Whether or not the Pastorals presuppose a Christian population of the size to necessitate multiple worshiping groups will be explored below.

In 2:9 the author turns to the subject of women in worship. It is possible, though not certain, that προσεύχεσθαι should be understood here, and that the women are also being exhorted to pray.[138] The explicit exhortation, however, is that women should adorn (κοσμεῖν) themselves "in becoming dress (ἐν καταστολῇ κοσμίῳ),[139] with modesty (αἰδοῦς) and prudence (σωφροσύνης). . . ." αἰδώς and σωφροσύνη are often paired as the virtues of women who exhibit proper reserve and self-control in sexual matters.[140] It thus appears that this is the author's emphasis here. By contrast, fashionable hairdos (πλέγμασιν),[141] gold jewelry, pearls, and expensive (πολυτελεῖς) clothes are singled out as inappropriate adornment for women in worship. Only well-to-do women could have been the object of this exhortation since only they could have afforded such ostentation.[142] The contrast of outward and inward adornment in women is a common Hellenistic topos,[143] although the

---

[137]Peterson, 266ff. Robert Banks, *Paul's Idea of Community* (Grand Rapids, MI: Eerdmans, 1980) 41-42, in commenting on the size of Paul's Corinthian community, suggests that no more than 40-45 people could have gathered in the entertainment room of the typical house of a moderately well-to-do family.

[138]Cf. Kähler, 149; Spicq, Dibelius/Conzelmann, ad loc.

[139]καταστολή can refer either to dress or to demeanor. If it means the latter here, then μετὰ . . . σωφροσύνης explicates (ἐν καταστολῇ κοσμίῳ). See Lock, Dibelius/Conzelmann, ad loc.

[140]Cf. Philo, *Spec. Leg.* 1.102, 3.51; and p. 135 above.

[141]πλέγματα refers to a fashionable style of plaiting the hair. See Kelly, ad loc.

[142]See Spicq, Kelly, ad loc. Cf. descriptions of wealthy women in Juvenal, *Sat.* 6.492; Petronius, *Sat.* 67.

[143]See Spicq, ad loc. Baltensweiler, 237, identifies the prohibition of expensive and ostentatious dress as a specifically Jewish characteristic. This is not so, however, as the following quotation from Plutarch, "Advice to the Bride and Groom" (*Mor.* 141E) indicates: "For as Crates used to say, 'adornment is that which adorns,' (κόσμος . . . ἐστιν . . . κοσμοῦν) 'and that adorns or decorates a woman which makes her more decorous (τὸ κοσμιώτεραν . . . ποιοῦν).' It is not gold or precious

specific application to worship is not a standard feature of the topos. Since the author places no special emphasis on this exhortation, it is unlikely that he viewed ostentatious dress among women in worship as a major problem.

V. 11 introduces new subject matter, although the context is still worship. Women must learn "in silence (ἐν ἡσυχίᾳ) in all subjection (ἐν πάσῃ ὑποταγῇ)." The import of this rule becomes clear in the following verse, in which the author insists, "I do not permit (οὐκ ἐπιτρέπω) a woman to teach (διδάσκειν) or to lord it over a man (αὐθεντεῖν ἀνδρός); rather she must remain in silence (ἐν ἡσυχίᾳ)." It is not completely clear whether the intent is to ban all speech by women in worship.[144] The main point, however, is that women be prohibited from exercising the teaching function in this setting. The author's choice of words here indicates that he regards women who teach in the public assembly as having transgressed the limits of their place as women in the order of things. Thus their activity as teachers is seen as "lording it over"[145] men, a posture which involves a reversal of the proper order. Women who learn in silence, by contrast, learn in subjection (ὑποταγή), a posture that reflects their subordinate station in relation to men. It should be remembered that teaching involved not only exposition of the doctrines of the faith, but also ethical exhortation on the subject of personal conduct. The author himself is engaging in such teaching activity in the present passage, where in the guise of Paul he gives practical directives, assuming the attitude of a superior (βούλομαι; οὐκ ἐπιτρέπω).[146] If women who taught in worship employed a similar

---

stones or scarlet that makes her such, but whatever invests her with that something which betokens dignity, good behavior and modesty (ἀλλ' ὅσα σεμνότητος εὐταξίας αἰδοῦς ἔμφασιν περιτίθησιν)."

[144]The similarities of this passage to 1 Cor 14:33bff. have often been noted. A few interpreters have detected a gentler tone in the present passage, in which ἡσυχία is enjoined on the woman rather than σιγή. It is argued that, while the latter means complete silence, the former can refer to calm, quiet behavior. Thus A. Schlatter, *Die Kirche der Griechen im Urteil des Paulus* (2d ed.; Stuttgart: Calwer, 1958) 87; Spicq, 389.

[145]αὐθέντης = δεσπότης. Thus αὐθεντεῖν = δεσποτεῖν. See Spicq, ad loc.; cf. Gayer, 133, n. 54; Leipholdt, 188.

[146]"I desire," does not really capture the force of βούλομαι here, which was used in this way to introduce legislative decrees in the secular world. See Spicq, Easton, Dibelius/Conzelmann, ad loc.; Jos. *Ant.*

style, it is not difficult to see how the author could have regarded them as "lording it over" men.

In vv. 13-15 the author adduces two reasons for the prohibition of v. 12, both of which have to do with the fundamental superiority of men over women. The first reason (v. 13) is simply that man was created before woman and thus occupies a superior place in the order of creation. Paul offers a similar argument in 1 Cor 11:8f., where he addresses the problem of proper attire for men and women in worship. The second reason (v. 14) is that is was not the man, but the woman who was "deceived" (ἐξαπατηθεῖσα). The reference is probably not simply to the account in Genesis, but to an apocryphal tradition in which Eve is seduced by the serpent.[147] This interpretation is suggested by the use here of ἐξαπατάω, which can refer to sexual transgression, rather than ἀπατάω, which is used in the Genesis account in the Septuagint. In addition, v. 15 states that a woman's salvation will come through child-bearing (διὰ τεκνογονίας),[148] which would be a form of expiation commensurate with the crime attributed to her.

Thus in vv. 11ff. the author argues as follows: women violate the fundamental order of things when they presume to become teachers in the church. Such teaching activity involves assuming a superior position in relation to the men of the congregation, but women were created to be subordinate to men, as is indicated by the fact that men were created first. Furthermore, women labor under the burden of an original sexual guilt that is to be expiated by childbearing, that is, by submitting to the proper role of a woman as a wife and mother.[149] A glance at the author's argumentation reveals that he has martialed the most devastating arguments available to oppose what he regards as a serious threat to the

---

XII.150, where it is used by Antiochus III in a decree ordering a settlement of Jews in Phrygia.

[147]Hanson has gathered the evidence for the currency of this tradition at the time of the writing of the Pastorals, in "Eve's Transgression," *Studies*, 64-77. The tradition is preserved in the *Prot. Jas.* 13:1 and is alluded to in *Ep. Diog.* 12:8. Cf. Baltensweiler, 237; Lock, Dibelius/Conzelmann, ad loc.

[148]The un-Pauline and un-Christian notion expressed here has led to various other attempts to explicate διὰ τεκνογονίας. Ellicott, Lock understand it as "through the (i.e. Jesus') birth." Holtz takes διά as having a descriptive/temporal force here, so that the idea is that the woman is saved in her life of bearing children.

[149]Cf. Kelly, Jeremias, ad loc.

church. There can be little doubt, then, that women really were teaching in public worship in the church of the Pastorals, and that serious conflict had erupted over this issue.

Age Groups in the Church (Titus 2:1ff.)

In this passage the household relationships have been replaced by relationships in the Christian community. The groups mentioned in 1 Tim 5:1-2, namely, older men, younger men, older women and younger women, are the object of somewhat more extended attention here.[150]

The use of πρεσβύτης, "old man," rather than πρεσβύτερος, in 2:2 makes it clear that the author is dealing with an age group and not an office.[151] The qualities urged upon old men (νηφαλίους, σεμνούς, σώφρονας) are to be found in various other lists in the Pastorals applied to different groups. Together they call for the dignified bearing and self-discipline demanded elsewhere of church officers (1 Tim 3:2, 8; Titus 1:8). In addition, old men should be "sound in faith, love, and endurance" (τῇ πίστει, τῇ ἀγάπῃ, τῇ ὑπομονῇ). The same triad appears together in a larger list in 1 Tim 6:11, and the same three virtues are included in a list in 2 Tim 3:10. They stand together as primary virtues of the Christian life.[152] "Sound" (ὑγιαίνοντας) is repeatedly used in the Pastorals to describe the authentic Christian teaching. Thus it is likely that the author also has in mind that the old men should be adherents of the "sound" teaching.[153] It is noteworthy that there is a concern for the soundness of the old men's faith, but that this concern is not repeated in the case of the other classifications.

The exact sense of the first phrase in 2:3 describing the behavior of old women, (εἶναι) ἐν καταστήματι ἱεροπρεπεῖς, is not clear. κατάστημα probably refers both to dress and more broadly to deportment.[154] ἱεροπρεπεῖς sometimes means "holy" and sometimes, "priestly." Lock suggests that the meaning is that the old women are to

---

[150]The section on slaves in vv. 9f. will not be discussed again here. See above pp. 140ff.

[151]See BAG, s.v.; *TDNT* VI, 682f.

[152]As Holtz notes, ad loc. Cf. the very similar if more famous triad, πίστις, ἐλπίς, ἀγάπη in 1 Cor 13:13.

[153]Cf. 1 Tim 1:10; 6:3; Tit 1:9; Lock, Brox, Spicq, ad loc.

[154]Cf. Ign. Trall. 3:2, on the bishop and also 3 Macc 5:45. For secular examples see Spicq, ad loc.

carry into life the demeanor of priestesses in a temple.[155] The warnings against slanderous talk (διαβόλους) and addiction to wine (οἴνῳ πολλῷ δεδουλωμένας) reflect what had apparently become a popular stereotype of "the old woman."[156] Perhaps the most interesting feature here is the assignment to old women of the responsibility for training younger women in proper matronly behavior. Thus, although women are excluded from teaching in the assembly, the elderly among them are expected to serve the community as καλοδιδάσκαλοι, "teachers of good things,"[157] within a certain strictly circumscribed sphere. There is no reason to believe that the author is urging some new pattern of behavior in the Christian community at this point.

The older women are to teach the younger women to be exemplary matrons (vv. 4-5). The contribution of the latter to the church is the same as that of the slaves: by keeping their proper place at home, they avoid giving the Christian faith a bad name among the general public.[158] The author's attitude toward older and younger women here is reminiscent of his attitude toward older and younger widows in 1 Tim 5:9ff. In the present section he appears to regard older women as fully socialized members of the Christian community, whom he can rely upon to assist in the socialization of younger women.

Younger men (v. 6) should "practice self-control" (σωφρονεῖν). In the case of younger men as in that of the younger women there is probably a sexual connotation.[159]

The exhortation to Titus in vv. 7f. apparently continues in this section. In this connection an important question is raised about the place of younger men in the community. V. 6, taken by itself, shows no interest in assigning any type of responsibility to the younger men. However, in vv. 7f. Titus is urged to be a model (τύπος) of good works whose leadership is characterized by adherence to the "sound speech" (λόγον ὑγιῆ)

---

[155]See BAG, s.v.; Lock, ad loc.

[156]See Spicq, ad loc., for examples from the inscriptions. Drunkenness among women was especially abhorred in Roman tradition.

[157]BAG, s.v.

[158]Cf. 1 Tim 6:1; Titus 2:10 on slaves; Barrett, Kelly, ad loc., and above, pp. 144f.

[159]See the discussion of 1 Tim 2:8ff. above; Kelly, ad loc. Jerome, followed by Nestle, *NEB*, and several other modern editions and translations reads the first words of v. 7, περὶ πάντων as part of this clause rather than the next, in which case "self-control in everything" is urged. See Dibelius/Conzelmann, Jeremias, Brox, ad loc.

with which no opponent could find fault. The author has previously exhibited such expectations of community leaders, and it is as a community leader that Titus is addressed here. Furthermore, the position of this exhortation immediately after v. 6 indicates that the author intended to picture Titus as belonging to the νεώτεροι.

Brox notes two passages in which Timothy's youth is similarly emphasized in connection with his leadership functions. In 1 Tim 4:12, Timothy is encouraged, "Let no one despise (καταφρονείτω) your youth (νεότητος)." Again in 1 Tim 5:1f., Timothy is portrayed as a younger man who addresses older men and women as parents and younger men and women as brothers and sisters. Brox concludes that the mention of the youthfulness of Timothy and Titus is probably not simply attention to biographical detail that belongs to the author's pseudepigraphical technique, but that the picture of Timothy and Titus as youthful office holders probably has current meaning for the author's situation. Brox suggests, mainly on the basis of 1 Tim 4:12, that office holders of the Pastorals must usually have been older men and that there may have been resistance to the authority of young office holders in the churches. The author would thus have been attempting to combat such resistance.[160]

Brox's conclusion from 1 Tim 4:12 that the official leadership generally came from among the older men is probably correct. As indicated above in the section on the leadership of the church, the passages on the qualifications for officers appear to assume this fact as well. It is not as clear that the author is seeking to bolster the authority of youthful leadership in his own day. 1 Tim 4:12 closely resembles 1 Cor 16:11, in which Paul urges the Corinthians not to despise (μή τις ἐξουθενήσῃ) Timothy. Thus 1 Tim 4:12 may simply be giving a biographical detail intended to lend an air of authenticity to the letter.[161] The other passages portraying Timothy and Titus as youthful may function similarly. On the whole it seems improbable that the author means through his portrait of Timothy and Titus to address or portray young leaders in his own day.

---

[160]Brox, 178f.; 296.

[161]On the author's painstaking efforts in this regard, see D. N. Penny, *The Pseudo-Pauline Letters of the First Two Centuries* (Ph.D. dissertation, Emory University, 1979), chapter III, "Personalia."

Wealth and the Wealthy (1 Tim 6:6-10; 17-19)

1 Tim 6:6-10 ostensibly continues a section in which false teachers are being attacked (6:3ff.).[162] The sections are connected by means of the theme of greed. In 6:5 it is suggested that the false teachers are motivated by a desire to reap a profit (πορισμός) from religion. In vv. 6-8 the way of self-sufficiency (αὐταρκεία) through which religion becomes profitable, is described. Then in vv. 9f. the topic is those who want to become wealthy (οἱ βουλόμενοι πλουτεῖν). The author condemns such aspirations as highly dangerous, predicting that those who persist in them will ultimately reap terrible consequences, variously described as a snare (παγίς), destruction (ἀπωλεία) and a falling away from the faith (ἀποπλανᾶσθαι ἀπὸ τῆς πίστεως). Such emphatic condemnation indicates that the author perceived such attitudes as a real problem in the congregations he addressed.

The passage in vv. 17-19 has a different group in view, namely, those who are already wealthy (οἱ πλούσιοι).[163] Persons in this category are to be urged "not to become haughty" (μὴ ὑψηλοφρονεῖν)[164] and not to place confidence in fleeting material possessions. Rather they should put their hope in God, "who endows us richly (πλουσίως) with all things."

The admonition against reliance on one's worldly possessions was a familiar topos in both Jewish and pagan tradition,[165] and in fact is employed in the gospels as well. Thus in Matt 6:19-21 Jesus' followers are exhorted not to store up (θησαυρίζειν) treasure on earth, but in heaven; and in Luke 12:33 they are told to sell their possessions (πωλήσατε τὰ ὑπάρχοντα) and give alms, and in so doing, to provide themselves with "an unfailing treasure in the heavens" (θησαυρὸν ἀνέκλειπτον ἐν τοῖς οὐρανοῖς). The possibility of righteous maintenance of wealth is not envisioned in either example. The way in which the

---

[162] Interpreters differ on how closely this section is connected with vv. 3-5. Kelly, e.g., views vv. 9f. as still descriptive of false teachers, while Hanson and Dibelius/Conzelmann, e.g., do not. Since nothing in vv. 9f. limits the description to false teachers, the latter view is probably to be preferred.

[163] Brox emphasizes this distinction, ad loc.

[164] Cf. Spicq, ad loc. ὑψηλοφροσύνη was widely viewed as an attitude to which wealthy people were susceptible, e.g., in Philo, *Mos.* 1:31; 1 Clem 59:3; Herm. m. 8:3.

[165] Cf. Lock, Spicq, ad loc.

topos is developed in 1 Tim 6:18 reflects a much more moderate attitude toward wealth. Here the wealthy (οἱ πλούσιοι) are not instructed to divest themselves of their possessions, but rather "to be wealthy (πλουτεῖν) in good works, to be generous (εὐμεταδότους) and ready to share (κοινωνικούς)." In this way they will be storing up wealth for the future (ἀποθησαυρίζειν εἰς τὸ μέλλειν). This view of the social role of the wealthy in the Christian community corresponds to the author's view of the role of privileged members of the community generally, especially in the case of office holders and slave owners.[166]

The author's moderate tone in this section stands in marked contrast to that in 6:9f. One could reasonably account for this difference on purely ethical grounds, by pointing out that the objection is not to wealth itself, but to the consuming desire for wealth. It is worthy of note, however, that this ethic encourages an essentially static social situation. Established wealth receives the tacit approval of leadership, while attempts to break into the circle of the wealthy from below meet with condemnation. Such a stance is consistent with the author's general social conservatism and with his concern that subordinate groups not overstep the bounds of their stations (τάγματα) in the social order.

The False Teaching and Its Adherents

Polemic against false teachers is interwoven among the ethical exhortations and church order material of the Pastorals.[167] Investigators of this material usually focus attention on the nature of the false teaching.[168] Here, by contrast, the following two questions hold the greatest

---

[166] Seneca, *Ben.* 4.5,26,28 and Philo, *Jos.* 43 show a similar outlook on wealth in their development of the topos. For a discussion of the ethical problem of wealth and poverty in the early church and the way in which it was approached, see Hengel, *Property and Riches.*

[167] For a summary, see Dibelius/Conzelmann, 51.

[168] R. J. Karris, "Background," especially pp. 557-60, has shown that the polemic against false teachers reflects to a great extent the traditional polemic against sophists. He isolates the elements in the description of the false teachers that are not attributable to this traditional polemic, in order to discover what the Pastorals reveal about actual characteristics of the false teachers. The results of Karris' investigation are consistent with the widely espoused theory that the false teachers of the Pastorals were proponents of an ascetic variety of gnostic

interest: (1) To whom among the membership did the false teaching appeal? (2) What, if any, social factors contributed to this appeal?

The author sometimes places the advent of the false teachers in the future, associating their activity with the trials of the last days (e.g., in 1 Tim 4:1ff.; 2 Tim 3:1ff.).[169] For the most part, however, he treats them and their activity as a present reality in the community (e.g., in 1 Tim 1:3ff.; 6:3ff.; 2 Tim 3:6; Titus 1:10ff.). It is not clear from the author's presentation whether the false teachers have all come from within the Christian community, or whether they represent a movement (or movements) involving elements external to the church. Whichever the case, false teaching has certainly found a following within the church of the Pastorals, as 1 Tim 1:5ff. illustrates:

> . . . the aim of our charge (τῆς παραγγελίας) is love that issues from a pure heart and a good conscience and sincere faith (πίστεως ἀνυποκρίτου). Certain persons (τινες) by swerving (ἀστοχήσαντες) from these have wandered (ἐξετράπησαν) away into vain discussion. . . .

The false teaching is not just a potential threat, but under its influence, members of the Christian community have actually "wandered away" from what the author regards as "sincere faith." Thus, whatever its origins, the false teaching has become a real internal problem of the household of God, causing serious divisions among the membership.

According to 2 Tim 3:6f., women figured prominently among the adherents of the false teaching. This passage is located in the middle of a section containing an otherwise conventional characterization of the false teachers as evil men of the last days (3:1-9). In 3:6f. the false teachers are accused of "creeping into households" (ἐνδύνοντες εἰς τὰς οἰκίας) and "snaring silly women" (αἰχμαλωτίζοντες γυναικάρια). Such women, the author asserts, are "always learning, but never able to arrive at knowledge of the truth." One is struck first of all by the use of ἐνδύνοντες and αἰχμαλωτίζοντες to describe the activity

---

teaching. Cf. R. Gayer, *Stellung*, 133f.; K. Wegenast, *Tradition*, 136ff.; Dibelius/Conzelmann, 65ff.; Brox, 166ff.

[169] On the assumption that the Pastorals were written pseudonymously a generation or more after Paul's death, the future reference in these passages would be explained as instances of pseudepigraphical prediction, in which "Paul" gives prophetic warning of difficulties with false teachers in the author's day. Cf. Barrett, Brox, Dibelius/Conzelmann, ad loc.

of the false teachers. ἐνδύνειν suggests a stealthy entry, while αἰχμαλωτίζειν normally refers to the taking of captives in war.[170] The resulting picture is one of a sneak attack on the households of the community. The sneak attack is directed at "silly women" (γυναικάρια),[171] who, according to the popular notion,[172] were viewed as particularly susceptible to outlandish religious impulses. In addition, the sarcastic description of these women as avid learners unable to achieve real knowledge recalls Juvenal's description of woman who fancy themselves as learned (*Sat.* 6. 434ff.). The author's adamant rejection of women as teachers in the church (1 Tim 2:10ff.) strongly suggests that he regarded all women as incapable of "knowledge of the truth" on the same level as men.

As Brox points out,[173] the author is at pains to emphasize that the false teachers succeed in "capturing" women only because they are γυναικάρια. One thus concludes that the false teachers of the Pastorals were in fact enjoying notable success in recruiting women to their cause and that the author was intent on discrediting their success by calling into question the good sense of the women involved.[174] His contempt for the false teachers and their converts cannot, however, conceal his alarm at the danger which they present to the households of the Christian community.[175]

The popularity of the false teaching among women was probably related to certain features of its content. In this connection it is of particular interest that prohibition of marriage was one of the prominent features of the false teaching (1 Tim 4:3).[176] This prohibition calls to

---

[170]On both words, see BAG, s.v.

[171]On γυναικάριον as a scornful diminutive of γυνή see Kelly, Dibelius/Conzelmann, ad loc.; BAG, s.v.

[172]See chapter II, p. 69.

[173]Ad loc.

[174]Cf. the similar conclusion of Karris on different grounds, "Background," 566.

[175]This sense of alarm is also registered in Tit 1:11, where the false teachers are accused of "turning whole households upside down" (ὅλους οἴκους ἀνατρέπουσιν). On ἀνατρέπω see Kelly, ad loc. Although women are not specifically mentioned here, it is probable that the author is envisioning a situation similar to that described in 2 Tim 3:6.

[176]This is one of the three concrete doctrines of the false teaching which are mentioned in the Pastorals. See Karris, "Background," 557ff. The Christian antecedents for such a variety of teaching are indicated in Gal 3:28, which proclaims the abolition of sexual differences in Christ.

mind the sexual asceticism of the apocryphal acts, and in particular the Acts of Paul, which stems from Asia Minor and may have been written as little as a generation after the Pastorals.[177] The "Paul" of the Acts of Paul preaches against marriage on the grounds that one must abstain from sexual intercourse in order to participate in the resurrection (chap. 11). Thecla, in obedience to Paul's preaching, refuses to marry her betrothed and after miraculously escaping being burned alive for her behavior, she sets off to find Paul and accompany him on his travels (chap. 20). She baptizes herself during a confrontation with wild beasts in a public arena (chap. 34); and eventually Paul commissions her to be a teacher of the word (chap. 41). Thus Thecla's rejection of marriage is accompanied by a degree of rebellion against the traditionally subordinate role of women in the household and in society at large.[178]

Considerable evidence exists to suggest that the sexual asceticism of the false teaching of the Pastorals contained similar tendencies toward female emancipation. There were women in the church of the Pastorals who were involved in public teaching (cf. 1 Tim 2:12). There were women of marriageable age who were rejecting the option of marriage, and, from the author's point of view, causing problems in the community (1 Tim 5:13f.). Furthermore, the author's vigorous advocacy of the matronly virtues of wifely subordination and motherhood strongly suggests that the women of the church were being exposed to such a variety of teaching (cf. 1 Tim 2:15; 5:14; Titus 2:4-5).

No other distinct social group in the church is identified by the author as particularly attracted to the false teaching. However, in Titus 1:10 he attributes a social characteristic to the proponents of the false teaching that provides an additional clue to their identity. V. 10 initiates a section (1:1-16) of polemic against false teachers. The previous section, which gives qualifications for the offices of elder and bishop, concludes with a reference to the bishop's role in defending the church against people who contradict sound doctrine (1:9). Vv. 10ff. emphasize that

---

As noted above, if this passage is quoted from a baptismal liturgy of the church, then we are dealing with an idea that was firmly rooted in the earliest Christian tradition and practice. See p. 142, n. 51 above.

[177] J. Rhode, "Pastoralbriefe und Acta Pauli," *Studia Evangelica* V (ed. F. L. Cross; TU 103; Berlin: Akademie Verlag, 1968) 304, sets the earlier limit for the *Acts of Paul* as 160.

[178] Meeks, "Image," 196, notes Thecla's symbolic appropriation of maleness by her wish to cut her hair and her wearing of men's clothes (Act. Pl. 25, 40).

there are "many" (πολλοί) such people and proceeds to describe them in greater detail.

Much of the description belongs to the traditional polemic against sophists as identified by Karris. However, the initial vice attributed to the false teachers in v. 10, namely that they are insubordinate (ἀνυπότακτοι), does not belong to this traditional polemic.[179] The same word is used in 1:6 to describe rebellious children, who by their behavior disqualify their fathers from office in the church. The author repeatedly uses ὑποτάσσεσθαι and its cognates to advance the notion that persons in subordinate groups should not challenge the authority of their superiors.[180] His charge against the proponents of the false teaching at this point, then, is that they are mounting an unjustifiable challenge from a subordinate position against a properly constituted authority, which in this case can only be the official leadership of the household of God.[181] If this analysis is correct, then the author is assuming that the proponents of the false teaching come from subordinate groups in the church rather than from among the official leadership itself. There is no reason to doubt that this assumption on his part corresponded in general to the actual situation, although one cannot rule out the possibility that a few among the established leadership may have espoused the false teaching.[182]

Thus the following picture emerges: The church of the Pastorals, as the author describes it, was characterized by an established leadership that ruled over subordinate groups as the οἰκοδεσπότης ruled over his wife, children, and servants. Access to leadership positions was controlled to a great degree by the established leadership. The adherents of the false teaching, insofar as they can be identified, generally belonged to subordinate groups, including men who were not among the official leaders and women, who, as a total group, were denied the opportunity to rise to leadership positions on the same level with men.

---

[179]Karris does not include the charge of insubordination among the special features of the polemic of the Pastorals. However, he does not identify this charge as a feature of the traditional polemic either.

[180]So women and men in 1 Tim 2:8ff., slaves and masters in Titus 2:9; and the community as a whole to the worldly rulers in Titus 3:1.

[181]Cf. Kelly, Brox, ad loc.

[182]The author's insistence that church officers be firmly grounded in the true faith (1 Tim 3:9; Titus 1:9) as well as his cautionary remarks about making a recent convert a bishop (1 Tim 3:6) suggest this possibility.

In the case of women, the appeal of the false teaching must have consisted at least partially in the fact that it offered them both emancipation from a subordinate position in the household and recognition and leadership opportunities which they were denied as a subordinate group in the church. Thus, in this case, social tensions inherent in the social structure of the church contributed to the appeal of the false teaching among a particular social group within the membership.

The situation is not as clear in the case of the men whom the author describes as ἀνυπότακτοι. Probably the false teaching appealed to ambitious men in the church who were excluded from official leadership positions, in part, because it provided them with a vehicle for asserting themselves against the official leadership. However, two considerations engender a sense of caution at this point. Firstly, the Pastorals contain abundant material attesting to social tensions involving the position of women in the church, but no unequivocal additional evidence of social tensions involving men with thwarted leadership ambitions. Secondly, because of the tendencies toward female emancipation in the false teaching, its potential appeal to women kept in subordinate positions is evident; but nothing has emerged to suggest that the content of the false teaching as such would have held any special appeal for men excluded from official leadership positions. Thus the interpretation arrived at here is offered tentatively, because its evidential base is extremely narrow.

OVERALL ASSESSMENT: SOCIAL STRUCTURE, SOCIAL STATUS, AND SOCIAL TENSIONS IN THE CHURCH OF THE PASTORALS

The church of the Pastorals emerges as a social entity of considerable size and diversity, and as a community with substantial personal and financial resources. The church membership covered the spectrum of urban social strata. The leaders of the church were a group that consisted in large part of prosperous householders. They tended to be older men, although young men may have occasionally entered their ranks. Some of the leaders no doubt came from among the "wealthy" of 1 Tim 6:17ff. Exactly what would have constituted wealth in the author's eyes is uncertain; however, the women of 1 Tim 2:9f., who wore elaborate hair styles, expensive jewelry and fine clothes must have belonged either to the social stratum of the municipal aristocracies, or to that of the aspirants to these aristocracies.

Below the level of the leadership the membership of the church covered a wide socio-economic range. Well-to-do πισταί, if the parallels from Acts and from Paul's letters are any indication, were probably on a socio-economic level equal or superior to that of most of the official leaders. The πισταί supported and probably housed widows who would otherwise have to have been supported by the church. Some widows were in fact being supported from the church's funds. Such widows had probably come from a level of society in which dowry, property holdings and the like would have been minimal or non-existent. The children and grandchildren of some widows apparently could have supported them but were reluctant to do so. Perhaps other families had experienced a severe strain on their finances in the attempt to provide such support and thus had discontinued it. Other widows (perhaps the πισταί) probably supported themselves. There is no mention of church members who were freedmen or freedwomen; however, slaves from both pagan and Christian households belonged to the church. In addition, there were entrepreneurs (1 Tim 6:6ff.), perhaps both free and slave, who were attempting to advance into the circle of the wealthy.

There are a number of other indications of the size and diversity of the church of the Pastorals. There were three classifications of major offices in the church. One group at least among the officers received financial compensation for their work. There was also an office of widows. Either directly or indirectly through its individual members the church was supporting what was, one gains the impression, a large group of widows.[183] Thus the financial resources of this Christian community must have been considerable. Although the leadership tended to be drawn from among older adults, both young men and young women were probably present in the church in significant numbers. At any rate there were enough young widows among the membership that the leadership was becoming uneasy about their presence and their activities, if the author's attitude may be taken as characteristic. Finally, the size of the membership is suggested by the possibility that it may have been large enough that it met for worship in several different groups in the same city.

The official leadership had succeeded in concentrating much of the authority and power in this rather large and diverse Christian community

---

[183]In Lucian's description widows appear as a particularly prominent group among the early Christians (*Peregrinus* 12). His outsider's eye may fall on a characteristic feature of Christian groups that from the insider's viewpoint was normally not so obvious.

in its own hands, exercising teaching, pastoral and disciplinary functions. It had also been able to consolidate the authority of office and the authority of charisma, if the descriptions of Timothy's ordination may be trusted here. Furthermore, the leadership appears to have been able for the most part to control access to its own ranks.

The author of the Pastorals, who identifies with the leadership, conceptualizes the church as a great household with its many and diverse ranks of servants and its οἰκοδεσπότης firmly entrenched in his patriarchal authority.[184] This comparison is in many ways apt, since it evokes the size and complexity as well as the authority structure of the church of the Pastorals. However, the author presents the image of the household not only for descriptive, but also, and more importantly, for prescriptive purposes. In the traditional patriarchal household the householder is expected to exercise his authority in competent fashion, keeping those in subordinate stations properly subject to him and representing his household in the larger community. The other members of the household, typically, women, children and servants, are expected to acknowledge their subordinate positions and to behave accordingly. In the church, the author is suggesting, authority is properly concentrated in the hands of an official leadership that is expected to govern effectively and to represent the church to the world. As in the household, women, slaves, children and young men properly belong to subordinate stations. They should know the limits of these stations and keep within these limits.

The significance of the author's prescription of proper behavior in the household of God becomes clearer in relation to several other factors in the social life of the church. It will be recalled that the prevailing domestic ideal in the church of the Pastorals reflected the dominant social values of the larger society, namely, prosperity and propriety. The social life of the church as a whole was dominated by the same values. In the first place, the church, as represented by the author of the Pastorals, values highly the good opinion of the larger society. Thus there is concern that women and slaves not give occasion by insubordinate behavior for the Christian faith to be blasphemed by outsiders. The same concern is present in the author's advice that the office of bishop be filled by men

---

[184]It is interesting that in the Ephesian *Haustafel* the reverse process has occurred, i.e., the household relationship of husband and wife has been conceptualized on the model of Christ and the church (Eph 5:22ff.). By contrast, the author of the Pastorals never uses the structure of the church as a conceptual model for the structure of the household.

who possess a good reputation in society at large. Of course, this concern in itself would not necessarily indicate that the church shared the values of the larger society. It might simply reflect the church's prudence in attempting to develop and maintain a favorable public image. No doubt this is in part the case. That something more is involved as well can be seen when the social values associated with office in the church are considered. The author, as a representative of the viewpoint of the official leadership, espouses the aristocratic social values associated with leadership circles in the municipalities of the Hellenistic-Roman world. Municipal office is undertaken by the well-to-do, who expend their own resources on behalf of the πόλις. In the process they demonstrate both their prosperity and their liberality, and in so doing enhance their own social standing. In the church of the Pastorals, office is similarly regarded by those who hold or aspire to it. It is a good work which well-to-do members undertake for the benefit of the Christian community and which enhances their social standing in the community. Thus in the church of the Pastorals one is normally rewarded socially for being male, prosperous, respectable and a competent household manager.

Persons who do not fit this description experience a corresponding social devaluation. Thus, in an earlier day well-to-do and independent women like Lydia and Tabitha had provided significant leadership to the church. The πισταί of the Pastorals, however, who probably could have provided similar leadership, barely receive mention in the Pastorals and only in connection with their involvement in the bothersome (to the author) duty of caring for poor widows. One can easily imagine the frustration of such women at the constriction of their roles within the community. Perhaps some of them were among the teachers whom the author wanted to silence. Older widows are honored for their past life and single-minded devotion to the Lord. Younger widows, by contrast, are encouraged to forego this religious ideal in favor of the matron's role. There is an office of widows by which those who meet certain requirements are recognized, yet on the whole widows seem to be regarded as a burden to the church. The prevailing attitude toward them is one of ambivalence, a peculiar mixture of reverence and resentment, if not contempt. Slaves are viewed with suspicion and contempt according to the popular stereotype (Titus 2:9-10). The author is so incapable of reasoning from the slave's point of view that he can urge slaves of Christian masters to obedience on the grounds that the latter are paragons of Christian beneficence.

Nevertheless, there is evidence that the social values of the established leadership enjoyed wide acceptance among the general membership. In particular, the acceptance of prosperity as a social value is seen in the ostentatious dress of women in public worship and in the entrepreneurs in the community whom the author attacks in 1 Tim 6:6ff. It is interesting that in these cases, when the value of prosperity is accepted with too great an enthusiasm, the leadership disapproves. Perhaps the reason is that in both cases the espousal of the value of prosperity is not balanced sufficiently by the attendant value of propriety. The response of the leadership to the entrepreneurs also has the effect of preserving the status of the established leadership against would-be social climbers.

All this is not to say that there were no social rewards for people in subordinate roles. In fact, members of the church outside the circle of the official leadership often had opportunities for responsibility and recognition in the life of the community. Teaching in the assembly was apparently open to all men. Old men especially were expected to be exemplary in their adherence to the faith. Some women had also been teaching in worship, a development which the author, probably supported by a portion of the official leadership, strongly opposed (see p. 169). Older women were assigned a special responsibility for the training of younger women in their proper roles. Official widows must have had certain responsibilities, although what these were is not clear. πισταί supported needy widows and probably engaged in other benevolent works. Even destitute widows had a special duty to engage in intercessory prayer. The groups that ordinarily had the most meager responsibilities in the life of the community were younger women (except as widows--and here their contribution was being seriously questioned), slaves, younger men and children. Slaves and younger women could contribute to the life of the community by not damaging the church's reputation with outsiders through their behavior. Younger men and children appear to have been accorded no particular responsibilities in this context. As a consolation younger women could look forward to the possibility of becoming honored οἰκοδέσποιναι; and younger men could look forward to the possibility of entering leadership positions as they grew older, if they met the qualifications for office. These features of the social life of the community no doubt served to reduce social tensions and preserve the established structures.

However, although social tensions could be reduced in this way, they could not be eliminated. These tensions were based in the social structure of the community, but were fueled and shaped by certain ideas present in the church since the first generation. The position of slaves in the church had worsened noticeably in comparison with the situations represented by the earlier *Haustafeln.*[185] In fact, the position of slaves in the church of the Pastorals appears to be nearly that of slaves in the *Apostolic Tradition* of Hippolytus, in which slaves of Christian masters must gain their master's permission in order to join the church (16:4). At the same time slaves in the church of the Pastorals were being exposed to the teaching that all Christians were ἀδελφοί. Thus the social attitudes which they faced directly contradicted the liberating, affirmative message which they heard. It is no wonder, then, that slaves of Christian masters were in some cases rejecting the subservient role they were expected to play. Yet, slave insubordination is dealt with by the author in cursory fashion as a minor problem. Therefore, one concludes that slaves in the church were not rebelling in a major way against the existing structures.

A major conflict had developed, however, over the role of women in domestic life and in the life of the church. On the one hand, this conflict reflected pervasive tensions abroad in Hellenistic-Roman society. On the other hand, as in the case of slaves, this conflict took shape in relation to certain ideas and ideals present in Christian teaching. According to the traditional values, propriety and proper order demanded the subordination of women in the household and in society at large. At the same time feminine emancipatory tendencies were to be seen in various forms throughout the society. Such tendencies had emerged in the first generation of the church in a single sexual standard for men and women.[186] In the church of the Pastorals this single standard took the form of a twin ideal, foreshadowed in Paul's advice to widows in 1 Corinthians, namely the ideal of the μιᾶς γυναικὸς ἀνήρ and the ἑνὸς ἀνδρὸς γυνή. This ideal, with its ascetic tendencies, led to an overt social conflict in the case of younger widows. Such women, in living out the role of the ἑνὸς ἀνδρὸς γυνή, were engaging in activities that appeared to the author of the Pastorals as too radical a departure from the traditional feminine role, and perhaps as a threat to the traditional households of the church. One imagines such women on the model of the energetic, emancipated Thecla of the *Acts of Paul.*

The emancipatory tendencies present here were being fueled in addition by a more thoroughgoing brand of ascetic teaching that was being championed in the church of the Pastorals by certain opponents of the

---

[185]See p. 144, n. 56.
[186]See p. 131, n. 12.

author and the established leadership. Some of these opponents may have been outsiders who were, in a sense, invading the church, as the author's imagery (2 Tim 3:6) suggests. However, at least some of them were men in the church who were not part of the established leadership. These opponents, labelled by the author as false teachers, were promulgating a gnosticizing form of Christian teaching which rejected marriage altogether, and which in this connection probably also recognized no spiritual or social differences between women and men who were believers. The latter idea was now newly imported, but had probably been expressed as a part of the church's baptismal liturgy since the first generation of the church. The rejection of marriage altogether should perhaps be understood as in part a reaction against the rigid, subordinating social structure of the church. At any rate, the appeal of this teaching to women in the church of the Pastorals is understandable. In this connection, it is reasonable to suppose that the women who were teaching in the worship assemblies of the church were proponents of this ascetic/gnostic brand of Christianity. Thus one can see why the author of the Pastorals, as a representative of the established leadership, would feel it necessary to condemn this activity in such harsh terms as he does in 1 Tim 2:12ff.

The author of the Pastorals is alarmed by the vitality of this movement within his church. He perceives it correctly as a threat to the established order, and fears, no doubt again correctly, that such radicalism will damage the public reputation of the church and thus endanger it. The purpose for which the author employs the image of the Household of God in this context is now clear. He intends to bolster a hierarchical social structure in the church that is being threatened by disruptive forces. The social structure which he is defending has in large part given rise to the disruptive forces, yet they are being fed by certain ideas already present in Christian tradition. He responds by promoting an image of the church that legitimates the established hierarchical structure. In this way he hopes to suppress the forces that threaten it and the radical social values which they represent.

BIBLIOGRAPHY

Abbott, F. F. and Johnson, A. C. *Municipal Administration in the Roman Empire*. Princeton: Princeton University Press, 1926.

Afanasieff, N. "L'assemblee eucharistique dans l'eglise ancienne." *Kleronomia* 6 (1974) 1-34.

Alföldy, G. "Consuls and Consulars under the Antonines." *Ancient Society* 7 (1976) 263-99.

__________. *Römische Sozialgeschichte*. Wiesbaden: Franz Steiner, 1975.

The Apostolic Fathers. 2 vols. Translated by K. Lake. LCL. Cambridge, MA: Harvard University Press, 1912-13.

The Apostolic Tradition of Hippolytus. Translated by B. S. Easton. New York: Macmillan, 1934.

Aristophanes. *Wasps*. With English translation by Benjamin B. Rogers. LCL. Cambridge, MA: Harvard University Press, 1924.

Aristotle. *Politics*. Vol. 1. Translated by H. Rackham. LCL. London: Heinemann, 1932.

Arnold, W. T. *The Roman System of Provincial Administration to the Accession of Constantine the Great*. New edition revised from the author's notes by E. S. Shuckburgh. Oxford: B. H. Blackwell, 1906.

Athenagoras: Legatio and De Resurrectione. Edited and translated by W. R. Schoedel. Oxford: Clarendon, 1972.

Avigad, N. "How the Wealthy Lived in Herodian Jerusalem." *BARev* 2 (1976) 23-25.

The Babylonian Talmud. 39 vols. in 64. Edited by I. Epstein. New York: Rebecca Bennet Publications, 1959.

Baer, Richard A., Jr. *Philo's Use of the Categories Male and Female*. Leiden: Brill, 1970.

Balch, David. *"Let Wives Be Submissive. . . ." The Origin, Form and Apologetic Function of the Household Duty Code (Haustafel) in I Peter*. Ph.D. dissertation, Yale University, 1974.

Balsdon, J. P. V. D. *Roman Women: Their History and Habits*. London: The Bodley Head, 1962.

Baltensweiler, H. *Die Ehe im Neuen Testament.* ATANT LII. Zurich: Zwingli Verlag, 1967.

Banks, Robert. *Paul's Idea of Community: The Early House Churches in Their Historical Setting.* Grand Rapids: Eerdmans, 1980.

Baron, S. W. *A Social and Religious History of the Jews.* Vol. 1-2. Second Edition. New York: Columbia University Press, 1952-53.

Barrett, C. K. "Jews and Judaizers in the Epistles of Ignatius." *Jews, Greeks and Christians.* Edited by R. Hamerton-Kelly. Leiden: Brill, 1976. Pp. 220-44.

_________. *The Pastoral Epistles in the New English Bible with Introduction and Commentary.* Oxford: Clarendon, 1963.

_________. "Pauline Controversies in the Post-Pauline Period." *NTS* 20 (1973-74) 229-45.

_________. "Titus." *Neotestamentica et Semitica: Studies in Honour of Matthew Black.* Edited by E. E. Ellis and M. Wilcox. Edinburgh: T. & T. Clark, 1969. Pp. 1-14.

Barrow, R. H. *Slavery in the Roman Empire.* New York: Barnes and Noble, 1968.

Bartchy, S. S. *Mallon Chrēsai.* Missoula: University of Montana Press, 1973.

Bartsch, H. W. *Die Anfänge urchristlicher Rechtsbildungen.* Hamburg: Herbert Reich, 1965.

Bauer, W. *A Greek-English Lexicon of the New Testament and Other Early Christian Literature.* Translated by W. F. Arndt and F. W. Gingrich from the fourth German edition. Chicago: University of Chicago Press, 1957.

Beebe, H. K. "Domestic Architecture and the New Testament." *BA* 38 (1975) 89-103.

Beker, J. Chr. "The Pastoral Letters." *IDB* III.

Benko, S. and O'Rourke, J. J. *The Catacombs and the Colosseum: The Roman Empire as the Setting of Primitive Christianity.* Valley Forge: Judson Press, 1971.

Berger, P. L. and Luckman, T. *The Social Construction of Reality.* New York: Doubleday, 1967.

Bernard, J. H. *The Pastoral Epistles.* The Cambridge Greek New Testament, 1922.

Best, E. F. "Cicero, Livy and Educated Roman Women." *Classical Journal* 65 (1970) 199-204.

_________. "I Peter and the Gospel Tradition." *NTS* 16 (1969-70) 95-113.

_________. "I Peter 2:4-10--A Reconsideration." *NovT* 11 (1969) 70-93.

Betz, H. D. *Galatians.* Hermeneia. Philadelphia: Fortress, 1979.

_________. "The Literary Composition and Function of Paul's Letters to the Galatians." *NTS* 21 (1975) 353-79.

Beyer, H. W. et al. *Die kleineren Briefe des Apostels Paulus.* Fifth edition. Göttingen: A. Oepke, 1949.

Bjerkelund, C. J. *Parakalo: Form, Function und Sinn der parakalo-Sätze in den paulinischen Briefen.* Oslo: Universitetsforlaget, 1967.

Blanchetiere, F. "Juifs et non-Juifs--essai sur la diaspora en Asie Mineur." *RHPR* 54 (1974) 367-82.

Blanck, H. *Einführung in das Privatleben der Griechen und Römer.* Darmstadt: Wissenschaftliche Buchgesellschaft, 1976.

Bömer, F. *Untersuchungen über die Religion der Sklaven im Griechenland und Rom.* Vol. 1. Wiesbaden: Franz Steiner Verlag, 1957.

Boers, H. "Form Critical Study of Paul's Letters." *NTS* 22 (1976) 140-58.

Bopp, L. *Das Witwentum als organische Gliedschaft im Gemeinschaftsleben der alten Kirche.* Mannheim: N. Wohlgemuth, 1950.

Bousset, W. *Kyrios Christos.* Translated by J. E. Steely. Nashville: Abingdon, 1970.

Bowersock, G. *Augustus and the Greek World.* Oxford: Clarendon, 1965.

Bradley, D. G. "The Topos as a Form in the Pauline Parenesis." *JBL* 72 (1953) 238-46.

Brox, N. *Die Pastoralbriefe.* Regensburg: Verlag Friedrich Pustet, 1969.

Buckland, W. W. *Roman Law of Slavery.* Cambridge, 1908.

Buckler, W. H. "Labor Disputes in Asia." *Anatolian Studies Presented to Sir Wm. Ramsay.* Manchester, 1917. Pp. 27-50.

Bultmann, Rudolf. *The Theology of the New Testament.* 2 vols. Translated by K. Grobel. New York: Scribner's, 1955.

Burck, E. *Die Frau in der griechisch-römischen Antike.* Munich: Heimeran, 1969.

Burke, P. "The Monarchical Episcopate at the End of the First Century." *JES* 8 (1970) 499-518.

Burton, E. *A Critical and Exegetical Commentary on the Epistle to the Galatians.* Edinburgh: T. & T. Clark, 1921.

Cadbury, H. J. *The Book of Acts in History.* London: A. & C. Black, 1955.

Campenhausen, H. von. *Ecclesiastical Authority and Spiritual Power.* Translated by J. A. Baker. Stanford: Stanford U. Press, 1969.

_________. *The Formation of the Christian Bible.* Translated by J. A. Baker. Philadelphia: Fortress Press, 1972.

_________. *Polykarp von Smyrna und die Pastoralbriefe.* Heidelburg: Carl Winter, Universitätsverlag, 1951.

Cancik, H. *Untersuchungen zu Senecas Epistulae morales.* Hildesheim, 1967.

Carcopino, J. *Daily Life in Ancient Rome.* Translated by E. Lorimer. New Haven: Yale University Press, 1940.

Carrington, P. *The Primitive Christian Catechism.* Cambridge: Cambridge University Press, 1940.

Case, S. J. *The Social Origins of Christianity.* Chicago: University of Chicago Press, 1923.

Cicero. *De officiis.* Translated by W. Miller. LCL. London: Heinemann, 1913.

Conzelmann, H. *I Corinthians.* Edited by G. W. MacRae. Translated by J. W. Leitch. Bibliography and references by J. W. Dunkly. Hermeneia: Philadelphia: Fortress Press, 1975.

Corbett, P. E. *The Roman Law of Marriage.* Oxford: Clarendon, 1930.

Crouch, J. E. *The Origin and Intention of the Colossian Haustafel.* Göttingen: Vandenhoeck und Ruprecht, 1972.

Daube, D. *The New Testament and Rabbinic Judaism.* London: University of London, Athlone Press, 1956.

Day, John. *An Economic History of Athens under Roman Domination.* New York, 1942.

Deissmann, A. *Light from the Ancient East.* Translated by L. R. M. Strachan. New York: Doran, 1927.

Delling, G. "τάσσω." *TDNT* VIII.

_________. "Zur Taufe von Häusern" im Urchristentum." *NovT* 7 (1965) 285-311.

_________, ed. *Bibliographie zur jüdisch-hellenistischen und inter-testamentarischen Literature:* 1900-1965. Berlin: Akademie-Verlag, 1969.

Demarolle, J.-M. "Les femmes chretiennes vues par Porphyre." *JAC* 13 (1970) 42-47.

Demosthenes. 7 vols. Translated by J. H. Vince et al. LCL. London: Heinemann, 1926-49.

Dibelius, Martin. *From Tradition to Gospel.* Translated from the revised second edition by B. L. Woolf. Cambridge: James Clark & Co. Ltd., 1971.

_________. *James: A Commentary on the Epistle of James.* Revised by H. Greeven. Translated by M. A. Williams. Hermeneia: Philadelphia: Fortress Press, 1976.

Dibelius, Martin and Conzelmann, Hans. *The Pastoral Epistles: A Commentary on the Pastoral Epistles.* Translated by P. Buttolph and A. Yarbro. Edited by H. Koester. Hermeneia. Philadelphia: Fortress Press, 1972.

Dickey, S. "Some Economic and Social Conditions of Asia Minor Affecting the Expansion of Christianity." S. J. Case, ed. *Studies in Early Christianity.* New York: Century, 1928. Pp. 393-416.

Didascalia Apostolorum. Translated by R. H. Connolly. Oxford: Clarendon, 1929.

Dill, Samuel. *Roman Society from Nero to Marcus Aurelius.* New York: Meridian Books, 1956.

Dio Cassius. *Roman History.* Vol. 5. Translated by E. Cary. LCL. London: Heinemann, 1914.

Dio Chrysostom. *Orations.* Vol. 3. Translated by J. W. Colson and H. L. Crosby. LCL. Cambridge, MA: Harvard University Press, 1932-51.

Diodorus Siculus. *Library of History.* Vol. 1. Translated by C. H. Oldfather et al. LCL. Cambridge, MA: Harvard University Press, 1933-57.

Dionysius of Halicarnassus. *The Roman Antiquities*. Vol. 1. Translated by E. Cary. LCL. London: Heinemann, 1937.

Dittenberger, W., ed. *Orientis Graeci inscriptionis selectae*. 2 vols. Hildesheim: G. Olms, 1960.

Dobschütz, E. von. *Christian Life in the Primitive Church*. Edited by W. D. Morrison. Translated by G. Bremer. New York: G. P. Putnam's Sons, 1904.

Donfried, Karl P. "False Presuppositions in the Study of Romans." *CBQ* 36 (1974) 332-55.

Dornier, P. *Les Epîtres pastorales*. Paris: J. Gabalda, 1969.

Doty, W. G. *Letters in Primitive Christianity*. Philadelphia: Fortress Press, 1977.

Downey, G. *A History of Antioch in Syria from Seleucus to the Arab Conquest*. Princeton: Princeton University Press, 1961.

Duff, A. M. *Freedmen in the Early Roman Empire*. Revised edition. New York: Barnes and Noble, 1958.

Duncan-Jones, R. *The Economy of the Roman Empire*. Cambridge: Cambridge University Press, 1973.

Easton, B. S. *The Pastoral Epistles*. New York: Charles Scribner's Sons, 1947.

Ellicott, C. J. *The Pastoral Epistles of St. Paul*. 5th edition. London: Longmans, Green & Co., 1883.

Ellis, E. E. "The Authorship of the Pastorals: A Resume." *EvQ* 32 (1960) 151-61.

Epictetus. *Discourses*. 2 vols. Translated by W. A. Oldfather. London: Heinemann, 1926.

Erdman, C. R. *The Pastoral Epistles of St. Paul*. Philadelphia: Westminster Press, 1966.

Falconer, R. *The Pastoral Epistles*. Oxford: Clarendon, 1937.

Falk, Z. W. *Introduction to Jewish Law of the Second Commonwealth*. 2 vols. Leiden: Brill, 1979.

Ferguson, E. "Selection and Installation for Office in Roman, Greek and Jewish Antiquity." *ThL* 30 (1974) 273-84.

Filson, F. "The Significance of the Early House Churches." *JBL* 58 (1939) 109-12.

Finley, M. I. *The Ancient Economy*. Berkeley: University of California Press, 1973.

_________. "Between Slavery and Freedom." *Comparative Studies in Society and History* 6 (1964) 233-49.

_________. "Was Greek Civilization Based on Slave Labor?" *Historia* 8 (1959) 146-64.

_________, ed. *Slavery in Classical Antiquity*. Cambridge: W. Heffer, 1960.

Fischel, H. A. *Rabbinic Literature and Greco-Roman Philosophy*. Leiden: Brill, 1973.

Fischer, J. A. "Pauline Literary Forms and Thought Patterns." *CBQ* 39 (1977) 209-23.

Floor, L. "Church Order in the Pastoral Epistles." *Neot* 10 (1976) 81-91.

Foerster, W. "εὐσεβεία" in den Pastoralbriefen." *NTS* 5 (1959) 213-18.

_________. "σέβομαι." *TDNT* VII.

Forbes, C. A. "The Education and Training of Slaves in Antiquity." *TAPA* 86 (1955) 321-60.

Frank, Tenney. *An Economic Survey of Ancient Rome*. Vols. 2, 4, and 5. Baltimore: The Johns Hopkins University Press, 1938.

Frey, J.-B. "La signification des terms *monandros* et *univira*." *RSR* 20 (1930) 48-60.

Friedländer, L. *Roman Life and Manners under the Early Empire*. 4 vols. Translated by L. A. Magnus. New York: Dutton, 1913.

Funk, R. W. "Apostolic Parousia: Form and Significance." *Christian History and Interpretation*. Studies Presented to John Knox. Edited by W. R. Farmer et al. Cambridge: Cambridge University Press, 1967. Pp. 249-68.

Furnish, V. P. *Theology and Ehics in Paul*. Nashville: Abingdon Press, 1968.

Gagé, J. *Les classes sociales dans l'Empire romain*. Paris, 1964.

Gager, J. G. *Kingdom and Community*. Englewood Cliffs: Prentice-Hall, 1975.

Gaiser, K. *Für und wider die Ehe*. Munich: Heimeran, 1974.

Galen on the Passions and Errors of the Soul. Translated by P. W. Harkins. Columbus, OH: Ohio State University Press, 1963.

Garnsey, P. "Aspects of the Decline of the Urban Aristocracy in the Empire." *ANRW*. Part 1, Vol. 1. Pp. 229-52.

_________. *Social Status and Legal Privilege in the Roman Empire*. Oxford: Clarendon, 1970.

Gayer, R. *Die Stellung des Sklaven in den paulinischen Gemeinden und bei Paulus*. Bern: Herbert Lang, 1976.

Gealy, F. D. *The Pastoral Epistles*. *IB*. Vol. 11.

Gelzer, M. *The Roman Nobility*. Translated by R. Seager. Oxford: Clarendon, 1969.

Goodenough, E. R. *The Jurisprudence of the Jewish Courts in Egypt*. New Haven: Yale University Press, 1929.

_________. "The Political Philosophy of Hellenistic Kingship." *Yale Classical Studies* 1 (1928) 53-102.

_________. *The Politics of Philo Judaeus*. New Haven: Yale University Press, 1938.

Goodsell, W. *A History of the Family as a Social and Educational Institution*. New York: Macmillan, 1930.

Goppelt, L. "Prinzipien neutestamentlicher Sozialethik nach dem 1. Petrusbrief." *Neues Testament und Geschichte*. Oscar Cullmann zum 70. Geburtstag. Hrsg. H. Baltensweiler und B. Reicke. Tübingen: J. C. B. Mohr (Paul Siebeck), 1972. Pp. 285-96.

Gordon, M. L. "The Freedman's Son in Municipal Life." *JRS* 21 (1931) 65-77.

Graham, R. W. "Women in the Pauline Churches." *Lexington Theological Quarterly* 11 (1976) 25-34.

Grant, R. M. *Early Christianity and Society*. New York: Harper and Row, 1977.

Greeven, H. "Zu den Aussagen des NT über die Ehe." *ZEE* 1 (1957) 109-25.

Gryson, R. *Ministry of Women in the Early Church*. Translated by J. Laporte and M. Hall. Collegeville: Liturgical Press, 1976.

Gülzow, H. *Christentum und Sklaverei in den ersten drei Jahrhunderten.* Bonn: Rudolf Habelt Verlag, 1969.

Guthrie, Donald. *The Pastoral Epistles.* Grand Rapids: Eerdmans, 1957.

Hadas, M. *Three Greek Romances.* Garden City: Doubleday, 1953.

Haenchen, E. *The Acts of the Apostles: A Commentary.* Translated by B. Noble and G. Shinn under the supervision of H. Anderson, with the translation revised and updated by R. McL. Wilson. Philadelphia: Westminster Press, 1971.

Hammond, M. *The City in the Ancient World.* Cambridge, MA: Harvard University Press, 1972.

Hands, A. R. *Charities and Social Aids in Greece and Rome.* Ithaca: Cornell University Press, 1968.

Hansen, E. V. *The Attalids of Pergamon.* Cornell Studies in Classical Philology 29. Ithaca: Cornell University Press, 1947.

Hanson, A. T. *The Pastoral Epistles.* Cambridge: Cambridge University Press, 1966.

__________. *Studies in the Pastoral Epistles.* SPCK, 1968.

Hanson, R. P. C. *Tradition in the Early Church.* Philadelphia: Westminster Press, 1963.

Harnack, A. von. *The Constitution and Law of the Church in the First Two Centuries.* New York: G. P. Putnam's Sons, 1910.

Harrison, A. R. W. *The Law of Athens.* 2 vols. Oxford: Clarendon, 1968.

Hatch, E. *The Organization of Christian Churches.* 2nd ed. revised. London: Rivingston, 1882.

Hauck, F. and Schulz, S. "πορνή." *TDNT* V.

Heinen, H. "Zur Sklaverei in der hellenistischen Welt." *Ancient Society* 7 (1976) 127-49; 8 (1977) 121-54.

Hengel, M. *Property and Riches in the Early Church.* Translated by J. Bowden. Philadelphia: Fortress Press, 1974.

Hennecke, E. and Schneemelcher, W., eds. *New Testament Apocrypha.* 2 vols. Translated by R. McL. Wilson. Philadelphia: Westminster Press, 1963.

Highet, G. *Juvenal the Satirist.* Oxford: Clarendon, 1954.

Holtz, G. *Die Pastoralbriefe*. THKNT 13, 1965.

Hombert, M. and Preaux, C. *Recherches sur le recensement dans l'Egypte romaine*. Lugdunum Batavorum: Brill, 1952.

Homo, L. *Rome imperiale et l'urbanisme dans l'antiquite*. Paris: Michel, 1951.

Hopkins, K. *Conquerors and Slaves*. Cambridge: Cambridge University Press, 1978.

__________. "The Probable Age Structure of the Roman Population." *Population Studies* 20 (1966-67) 245-64.

Iamblichus. *De vita Pythagorica*. Edited by A. Nauck. Amsterdam: Verlag Adolf M. Hakkert, 1965.

Isaeus. Translated by E. S. Foerster. LCL. London: Heinemann, 1927.

Isocrates. Vol. 1. Translated by G. Norlin. LCL. London: Heinemann, 1928.

Jeremias, J. *Die Briefe an Timotheus und Titus*. 4th edition. Das Neue Testament Deutsch, 1947.

Johnson, S. E. "The Emergence of the Christian Church in the Pre-Catholic Period." H. R. Willoughby, ed. *The Study of the Bible Today and Tomorrow*. Chicago: University of Chicago Press, 1947. Pp. 345-65.

Jones, A. H. M. *The Roman Economy*. Oxford: Blackwell, 1974.

__________. *Were Ancient Heresies Disguised Social Movements?* Philadelphia: Fortress Press, 1966.

Josephus. 9 vols. Translated by H. St. J. Thackery et al. LCL. Cambridge, MA: Harvard University Press, 1926-65.

Judge, E. A. "The Early Christians as a Scholastic Community." *JRelS* 1 (1960-61) 1-8; 124-37.

__________. "St. Paul and Classical Society." *JAC* 15 (1972) 19-36.

__________. *The Social Pattern of Christian Groups in the First Century*. London: Tyndale, 1960.

Juncker, A. *Die Ethik des Apostels Paulus*. Vol. 2. Halle: Verlag von Max Niemeyer, 1919.

Juvenal and Persius. Translated by G. G. Ramsay. LCL. London: Heinemann, 1918.

Kähler, E. *Die Frau in der paulinischen Briefen*. Frankfurt: Gotthelf, 1960.

Käsemann, E. "Ministry and Community in the New Testament." *Essays on New Testament Times*. Translated by W. J. Montague. SBT 41. London: SCM Press, 1960. Pp. 63-94.

_________. "Worship and Everyday Life." *New Testament Questions of Today*. Translated by W. J. Montague. Philadelphia: Fortress, 1969. Pp. 188-95.

Kajanto, I. "On Divorce among the Common People of Rome." *Revue des etudes latines* 47 (1970) 99-113.

Kamlah, E. *Die Form der katalogischen Paränese im Neuen Testament*. WUNT 7, 1964.

_________. "ὑποτάσσεσθαι in den neutestamentlichen Haustafeln." *Verborum Veritas*. Festschrift für Gustave Stählin zum 70. Geburtstag. Hrsg. O. Bocher und K. Haacker. Wuppertal: Theologischer Verlag Brockhaus, 1970. Pp. 237-43.

Karris, R. J. "The Background and Significance of the Polemic of the Pastoral Epistles." *JBL* 92 (1973) 549-64.

_________. *The Function and Sitz im Leben of the Paraenetic Elements in the Pastoral Epistles*. Th.D. dissertation, Harvard University, 1971.

_________. "Rom 14:1-15:3 and the Occasion of Romans." *CBQ* 35 (1973) 155-78.

Kaser, Max. *Roman Private Law*. Translated by Rolf Dannenbring. Durban: Butterworth's, 1968.

Kautsky, Karl. *Foundations of Christianity: A Study of Christian Origins*. Authorized translation from the 13th edition. New York: International Publishers, 1925.

Kelly, J. N. D. *A Commentary on the Pastoral Epistles*. New York: Harper and Row, 1963.

Kienast, D. "Ein vernachlässigtes Zeugnis für die Reichspolitik Trajans: Die zweite tarsische Rede des Dion von Prusa." *Historia* 20 (1971) 62-80.

Kippenberg, H. G. "Versuch einer soziologischen Verortung des antiken Gnostizismus." *Numen* 17 (1970) 211-31.

Kittel, G. "Das kleinasiatische Judentum in der hellenistisch-römischen Zeit." *ThLZ* 69 (1944) 9-20.

Koester, H. "φύσις." *TDNT* IX.

Kraeling, K. "The Jewish Community at Antioch." *JBL* 51 (1932) 130-60.

Kreissig, H. "Zur sozialen Zusammensetzung der frühchristlichen Gemeinden im ersten Jahrhundert u. Z." *Eirene* 6 (1927) 91-100.

Lacey, W. K. *The Family in Classical Greece*. London: Thames and Hudson, 1968.

Leaney, A. R. C. *The Epistles to Timothy, Titus and Philemon*. London: SCM Press, 1960.

Leenhardt, F. J. and Blanke, F. *Die Stellung der Frau im NT und in der alten Kirche*. Zurich, 1949.

Leipholdt, J. *Die Frau in der antiken Welt und im Urchristentum*. 2nd edition. Leipzig: Koehler und Amelang, 1955.

Lemaire, A. "Pastoral Epistles: Redaction and Theology." *BTB* 2 (1972) 25-42.

Leon, H. J. *The Jews of Ancient Rome*. Philadelphia: Jewish Publication Society of America, 1960.

Levick, B. M. *Roman Colonies in Southern Asia Minor*. Oxford: Clarendon, 1967.

Levin, S. "St. Paul's Ideology for the Urbanized Roman Empire." *Concordia Theological Monthly* 39 (1968) 607-11.

Levy, I. "Etudes sur la vie municipale en Asia mineure au temps des Antonins." *Revue des etudes grecques* 8 (1895) 203-50; 12 (1899) 255-89; 14 (1901) 350-71.

Lightman, M. and Zeisel, W. "*Univira*: An Example of Continuity and Change in Roman Society." *CH* 46 (1977) 19-32.

Linton, O. *Das Problem der Urkirche in der neueren Forschung*. Uppsala: Almsqvist & Wiksells, 1932.

Lock, W. A. *A Critical and Exegetical Commentary on the Pastoral Epistles*. Edinburgh: T. & T. Clark, 1924.

Lohfink, G. "Normitivität der Amstvorstellungen in den Pastoralbriefen." *TQ* 157 (1977) 93-106.

Lohmeyer, E. *Die Briefe an die Kolosser und an Philemon*. Göttingen: Vandenhoeck & Ruprecht, 1954.

__________. *Soziale Fragen im Urchristentum*. Leipzig, 1921; reprint ed., Darmstadt: Wissenschaftliche Buchgesellschaft, 1973.

Luck, U. "ὕβρις." *TDNT* VII.

Lucian. Vol. 5. Translated by A. M. Harmon. LCL. Cambridge, MA: Harvard University Press, 1936.

Lyall, F. "Roman Law in the Writings of Paul--The Slave and the Freedman." *NTS* 17 (1970-71) 73-79.

Lysias. Vol. 1. Translated by W. R. M. Lamb. LCL. London: Heinemann, 1930.

McEleney, N. J. "The Vice Lists of the Pastoral Epistles." *CBQ* 36 (1974) 203-19.

McKay, A. G. *Houses, Villas and Palaces in the Roman World*. Ithaca: Cornell University Press, 1975.

MacMullen, R. *Enemies of the Roman Order*. Cambridge, MA: Harvard University Press, 1966.

__________. *Roman Social Relations*. New Haven: Yale University Press, 1974.

Maehlum, H. *Die Vollmacht des Timotheus nach den Pastoralbriefen*. Basel: Friedrich Reinhardt, 1969.

Magie, D. *Roman Rule in Asia Minor*. Princeton: Princeton University Press, 1950.

Malherbe, A. J. *Social Aspects of Early Christianity*. Baton Rouge: Louisiana State University Press, 1977.

Marquardt, J. *Das Privatleben der Römer*. Leipzig, 1886.

Marshall, A. J. "Roman Women and the Provinces." *Ancient Society* 6 (1975) 109-28.

Martial. *Epigrams*. 2 vols. Translated by W. Ker. LCL. London: Heinemann, 1925.

Martin, R. P. *The Family and the Fellowship*. Grand Rapids: Eerdmans, 1979.

Maxey, Mima. *Occupations of the Lower Classes in Roman Society*. Chicago: University of Chicago Press, 1938; reprinted in *Two Studies on the Roman Lower Classes*. New York: Arno Press, 1975.

Meeks, W. A. "The Image of the Androgyne: Some Uses of a Symbol in Earliest Christianity." *HR* 13 (1974) 165-208.

Merk, O. "Glaube und Tat in den Pastoralbriefen." *ZNW* 66 (1975) 91-102.

Michel, O. "οἶκος." *TDNT* V.

Millar, F. *A Study of Cassius Dio*. Oxford: Clarendon, 1964.

Miltner, F. *Ephesos*. Vienna: Verlag F. Deutke, 1958.

Monumenta Asiae Minoris antiqua. 8 vols. Published in association with the American Society for Archeological Research in Asia Minor by Manchester University Press, 1928-62.

Moore, G. F. *Judaism in the First Centuries of the Christian Era*. 3 vols. Cambridge, MA: Harvard University Press, 1927-30.

Morrison, Clinton. *The Powers That Be*. London: SCM Press, 1960.

Morrow, G. R. *Plato's Law of Slavery in Its Relation to Greek Law*. Urbana: University of Illinois Press, 1939.

Mossé, Claude. *The Ancient World at Work*. Translated by J. Lloyd. London: Chatto and Windus, 1969.

Motto, A. L. "Seneca on Women's Liberation." *Classical World* 65 (1972) 155-57.

Müller-Bardorff, J. "Zur Exegese von I Tim. 5:3-16." *Gott und die Götter. Festgabe für Erich Fascher*. Berlin: Evangelische Verlagsanstalt, 1958. Pp. 113-33.

Nicolet, C., ed. *Recherches sur les structures sociales dans l'Antiquite classique*. Paris, 1970.

Nock, A. D. *Conversion*. London: Oxford University Press, 1933.

Norman, A. F. "Gradations in Later Municipal Society." *JRS* 48 (1958) 79-85.

Oepke, A. *Der Brief des Paulus an die Galater*. 2nd edition. Berlin: Evangelische Verlagsanstalt, 1960.

__________. "γυνή." *TDNT* I.

__________. "Der Dienst der Frau in der urchristlichen Gemeinde." *Neue Allgemeine Missionszeitschrift* 16 (1939) 81-86.

__________. "παῖς." *TDNT* V.

Osbourne, G. R. "Hermeneutics and Women in the Church." *Journal of the Evangelical Theological Society* 20 (1977) 337-52.

Oster, R. "The Ephesian Artemis as an Opponent of Early Christianity." *JAC* 19 (1976) 24-44.

Packer, J. E. "Housing and Population in Imperial Ostia and Rome." *JRS* 57 (1967) 80-95.

_________. *The Insulae of Imperial Ostia*. Memoirs of the American Academy of Rome 31 (1971).

Parry, R. St. J. *The Pastoral Epistles*. Cambridge: Cambridge University Press, 1920.

Pelser, G. M. M. "Women and Ecclesiastical Ministries in Paul." *Neot* 10 (1976) 92-109.

Penny, D. N. *The Pseudo-Pauline Letters of the First Two Centuries*. Ph.D. dissertation, Emory University, 1979.

Perelman, Ch. and Olbrechts-Tyteca, L. *The New Rhetoric: A Treatise on Argumentation*. Notre Dame: University of Notre Dame Press, 1971.

Petersen, J. M. "House Churches in Rome." *VC* 23 (1969) 264-72.

Petronius. Translated by M. Heseltine. LCL. London: Heinemann, 1913.

Philo. 10 vols. Translated by F. H. Colson. LCL. Cambridge, MA: Harvard University Press, 1929-62.

Plato. *Laws*. 2 vols. Translated by R. G. Bury. LCL. Cambridge, MA: Harvard University Press, 1914.

Pleket, H. W., ed. *Epigraphica II: Texts on the Social History of the Greek World*. Leiden: Brill, 1969.

Pliny. *Letters and Panegyricus*. 2 vols. Translated by B. Radice. LCL. London: Heinemann, 1969.

Plümacher, E. *Lukas als hellenistischer Schriftsteller*. Göttingen: Vandenhoeck und Ruprecht, 1972.

Plutarch's Lives. 11 vols. Translated by B. Perrin. LCL. London: Heinemann, 1914-26.

Plutarch's Moralia. 14 vols. Translated by F. C. Babbit, et al. LCL. London: Heinemann, 1927.

Polybius. *The Histories*. Vol. 5. Translated by W. R. Paton. LCL. London: Heinemann, 1922.

Pomeroy, S. B. *Goddesses, Whores, Wives and Slaves. Women in Classical Antiquity*. New York: Schocken, 1975.

_________. "The Relationship of the Married Woman to Her Blood Relatives in Rome." *Ancient Society* 7 (1976) 215-37.

_________. "Selected Bibliography on Women in Antiquity." *Arethusa* 6 (1973) 125-37.

Preaux, C. Le status de la femme a l'Epoque hellenistique, principalment en Egypte." *Recouils de la Societe Jean Bodin*. Vol. 2.: *La femme* (1959) 19-33; 92-109.

Preisker, H. *Christentum und die Ehe in den ersten drei Jahrhunderten*. Berlin: Trowitzsch und Sohn, 1927.

Pseudo-Phocylides. *The Sentences of Pseudo-Phocylides*. Introduction, translation and commentary by P. W. van der Horst. Leiden: Brill, 1978.

Ramsay, W. M. "The Jews in the Graeco-Asiatic Cities." *Expositor*, Series 6,5 (1902) 19-32; 92-109.

_________. *The Social Basis of Roman Power in Asia Minor*. Aberdeen: Aberdeen University Press, 1941.

Rawson, B. "Family Life Among the Lower Classes at Rome in the First Two Centuries of the Empire." *Classical Philology* 61 (1966) 71-83.

_________. "Roman Concubinage and other *de facto* Marriages." *TAPA* 104 (1974) 279-305.

Reekmans, J. "Juvenal's View on Social Classes." *Ancient Society* 2 (1971) 117-61.

Reid, J. *The Municipalities of the Roman Empire*. Cambridge: Cambridge University Press, 1913.

Reinhold, M. "Usurpation of Status and Status Symbols in the Roman Empire." *Historia* 20 (1971) 275-302.

Rengstorf, K. H. "διδάσκω." *TDNT* II.

_________. *Mann und Frau im Urchristentum*. Köln: Westdeutsche Verlag, 1954.

Richter, D. C. "Women in Classical Times." *Classical Journal* 67 (1971) 1-8.

Rohde, J. "Pastoralbriefe und Acta Pauli." Edited by F. L. Cross. *Studia Evangelica* V. TU 103 (1968) 303-10.

Rordorff, W. "Was wissen wir über die christliche Gottesdiensträume?" *ZNW* 55 (1964) 110-28.

Rose, H. J. "The Religion of a Greek Household." *Euphrosyne* 1 (1957) 95-116.

Rosen, H. B. "Motifs and Topoi from the New Comedy in the New Testament." *Ancient Society* 3 (1972) 245-57.

Rostovtzeff, M. *Social and Economic History of the Roman Empire.* 2 vols. Revised by P. M. Fraser. Oxford: Clarendon, 1957.

Safrai, S. and Stern, M., eds. *The Jewish People in the First Century.* Vol. 2. CRINT, Section 1, 1976.

Ste. Croix, G. E. M. de. "Early Christian Attitudes to Property and Slavery." D. Baker, ed. *Church, Society and Politics.* London: Blackwell, 1975.

Salmon, P. *Population et depopulation dans l'Empire romain.* Bruxelles: Latomus, 1974.

Sampley, J. P. *"And the Two Shall Become One Flesh": A Study of Traditions in Ephesians 5:21-33.* NTS Monograph Series, 1971.

Sand, A. "Witwenstand und Ämterstructuren in den urchristlichen Gemeinden." *Bibleb* 12 (1971) 186-97.

Sanders, J. T. "The Transition from Opening Epistolary Thanksgiving to Body in the Letters of the Pauline Corpus." *JBL* 81 (1962) 348-62.

Saucy, R. L. "The Husband of One Wife." *Bibliotheca Sacra* 131 (1974) 229-40.

Schlatter, A. *Die Kirche der Griechen im Urteil des Paulus.* 2nd edition. Stuttgart: Calwer, 1958.

Schlier, H. *Die Zeit der Kirche.* Freiburg: Herder, 1956.

Schmithals, W. *Gnosticism in Corinth.* Translated by J. E. Steely. Nashville: Abingdon, 1971.

Schneider, Carl. *Kulturgeschichte des Hellenismus.* 2 vols. Munich: C. H. Beck, 1967-69.

Schrage, W. "Zur Ethik der NT Haustafeln." *NTS* 21 (1974) 1-22.

Schubert, P. "Form and Function of the Pauline Letters." *JR* 19 (1939) 365-77.

_________. *Form and Function of the Pauline Thanksgivings*. BZNW 20. Berlin: A. Töpelmann, 1939.

Schulze, W. A. "Ein Bischof sei eines Weibes Mann." *KD* 4 (1958) 287-300.

Schweizer, E. *Church Order in the New Testament*. London: SCM Press, 1961.

_________. "Traditional Ethical Patterns in the Pauline and Post-Pauline Letters and Their Development." E. Best and R. McL. Wilson, eds. *Text and Interpretation*. Studies in the New Testament Presented to Matthew Black. Cambridge: Cambridge University Press, 1979. Pp. 195-209.

_________. "Die Weltlichkeit des neuen Testaments--die Haustafeln." H. Donner, R. Hanhart and R. Smend, eds. *Beiträge zur alttestamentlichen Theologie*. Festschrift für Walther Zimmerli zum 70. Geburtstag. Göttingen: Vandenhoeck und Ruprecht, 1977. Pp. 397-413.

Scott, E. F. *The Pastoral Epistles*. London: Hodder and Stoughton, 1936.

Scroggs, R. "Marriage in the New Testament." IDB Sup.

_________. "Paul and the Eschatological Woman." *JAAR* 40 (1972) 283-303.

Seeberg, A. *Der Katechismus der Urchristenheit*. Leipzig, 1903; reprint ed. Theologische Bücherei 26. Munich, 1966.

Seneca. *Epistulae Morales*. 3 vols. Translated by R. M. Gummere. LCL. London: Heinemann, 1917.

_________. *Moral Essays*. 3 vols. Translated by J. W. Basore. LCL. London: Heinemann, 1932.

Sherwin-White, A. N. *The Roman Citizenship*. Oxford: Clarendon, 1939.

_________. "Roman Citizenship. A Survey of Its Development into a World Franchise." *ANRW* I, 2. Pp. 23-58.

_________. *Roman Society and Roman Law in the New Testament*. Oxford: Clarendon, 1963.

Simpson, E. K. *The Pastoral Epistles*. London: Tyndale, 1954.

Smallwood, E. M. *The Jews under Roman Rule*. Leiden: Brill, 1976.

Smith, J. Z. "The Social Description of Early Christianity." *Religious Studies Review* 1 (1975) 19-25.

Spencer, A. D. B. "Eve at Ephesus." *Journal of the Evangelical Theological Society* 17 (1974) 215-22.

Sperber, D. "Costs of Living in Roman Palestine." *Journal of the Economic and Social History of the Orient* 8 (1965) 248-71.

Spicq, C. *Les Épîtres pastorales*. 2 vols. 4th revised edition. Paris: J. Gabalda, 1969.

Stählin, G. "χήρα." *TDNT* IX.

Stenger, W. "Timotheus und Titus als literarischen Gestalten. Beobachtungen zur Form und Function der Pastoralbriefe." *Kairos* 16 (1974) 252-67.

Stobaeus. *Anthologium*. 5 vols. C. Wachsmuth and O. Hense, eds. Berlin: Weidmann'sche Verlagsbuchhandlung, 1958.

Strack, H. L. and P. Billerbeck. *Kommentar zum neuen Testament aus Talmud und Midrasch*. Vol. 3. Munich: C. H. Beck'sche Verlagsbuchhandlung. 1922-28.

Strobel, A. "Der Begriff des 'Hauses' im griechischen und römischen Privatrecht." *ZNW* 56 (1965) 91-100.

Szilagy, J. "Prices and Wages in the Western Provinces of the Roman Empire." *Acta Antiqua* 11 (1963) 325-89.

Talbert, Charles. "Tradition and Redaction in Romans 12:19-21." *NTS* 16 (1969-70) 83-94.

Tanzer, H. H. *The Common People of Pompei*. Baltimore: Johns Hopkins, 1939.

Tarn, W. W. *Hellenistic Civilization*. London: E. Arnold, 1927.

Taubenschlag, R. *The Law of Greco-Roman Egypt in the Light of the Papyri: 332 B.C.--640 A.D.* 2nd edition. Warsaw: Panstowe Wydawnictwo Naukowe, 1955.

Tcherikover, V. A. *Hellenistic Civilization and the Jews*. Translated by S. Applebaum. Philadelphia: Jewish Publication Society, 1959.

Tcherikover, V. A. and Fuks, A., eds. *Corpus Papyrorum Judaicarum*. 2 vols. Cambridge, MA: Harvard University Press, 1957-60.

Temporini, H. ed. *Aufstieg und Niedergang der römischen Welt*. 19 vols. Berlin: De Gruyter, 1972-.

Tertullian. *Treatises on Marriage and Re-marriage.* Translated and annotated by W. P. Le Saint. Westminster, MD: Newman Press, 1951.

Theissen, G. "Legitimation und Lebensunterhalt: Eine Beitrag zur Soziologie urchristlicher Missionäre." *NTS* 21 (1975) 192-221.

_________. *Sociology of Early Palestinian Christianity.* Translated by J. Bowden. Philadelphia: Fortress Press, 1978.

_________. "Soziale Integration und sakramentale Handeln: Eine Analyse von I Kor. 11:17-34." *NovT* 16 (1974) 179-206.

_________. "Soziale Schichtung in der korinthischen Gemeinde." *ZNW* 65 (1974) 232-72.

_________. "Die soziologische Auswertung religioser Überlieferungen." *Kairos* 17 (1975) 284-99.

_________. "Die Starken und Schwachen in Korinth. Soziologische Analyse eines theologischen Streites." *ET* 35 (1975) 155-72.

_________. "Theoretische Probleme religionssoziologischer Forschung und die Analyse des Urchristentums." *Neue Zeitschrift für systematische Theologie und Religionsphilosophie* 16 (1974) 205-31.

Thuren, J. "Die Structure der Schlussparänese I Tim. 6:3-12." *TZ* 26 (1970) 241-53.

Treggiari, S. "Domestic Staff at Rome in the Julio-Claudian Period, 27 B.C. to 68 A.D." *Histoire sociale; Revue canadienne* 6 (1973) 241-55.

_________. "Libertine Ladies." *Classical World* 64 (1971) 196-98.

_________. *Roman Freedmen during the Late Republic.* Oxford: Clarendon, 1969.

Troeltch, E. *The Social Teaching of the Christian Churches.* Vol. 1. Translated by O. Wyon. London: George Allen and Unwin, 1931.

Trummer, P. "Einehe nach den Pastoralbriefen." *Biblica* 51 (1970) 471-84.

Turner, J. H. *The Structure of Sociological Theory.* Homewood, IL: Dorsey Press, 1974.

Unnik, W. C. van. "The Teaching of Good Works." *NTS* 1 (1954) 92-110.

Vatin, C. *Recherches sur le mariage et la condition de la femme mariée a l'Epoque hellenistique.* Paris: E. de Boccard, 1970.

Vogt, J. *Ancient Slavery and the Ideal of Man*. Translated by T. Wiedemann. Cambridge, MA: Harvard University Press, 1975.

Weaver, P. R. C. *Familia Caesaris. A Social Study of the Emperor's Freedmen and Slaves*. Cambridge: Cambridge University Press, 1972.

Wegenast, K. *Das Verständnis der Tradition bei Paulus und in den Deuteropaulinien*. Neukirchen: Neukirchener Verlag, 1962.

Weidinger, K. *Die Haustafeln. Ein Stück urchristlicher Paränese*. UNT 14. Leipzig, 1928.

Welles, C. B. *Royal Correspondence in the Hellenistic Period*. New Haven, 1934; reprint ed., Chicago: Ares Publishers, 1974.

Westermann, W. L. *The Slave Systems of Greek and Roman Antiquity*. Philadelphia: American Philosophical Society, 1955.

Wilson, R. McL. "How Gnostic Were the Corinthians?" *NTS* 19 (1972) 65-72.

Wiseman, T. P. "The Definition of 'Eques Romanus' in the Late Republic and Early Empire." *Historia* 19 (1970) 67-83.

Wolff, H. J. "Marriage Law in Ancient Athens." *Traditio* 2 (1944) 43-95.

_________. *Written and Unwritten Marriages in Hellenistic and Postclassical Roman Law*. Haverford, PA: American Philological Association, 1939.

Wuellner, W. "Paul's Rhetoric of Argumentation in Romans: An Alternative to the Donfried--Karris Debate over Romans." *CBQ* 38 (1976) 330-51.

_________. "The Sociological Implications of I Cor. 1:26-28 Reconsidered." *Studia Evangelica* IV; TU 112 (1973) 666-72.

Xenophon. 7 vols. Translated by C. L. Brownson, O. J. Todd and E. C. Marchant. LCL. London: Heinemann, 1918-23.

Xenophon Ephesius. *Ephesiacorum*. Edited by A. D. Papanikolaou. Leipzig: Teubner, 1973.